Slash of the Titans: The Road to Freddy vs Jason © 2017 by Dustin McNeill

ISBN-13: 978-0692033494

ISBN-10: 0692033491

Published by Harker Press

SLASH

— OF THE —

TITANS

THE ROAD TO FREDDY vs JASON

By Dustin McNeill

*This book is dedicated to all the monster kids out there
who grew up envisioning this film years before they ever made it.*

Interview Directory

Table of Contents

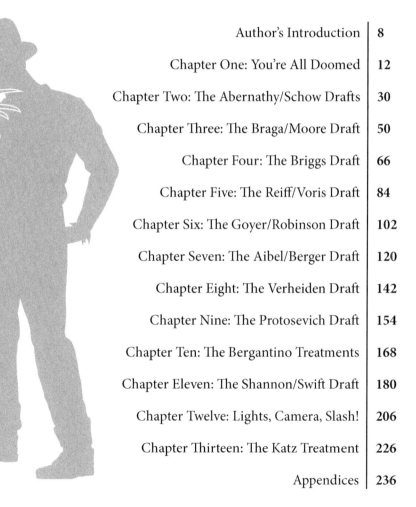

AUTHOR'S INTRODUCTION
"Welcome to my Nightmare."

Growing up, I was what you'd call a monster kid, proudly raised on the Universal classics. I didn't just watch them - I *studied* them. Once I'd explored every corner of that cinematic universe, I moved on to the more risqué Hammer films. Sure, the black-and-white Universal's were wonderfully gothic, but who could resist the blood-red allure of the Hammer's in "terrifying technicolor?" In fourth-grade, I became aware of horror's more modern monsters, namely Michael Myers, Freddy Krueger, and Jason Voorhees. These were nothing like the Universal's and Hammer's. These were *scary*. I got the sense my parents were not going to let me rent these tapes anytime soon, but I simply had to see them - all of them.

I spent that October scouring my local newspaper's television listings for these slasher flicks. I meticulously programmed my family's VCR to record at least a dozen of them, my introductions to franchises like *Halloween, Nightmare on Elm Street,* and *Friday the 13th.* At this age, such films were all beyond terrifying. I can honestly remember being grateful for the commercials just for a break in the tension. Watching a bloodless vampire bite wasn't that scary, but I'll never forget the first time I saw Freddy Krueger suck Johnny Depp into his bed, purée him, and spray his remains all over the room. That was the stuff nightmares are made of.

By the following October, I was hooked on these new franchises and determined to dress up as Freddy for Halloween. I saved my allowance for what seemed like ages until I had enough to buy a mask and glove. Some of you may remember this particular piece, which was based on the *New Nightmare look*, with its awkwardly cut eyeholes just above Freddy's own bulging peepers. My toddler-sister was deathly afraid of this mask, a visceral fear that I fully confess to having exploited regularly. I often left it in the doorway to my room to ensure she wouldn't mess with my stuff while I was at school. Years later, I would follow up on this trauma by taking her to *A Nightmare on Elm Street* as her first big screen R-rated movie. I'd like to think the experience was somehow therapeutic.

I remained a monster kid at heart heading into my teenage years. By my remembrance, 2003 was a pretty great year for horror. There were so many franchises returning on screens both big and small. We had new entries in ongoing series like *Re-Animator, Texas Chainsaw Massacre, Final Destination, Puppet Master, Ju-on: The Grudge,* and *Leprechaun.* We were also introduced to *House of 1,000 Corpses, Wrong Turn, Dead End,* and *Haute Tension.* Best of all? On August 15, New Line finally unleashed the long-awaited *Freddy vs Jason* in theaters. Who could even believe this was finally happening? *Freddy vs Jason* seemed far more like schoolyard conjecture than an actual production. How often had my friends and I speculated on which slasher might win in a fight to the death? For us, it was all about the particulars. Is this human-Jason or zombie-Jason? Can Freddy turn into that snake creature from *Dream Warriors*? Is Jason using his machete or that weed-wacker thing from *New Blood*? Is this reality-Freddy or dreamscape-Freddy? And who gets home field advantage?

Your mileage may vary, but I had a fantastic time with *Freddy vs Jason*. In fact, I went to see it opening weekend on Friday, Saturday, and Sunday. There was just so much to like! Robert Englund was back and still at the top of his Freddy game. The titans didn't fight just once, but multiple times. They even stole each other's signature weapons to use in battle! We had the return of Mrs. Voorhees (sort of) and got a brief look at Springwood Slasher-era Freddy. The movie took us back to both Elm Street and Camp Crystal Lake. Of course, it majorly sucked that Kane Hodder wasn't playing Jason, but I thought the new guy did a terrific job. There was also the joyous thrill of finally seeing one of these movies on the big screen, which was a far cry from watching edited versions taped off late night cable.

We horror fans are an awfully curious bunch. It's not enough simply to watch and enjoy these movies. We want to know how they were made. We want to learn about the mythologies. We want to see shooting scripts, workprints, and deleted scenes. Most of you reading this can probably remember a time before the internet when it wasn't so easy to read up on your favorite scary movies. The best you could hope for growing up was finding back issues of *Fangoria* or *Gorezone*. Having said that, getting a two-disc Platinum Edition DVD for *Freddy vs Jason* was a huge thrill. Suddenly, we had filmmaker commentaries, featurettes, deleted scenes, and storyboards. What more could there possibly be to say on the subject of *Freddy vs Jason*? Quite a lot, it turns out. First came Peter Bracke's lavish *Crystal Lake Memories: The Complete History of Friday the 13th* coffee table book in 2006. Then came Daniel Farrands' *His Name was Jason: 30 Years of Friday the 13th* documentary in 2009. Farrands teamed with co-director Andrew Kasch to give us *Never Sleep Again: The Elm Street Legacy* the following year and later wildly outdid himself with an eponymous documentary adaptation of Bracke's book in 2013. What a glorious time to be a horror fan with these incredible resources at our disposal.

I first learned of *Freddy vs Jason*'s troubled development in the pages of *Fangoria* magazine. The article was by future *Sharknado* director Anthony C. Ferrante. As it turned out, New Line Cinema had spent nearly a decade trying to find the right screenplay for the crossover. That revelation stunned me. *Ten years?* Let's not kid ourselves, *The Godfather* this wasn't! This was a fun popcorn movie, a rompy slasher throwdown. Nothing about the film suggested it should have taken so long to develop. The book and documentaries above would shed further light on the subject, even including interviews with some of the original writers. This was all fascinating, but it wasn't the whole story. It was just enough to make me even more curious. So I began researching *Freddy vs Jason*'s history and immediately found a handful of unused screenplays online and several more available offline. These were intriguing reads, all wildly different from the 2003 film. I thought to myself, '*There might be an interesting 'What-if?' book in all of these unused drafts.*' Reaching out to the screenwriters only led me further down the rabbit hole to additional drafts and conspirators. And here we are.

Contained within this book is the story of *Freddy vs Jason*'s ten-year journey from script to screen. I'd like to think it's a fairly balanced account with perspectives from both the Freddy and Jason camps. Why was it so difficult finding the right script for this movie? In large part, the answer is because those three words - *Freddy vs Jason* - conjure up vastly different images in our minds. My vision for what the film should be and your own vision may be nothing alike. This was certainly the case for dozens of attached executives, producers, screenwriters, and directors throughout the years. To complicate matters further, this was a project with split creative control. No one person ever had the clout to force it into production. In retrospect, it's almost a miracle that *Freddy vs Jason* was ever made at all.

With all due to respect to Stokely, I can't say I agree with that or else I might've titled my book, *Slash of the Titans: The Most Shit Ideas You'll Be Glad They Didn't Use*. While there are a few groan-worthy moments among the unused drafts, they contain even more strokes of brilliance, ideas so rich that they could easily spin off into their own *Friday* and *Nightmare* entries. One huge difference between the 2003 film script and the preceding drafts involves creative risk. By design, the 2003 film plays it safe by not taking risks with the story or characters. The screenwriters sought to deliver us Freddy and Jason as we've always known them and they succeed at that goal. The many unused drafts, however, put forth a slew of bold ideas that range from murderous psycho cults to apocalyptic millennial prophecies to boxing matches in hell. To incorporate these concepts would've meant trying something new and different.

Which of these many ideas would have worked best in the eventual film? I suppose that's up to you to decide. If we've learned anything from twelve *Friday*'s and eight *Nightmare*'s, it's that there is no one right approach to either character. The titans are quite versatile that way. You can accuse these films of a lot of things, but stagnation isn't one of them. Take Jason, for example. We've seen him in comedy-horror (*Jason Lives*), grindhouse-horror (*A New Beginning*), supernatural-horror (*Jason Goes to Hell*) and sci-fi-horror (*Jason X*). Which one direction was right for *Freddy vs Jason* to head in? Again, that's up to you. Within this book you'll find plot information for ten different versions of the film. Maybe you prefer more humor. Or maybe you prefer none. Maybe you're into meta-horror like *New Nightmare*? Or maybe you'd rather the story continue on from previous sequels. These directions and more were all seriously considered.

In truth, I wrote *Slash of the Titans* as much for me to read as I did for all of you. Researching this subject has been a marvelously fun experience. Words cannot fully convey how exciting it was to interview genre legends like Sean Cunningham and Robert Englund for this project. As an ardent *Jason Goes to Hell* apologist, it was fantastic to speak with writer-director Adam Marcus. I must also express my enormous gratitude to the many *Freddy vs Jason* screenwriters for so candidly discussing their unrealized drafts, some of which are now more than twenty-years-old. These are among the most talented scribes you could ever hope to find this side of Elm Street. You may not recognize all of their names, but you will surely know their legendary film and television credits.

So lock your doors and grab your crucifix. It's time to begin. We're about to trace *Freddy vs Jason*'s history all the way from the project's earliest whispers to its red carpet premiere and beyond. I will warn you that exploring so many different versions of the same match-up can get confusing rather quickly. Feel free to consult the Appendices starting on page 236 if you need, which detail plotlines, screenwriters, protagonists, fight outcomes, and more.

Pleasant dreams,

Dustin McNeill

Chapter One
You're All Doomed

1980-1994

"I'll be first in line. In my heart I know it's gonna be terrible, but I'll still be there. [...] Everyone who goes will be like me, forking over for the ticket while knowing that the very idea is ludicrous, a setup job only a studio accountant could love, and yet…maybe it'll be good. Even if it's not, remember what Vern Tessio said in *Stand By Me* about a Superman/Mighty Mouse confrontation. No matter who wins, it'll be a good fight."

- Stephen King on *Freddy vs Jason* in Entertainment Weekly #724

SLASH OF THE TITANS

Freddy vs Jason. The idea was golden right from the start. Even the title seemed to roll off the tongue with ease. *Friday the 13th* and *A Nightmare on Elm Street* were, without question, the two most successful horror properties of the 1980s. They stood on nearly equal footing, having covered much of the same ground on their way to the top. Besides slaying the box office, they had each spun off a successful television show. They had been adapted into their own Nintendo games. They had even crossed over into rock-and-roll, Freddy with Dokken and Jason with Alice Cooper. With thirteen films between them as of 1990, where else was there to go if not up against one another?

The elder of the two franchises was *Friday the 13th*, which belonged to Paramount Pictures, one of the biggest and oldest studios in Hollywood. Although Jason was cinematically born unto Paramount, there was no denying they were a peculiar home for the series given how seldom they dipped into the horror genre. Paramount was far better known for their Oscar-winning dramas, comedies, and action-epics. Were it not for the phenomenal return-on-investment yields of the Jason films, they might never have ventured into the world of slasher films. Beginning in 1980, the studio churned out eight *Friday*'s in just ten years, making Jason the busiest horror icon of the decade.

Trailing *Friday* by four years, *A Nightmare on Elm Street* hit theaters in 1984 from distributor-turned-studio New Line Cinema. Founded in 1967 by Robert Shaye as an outlet for artistic and foreign films, New Line began rolling out its own projects a decade after inception. Seven years later, they landed a major hit with *Nightmare*'s surprisingly strong reception, which earned the studio a reputation as "The House That Freddy Built." Unlike Paramount with Jason, the ground floor of New Line's legacy was built squarely on *Elm Street*. Without this early horror hit, they might never have gone on to create blockbuster franchises like *Teenage Mutant Ninja Turtles, Rush Hour,* and *Lord of the Rings*. Starting in 1984, New Line produced five *Nightmare*'s before the end of the decade.

Tracing back who first thought of *Freddy vs Jason* is an impossible task. The answer is everyone. *Everyone* thought of *Freddy vs Jason*. Schoolchildren thought of it. Horror fans thought of it. Studio executives thought of it. The mere notion was so blatantly obvious, even to those who were not fans of the genre. But if we must find someone involved in the making of these films to credit with first publicly acknowledging the concept, we might go with *A Nightmare on Elm Street 2: Freddy's Revenge* screenwriter David Chaskin. He recalls remarking to a journalist about the crossover idea on that film's Los Angeles set during the summer of 1985. By that time, Jason had already hacked his way through three monstrously profitable sequels.

EARLY TALKS

The early history of *Freddy vs Jason* is a subject murkier than the crimson waters of Crystal Lake itself. We do know that preliminary discussions on the project first began at Paramount in 1986 following the successful release of *Friday the 13th Part VI: Jason Lives*. The topic arose from a discussion about the future of the *Friday* franchise between studio president Frank Mancuso Jr. and *Jason Lives* director Tom McLoughlin. Figuring that a match-up would be a surefire box office smash, the studio suit reached out to New Line with the concept.

Mancuso reportedly found the rival studio in agreement that *Freddy vs Jason* was a winning idea. There was but one unresolvable issue that prevented the project from going forward at that time. Like Paramount, New Line was only open to *Freddy vs Jason* so long as they could license their competitor's character to produce and distribute the picture themselves, a position neither party was willing to budge from. That arrangement meant that one studio would earn a flat licensing fee as the other reaped millions at the box office. This equal unwillingness to license out quickly resulted in a stalemate, ending the conversation. Retreating to their corners, Paramount began development on *Friday the 13th Part VII* as New Line continued with pre-production on *A Nightmare on Elm Street 3: Dream Warriors*.

New Line's staunch refusal to license out Freddy was validated the following year by *Dream Warriors'* stellar box office returns, which were more than twice what *Jason Lives* had earned. In fact, *Dream Warriors* grossed more than any prior film in either franchise. New Line would follow it up with *A Nightmare on Elm Street 4: Dream Master* in 1988, which proved to be an even *bigger* success. The original *Friday* may have outgrossed the original *Nightmare*, but Jason was no match for Freddy where the sequels were concerned. This trend would continue until the 2009/2010 reboots, which would see Jason finally eek out a victory over his arch-rival.

Paramount's plans for *Freddy vs Jason* were eventually rolled into *Friday the 13th Part VII: The New Blood*. The 1988 sequel retained the *Someone vs Jason* angle, swapping out New Line's dream slasher for new character Tina Shepard, a *Carrie*-esque teen with telekinetic abilities. In the film, Tina accidentally uses her powers to unleash a rotted-looking Jason from the depths of Crystal Lake, leading to a new slaughter. These powers also enable her to confront Jason near film's end and actually stand a fighting chance while doing so. Rather than the customary stalk-and-slash finale that concludes most *Friday*'s, *New Blood* climaxed with an explosive knock-down, drag-out fight between the two characters.

Two years after initial *Freddy vs Jason* talks had fizzled out, *Friday the 13th Part IV: The Final Chapter* director Joseph Zito attempted to revive the project with hopes of directing it. He was first moved to inquire about the possibility after noticing falling ticket sales for both franchises. Zito soon found that both Mancuso and Robert Shaye still had interest in making the film, but only if they could license the other studio's character and distribute the project themselves. Nothing had changed. The stalemate continued.

DOWNWARD TREND

Heading into the 1990's, there was growing concern that the franchises had peaked commercially and creatively. Paramount's most recent outing, *Friday the 13th Part VIII: Jason Takes Manhattan*, was simultaneously their biggest-budgeted and lowest-grossing effort to date. Going by the numbers, *Friday*'s box office prowess had technically been on the decline since *Part III*, but with returns typically hovering around or above $20 million, the studio had continued to feed the *Friday* machine.

Reviews for *Manhattan* were not particularly kind, either. With rising budgets and falling profits, Jason had become less appealing to the studio than ever before, especially in light of growing pushback from parent groups over film violence.

Paramount was not alone. New Line also appeared to be downward trending with their once flagship franchise. *A Nightmare on Elm Street 5: The Dream Child* grossed less than half of what its two predecessors had earned while drawing considerably worse reviews. Echoing other industry voices, *Variety* dismissed it as "a poorly constructed special effects showcase." Going for broke, the studio followed up two years later with *Freddy's Dead: The Final Nightmare*, which was widely promoted as the concluding chapter of the *Elm Street* saga. While that marketing ploy paid off at the box office with an improved gross, the reviews this time were even worse than on *Dream Chlld*. Even Freddy himself could not deny the drop in quality. "To be one hundred percent honest," Robert Englund wrote in his autobiography, "I'll admit that on *Nightmare 6*, we jumped the shark. The comedy might've become a little too broad, the fantasy might've become a little too trippy, and the violence might've become a little too cartoonish."

Decades before Freddy and Jason dominated the horror scene, Universal Pictures had experienced a similar drop in quality and profits with their signature horror properties. After four *Frankenstein* movies, the studio moved to pair the green behemoth with a fellow monster to reinvigorate the series and hopefully the box office. That picture was *Frankenstein Meets the Wolf-man*, which also marked the pairing of genre icons Bela Lugosi and Lon Chaney Jr. Universal's plan worked well enough to constitute a point of no return for single monster sequels with these characters. The solo adventures of Dracula, Frankenstein's monster, and the Wolf-man were now over for this era. The individual franchises had given way to a larger cinematic universe. One film later, the studio was advertising a whopping five monsters for the price of one in their publicity for *House of Frankenstein*. (For those counting, that number included Dracula, Frankenstein's monster, the Wolf-man, a mad scientist, and a hunchback.)

Yet that kind of monster mash was a long dead concept, possibly excepting the crossover exploits of Toho's *Godzilla* franchise. That domestic audiences had not seen this kind of horror gimmick in decades made it all the more special to attempt now with Freddy and Jason. The mere suggestion broke the established rules; modern horror heavies simply did not interact with each other that way. To pair the two highest-grossing slashers together would surely be a license to print money. No matter how you sliced it, *Freddy vs Jason* just made too much sense to ignore. But there was still the issue of Freddy being at New Line and Jason at Paramount.

In the wake of *Freddy's Dead* and *Jason Takes Manhattan*, prospects for a crossover sequel appeared grim. New Line had publicly committed - even if temporarily - to actually *stop* churning out *Nightmare* sequels. While Paramount had made no such declaration, they also had no immediate intention of mounting another *Friday*. With the franchises on pause, it would take the homecoming of a long absent franchise founder to reignite the fires of *Freddy vs Jason*.

A HOMECOMING AT CRYSTAL LAKE

Although Sean Cunningham had co-written, helmed, and produced the original *Friday the 13th*, he was not directly involved in the seven sequels that followed after. He instead spent the 1980s writing and directing genre pictures like *A Stranger is Watching* and *DeepStar Six*. Heading into the 1990s, he too felt that merging the *Friday* and *Nightmare* franchises was a smart move. His production team also liked the concept, which emboldened him to approach New Line about the possibility. The studio once again reaffirmed their interest in the project so long as *they* could be the one to produce and distribute it. That was good enough for Cunningham, who now needed to do what had previously been impossible: pry the rights to Jason away from Paramount.

Upon reconnecting with Paramount, Cunningham found a very different studio than the one he had previously known. Frank Mancuso Jr. was no longer in charge and the new regime seemed to have little regard for slashers. After taking into account the decreasing profits of *New Blood* and *Manhattan*, Paramount agreed to sell their rights. The catch was that their deal would only be for the Jason Voorhees character and related story elements, not the brand itself. This meant by way of Cunningham that New Line could now make any Jason film they wanted so long as they did not call it *Friday the 13th*. It was a breakthrough agreement and enough to finally move forward on *Freddy vs Jason*.

That the parent studio of *Friday the 13th* had grown disinterested in the series was a charge bolstered by the fact they were clearly in a state of transition at the time of Cunningham's approach. Heading into the '90s, both Paramount and New Line were shifting in their attitudes toward slashers. The former had unofficially abandoned the sub-genre with *Jason Takes Manhattan*, now looking ahead to more high-brow horrors like Stephen King adaptations and star-driven chillers. Paramount's horror output would slow to a dry-spell in the new decade with only three genre pictures released from 1993 to 2000. They would not greenlight another slasher film for two decades, not until the 2009 remake of *Friday the 13th* (or until their accountants realized the gross error of their ways). New Line, on the other hand, was increasing their investment in slashers by adding Leatherface to the in-house lineup in 1990.

At the outset of the deal that made *Freddy vs Jason* possible, the immediate future looked promising. The much anticipated crossover was finally poised to happen and in doing so would mark the triumphant return of Cunningham to the franchise he helped to create. In retrospect, he was the perfect candidate to breathe new life into *Freddy vs Jason* given his involvement not only with *Friday the 13th*, but with the original *Nightmare on Elm Street* as well. Little known to many horror fans is that Cunningham directed second unit material on the first *Nightmare* after having produced Wes Craven's *Last House on the Left* several years before. The list of filmmakers with a foot in both franchises is a short and exclusive one.

Cunningham's point of contact at New Line was then twenty-seven-year-old Michael De Luca, the company's president of production. De Luca had risen meteorically through the studio ranks, his first major credit three years prior as associate producer on *Leatherface: Texas Chainsaw Massacre III*. He would subsequently write and produce *Freddy's Dead: The Final Nightmare* along with several episodes of *Freddy's Nightmares*. A self-professed film nerd from Brooklyn, he would make realizing *Freddy vs Jason* a priority during his tenure at the studio. Whether or not being a creative force behind *Freddy's Dead* qualified or disqualified him to oversee *Freddy vs Jason* will depend upon your opinion of that particular entry. If nothing else, he had a clear passion for the material.

For most of *Freddy vs Jason*'s development, Cunningham and De Luca were the ultimate gatekeepers. No script could move forward without their joint approval. Although both were committed to making the best film possible, they had considerably different ideas as to what that might look like. Equal, however, was their dedication to the project and unwillingness to sign off on a vision they did not believe in. Freddy and Jason may have gotten star billing, but Cunningham and De Luca are the true titans of this story.

A NEW NIGHTMARE/A FINAL FRIDAY

Shortly after New Line wrangled Jason away from Paramount, the crossover slammed into a wall. As it turned out, Cunningham was not the only franchise elder revisiting old

"Face-off" glove by Mark Phillips.
(http://facebook.com/NightmaresUnlimited)

stomping grounds. After three sequels away, Wes Craven had decided upon a return trip to *Elm Street* in a deal made shortly after the Paramount agreement. Rather than greenlight competing Freddy projects, the studio put *Freddy vs Jason* on hold so that Craven could write and direct a new *Nightmare*, the seventh entry in that franchise. The sequel was scheduled to begin filming in October 1993 for release on Halloween the following year.

Craven had devised a clever twist for his aptly titled *New Nightmare* that would technically save New Line from accusations that they were reneging on the much publicized finality of *Freddy's Dead*. The new sequel would not feature the Freddy of the first six films, but rather a new evil that resides in our reality and takes the form of Freddy. Instead of terrorizing the youth of Elm Street, he would now haunt the the franchise's cast and crew. Series veterans Heather Langenkamp, Robert Englund, and John Saxon were enlisted to portray themselves alongside Craven himself in this art-imitating-life meta-sequel. Robert Shaye and Michael De Luca were also tapped for guest appearances, though the latter's cameo would wind up on the cutting room floor.

At the earliest indication that *Freddy vs Jason* was again on hold, Cunningham and De Luca agreed that their best course of action was to simultaneously produce another Jason movie to prevent the franchise from sitting dormant. By '92, Crystal Lake's most famous resident had been out of theaters for three years, his longest screen absence yet. To this end, Cunningham and De Luca developed *Jason Goes to Hell: The Final Friday*, which would film during the summer months of 1992 for an August 1993 release, beating *New Nightmare* to theaters by more than a year. Although the new title invoked *Friday the 13th*, it did not specifically include "*the 13th*," thereby avoiding violation of the Paramount deal. The project would mark the directorial debut of horror filmmaker Adam Marcus, who also helped write the film's story. (Two decades later, Marcus would return to New Line to co-write *Texas Chainsaw 3D*.)

Not unlike *New Nightmare*, *Jason Goes to Hell* explored a bold new direction for the series by re-writing existing mythology and subverting audience expectation at nearly every turn. The film opened with a shocking pre-credit sequence that saw a SWAT team utterly destroy Jason in a high-caliber raid on Camp Crystal Lake. His blown-apart remains are then taken to a morgue where his dark soul transfers to a coroner. From there, Jason goes body-hopping in search of a long lost sister through whom he can be reborn into his more familiar hockey-masked form. The ex-boyfriend of Jason's niece teams with a bounty hunter to stop him after the latter reveals that only a sacred dagger wielded by a Voorhees can *truly* send Jason to hell. By the end credits, the sequel had delivered on the promise of its title with angry demons bursting from the ground to drag Jason down into the underworld.

Jason Goes to Hell opened in second place at the domestic box office with a respectable $7.5 million weekend. The new sequel barely managed to outperform *Jason Takes Manhattan's* opening, yet cost only half of what *Manhattan* did to produce. New Line's promotional campaign went for some of the same marketing tactics that had worked well on *Freddy's Dead* by playing up the supposed finality of this *Final Friday*. Trailers and posters also trumpeted Cunningham's return to the franchise. ("The creator of the first returns to bring you the last!") Ultimately, the sequel achieved a nearly $16 million gross against a $2.5 million budget. Jason may not have been back to peak performance, but ticket sales were holding steady. Of the fourteen films New Line released in 1993, this new Jason outing ranked as their fourth highest-grossing.

The latest *Friday* may have managed to hold its own at the box office, but was no match for the barrage of scathing reviews, some of the worst the series had ever seen. The difference this time around was that they were coming from both critics and *Friday* fans alike, many of whom shunned this new direction. "For me, it was way past an embarrassment," Cunningham candidly shared in Peter Bracke's *Crystal Lake Memories*. "The body-morphing plot—it was a dismal idea. I suspected that early on, but the finished film completely proved it. I made many, many mistakes. Adam came to me and said, '*The last thing the fans want is to see Jason going through Camp Crystal Lake chopping up teenagers again*.' Of course, it was the only thing they wanted to see."

Time has been kind to *Jason Goes to Hell*, however. In the two decades since its release, the film has amassed a cult following of genre fans either discovering or rediscovering it on home video. Numerous critics and bloggers have made compelling cases for revisiting the film. It's even returned to the big screen on occasion with new theatrical screenings.

Despite its mixed-to-negative reception, *Jason Goes to Hell* concluded with a moment that managed to elevate even the most disappointed viewer out of their seat in excitement. The film's final shot zooms in on Jason's weathered mask in the dirt outside the Voorhees mansion. A familiar razor-gloved arm wearing an equally familiar red-and-green sweater bursts from the ground to claim it. This appendage clearly belongs to Freddy Krueger, who cackles menacingly as he drags Jason's mask down to hell. In reality, this arm belonged to returning Jason actor Kane Hodder, giving him the distinction of being the only person to play both Freddy and Jason in the same movie (or period, for that matter).

This may have looked like an in-film advertisement orchestrated by New Line, thought it was not. While the studio had been quietly developing *Freddy vs Jason*, they had no intention of using *Goes to Hell*'s ending as a lead-in to that project. There wasn't even yet a crossover script to lead into. The Freddy cameo came not from New Line's development team, but rather from *Final Friday* director Adam Marcus, who was simply trying to think of another fun in-joke to sneak into his movie. (Props from *Evil Dead II* and *Creepshow* also turn up in *Jason Goes to Hell*.) He pitched the idea to studio executives, who agreed to let him borrow an official *Nightmare* glove for the scene. The tease was approved in large part for being just enough to generate excitement without actually interfering with the direction of the still unwritten *Freddy vs Jason*. It also helped that New Line was able to include Freddy on the cheap without having to bring in Robert Englund.

Trailing the release of *Jason Goes to Hell* by roughly a year, Craven's *New Nightmare* hit theaters just before Halloween 1994 to essentially the opposite reception. The sequel pulled in some of the strongest reviews the franchise had seen in years. In fact, *New Nightmare* stands as the second best reviewed *Elm Street* on Rotten Tomatoes beyond the original, even besting the much loved *Dream Warriors*. The seventh film's warm reception was nowhere more evident than in Roger Ebert's positive notice. Known for savaging even great horror films throughout the years, Ebert gave the sequel three stars, complimenting Craven's "horror film within a horror film" as being "strangely intriguing." Unfortunately, the film's success with critics did not extend to its box office take.

New Nightmare opened toe to toe against *Pulp Fiction* and ultimately lost. Little could anyone have known that Quentin Tarantino's sophomore effort would become the first independent film to top $100 million at the domestic box office. The new Freddy outing grossed just $18 million domestically against a rumored $10 million budget. This meant *New Nightmare* had barely managed to outperform *Jason Goes to Hell* from a year earlier despite being released onto five hundred more screens and boasting a budget three times larger. Much like *Jason Takes Manhattan*, this latest *Nightmare* was simultaneously the biggest budgeted and lowest grossing series entry to date. The perception that these franchises were downward trending had now been reinforced.

MAKE IT GOOD

At long last, the road to *Freddy vs Jason* seemed clear of all obstacles. The necessary rights had all been secured. The titans had taken another lap around the box office and still proved viable. The actors who portrayed them, Robert Englund and Kane Hodder, were game to reprise their roles. Audiences wanted it. Theater owners were begging for it. All that was needed now was the right script, one that could win the joint approval of Michael De Luca and Sean Cunningham.

Many talented writers would submit drafts throughout *Freddy vs Jason*'s development. Some were seasoned horror fans, others not. Some preferred Freddy, others favored Jason. Some came onboard not being a fan of either. Some writers wished to read through the previously rejected screenplays, others did not. Their professional and personal backgrounds were as diverse as the directions they would take the crossover in. Even Wes Craven himself took a fruitless stab at bringing Freddy and Jason together (Craven to TV Guide in '02: "I just couldn't think of a way to do it that wouldn't be laughable.")

To the outside filmmaking world looking in, this was hardly a prestige project. Critics have often ill-regarded slasher films as low hanging creative fruit devoid of merit. To that mindset, combining two slashers into one script could only produce a movie twice as insufferable. One of *Freddy vs Jason*'s own former screenwriters would even deride the project as being "where you go when you admit to yourself that you've exhausted all possibilities," an admission that the franchises were on their "last gasp," but nothing could be farther from the truth. Despite all the cynical assumptions, *Freddy vs Jason*'s filmmakers genuinely wanted to make the best crossover film possible. Dismissing the project as a flagrant studio cash-grab is easy to do, but studio cash-grabs seldom take so long to find a workable screenplay. Such ventures typically rush through every phase of production, quality be damned, whereas *Freddy vs Jason* was the longest-gestating entry into either franchise. This was not a film that spent a decade in development hell due to studio politics or budget disputes, nor did it linger because Robert Englund was simply unavailable. The hold-up revolved entirely around finding a script that would please both De Luca and Cunningham, a wickedly difficult task.

Figuring out the story for *Freddy vs Jason* required careful planning. These were not simply characters from different franchises; they literally existed in different realms. Freddy and Jason operated on different planes of reality, which meant they were subject to different rules. Beyond those basics, there were endless details to consider. Would Freddy show up at Camp Crystal Lake? Or would Jason tromp down to Elm Street? Maybe the monsters would meet somewhere in the middle, but where was that exactly? (Pensylvania separates Ohio from New Jersey, so wouldn't that be Romero country?) And who would the victor be? Both win? Or both lose? Should the crossover feature returning characters or focus on a new cast? What condition are the monsters in at the beginning? How much should *Freddy vs Jason* adhere to existing continuities? Figuring these things out in the right combination constituted a daunting challenge for any screenwriter.

In an industry where success is so often measured by tickets sold, the case of *Freddy vs Jason* is curious. Taking so many years to find the right script demonstrates a level of restraint uncharacteristic of most big movie studios. Cunningham and De Luca could have, at any given point, dismissed their reservations and forged ahead with a random draft and it would have raked in millions. It's not as if the film's box office performance depended upon the script being good. This was *Freddy vs Jason*. Audiences were going to turn out for this fight no matter what. Yet New Line sought not to make just any *Freddy vs Jason*, but the best *Freddy vs Jason*. They were willing to invest both the time and money necessary to make that happen. The studio would spend more on the crossover's development alone than they would on each of the first three *Nightmare*'s.

How many outlines, treatments, and scripts were considered for *Freddy vs Jason* throughout its lengthy development? Too many to possibly count. New Line entertained pitches from scores of prospective screenwriters, not counting the many unsolicited script submissions. For the purposes of guiding this book, let us consider the findings of the Writer's Guild Arbitration Panel, which was tasked with deciding *Freddy vs Jason*'s final screenwriting credits. Officially, the project had sixteen screenwriters from 1993 to 2002, resulting in ten distinct visions for the film. *Slash of the Titans* will examine those ten screenplays with insights from eleven of the original writers, plus comments from cast, producers, directors, executives, and development staff.

NOTICE OF TENTATIVE WRITING CREDITS

Date: January 2, 2003

To: Writers Guild of America, Inc./West, 7000 West Third Street, Los Angeles, California 90048-4329
And
All Participating Writers (or to the current agent if that participant so elects)

NAMES OF PARTICIPATING WRITERS

Lewis Abernathy

Mark Protosevich

Jonathan Aibel
Glenn Berger

Ethan Reiff
Cyrus Voris

Rob Bottin

James Robinson

Brannon Braga

David Schow

Peter Briggs

Damian Shannon
Mark Swift

David S. Goyer

Mark Verheiden

Ronald Moore

Title of Photoplay: *FREDDY VS. JASON*

Executive Producers: Douglas Curtis Robert Shaye Stokely Chaffin Renee Witt

Producer: Sean Cunningham

Director: Ronny Yu

1

The WGA's full listing of *Freddy vs Jason* screenwriters (addresses removed for print).   21

AN ERRONEOUS HISTORY

The public record of *Freddy vs Jason*'s development is one wrought with misinformation. By and large, the project's evolutionary process played out behind closed doors. Although the film garnered numerous mentions in industry publications and genre magazines throughout the '90s, it was much more fervently covered online by websites like *Ain't It Cool News, Dark Horizons,* and *Corona's Coming Attractions.* With the internet still in its infancy, online reporting was not at all then what it is today. As such, phony updates on *Freddy vs Jason's* progress were commonplace. News was often either arrantly bogus or years out of date such as the mention of writers who had long departed the project. Other times, websites would miscredit an older storyline to a newer writer or vice versa. Another sham was that slashers like Michael Myers or Chucky would be joining the fight despite these characters belonging to rival studios. Further untruths included claims that Sean Cunningham sought to direct the match-up (he did not) or that Robert Englund would be executive producing (he expressed no such interest). Although New Line did not publicly respond to such erroneous reporting, Michael De Luca was occasionally known to comment in the talkbacks of *Ain't It Cool* to denounce the most far fetched claims.

There have also been a slew of *supposedly* attached writers and directors, people with no guild affiliation or prior credits of any kind and whom no one I spoke to from New Line can account for. In retrospect, claiming to have written an unused draft of *Freddy vs Jason* as a way of padding your resume might actually have worked, possibly eliciting a '*Who hasn't written an unused draft of Freddy vs Jason?!*' response. Then again, plenty of people have written unused drafts. We call these stories fan fiction, but, technically speaking, they're all unused drafts, aren't they?

Additionally, several established filmmakers found themselves attached to *Freddy vs Jason* despite having no involvement or interest whatsoever. One of these was UK-born effects maker and director Stephen Norrington, who was falsely reported to be helming the monster mash-up. Strangely, the *Blade* filmmaker's involvement with the project is still being reported on his Wikipedia page as of this writing, despite his own attempts to have it expunged from the listing. We cannot exclusively blame the internet for the circulation of bad *Freddy vs Jason* intel, however. Fake developments such as the Norrington story have also appeared in print media. Having said all that, my goal with *Slash of the Titans* is to only publish verified information, preferably sourced from the writers and filmmakers that have contributed to this chronicle. As much as I would love to include a chapter on David Lynch's rumored version of *Freddy vs Jason*, I must refrain since not even *The Onion* would confirm the remote possibility of his involvement.

INTERVIEW: Tom McLoughlin
Screenwriter/Director, *Friday the 13th Part VI: Jason Lives*

DUSTIN MCNEILL: Following *Jason Lives*, did you ever consider coming back to do another one? Or was it one and done?

TOM MCLOUGHLIN: Well, if I was going to do another, I would need to figure out what I could do differently than I did on *Jason Lives*. When I finished that movie, Frank Mancuso asked me if I was interested in doing another one and we kicked around some ideas together. This would have been sometime in 1986. He immediately brought up possibly doing *Freddy vs Jason* and my reaction was to ask how we could possibly work that out? They live in two different universes, but I guess you could find a way to do it. Then again, I was a big Universal Monster fan and I loved the whole notion of a bigger monster franchise like they did back then. So I told him I would think about it and went home. And he later came back to me and said, '*Nope. New Line has no interest in doing this right now.*'

I said, '*Well, if we're still in that school of thought, why not Cheech and Chong meet Jason? Paramount already has those characters!*'; He asked if I was kidding and I told him I was only half-kidding. I thought we might could do what we did with *Jason Lives*. We didn't make fun of Jason in that movie, though we certainly had humor. We would just up the humor and make fun of other things. Mancuso thought that would be too much comedy for the franchise. He felt strongly that fans were still upset over *Part V* not really having Jason in it. He also felt that we had just gotten the series back on track with *Jason Lives*. He said, '*Let's focus more on Jason and less on the comedy.*' So that was it. I tucked the idea way in the back of my head.

DM: You make a good point on how horror and comedy work together. Take *Abbott and Costello Meet Frankenstein*. That movie didn't degrade the monsters by making fun of them. For the most part, the humor was directed elsewhere.

TM: Exactly. So years go by and eventually they started to have discussions again about putting the two characters together. This was sometime in the '90s. I really had no idea what New Line was planning to do with it. My agent at the time said, '*This is something you've got a passion for. You should at least go in and pitch your idea about it.*' Enough time had passed that I thought I could go back in and take the same approach I took with *Jason Lives*. I should also say that I never really saw *Part VI* as a comedy. I just wanted the basic characters to be really likable and have some fun with the genre. I also wanted there to be all types of nods that fans would recognize. You know, have a Carpenter Street or Cunningham Drive. I named Sheriff Garris in that movie after my friend, filmmaker Mick Garris.

At first, I figured I could go in with those same sensibilities, but that something else was still needed. Putting those characters together is a really unusual blend. You've got Jason who exists in the real world and Freddy who exists in the dream realm. I kept thinking you would need a third thing that somehow allows them to come together. But what is that thing?

DM: Not Cheech and Chong?

TM: No, it needed something much darker than that. There was, at that time, a lot of discussion about the effects that horror movies were having on people who were a little off in some way. I had seen a documentary where this kid had killed his friend's mother and when they interviewed him about it, he said he thought he was Jason. He hid behind that identity as a way to commit a horrible act. I thought you could possibly make something of that, maybe set *Freddy vs Jason* in an institution. We could focus on two particularly deranged individuals who have identified so strongly with Freddy and Jason that they become those characters. With that approach, the audience would be constantly questioning what was real and not real. That was interesting to me.

I don't remember who I met with at New Line, but I went in with all my notes to pitch this and got a quick '*No, that's not really where we want to go with it.*' They told me that they already had some idea of where they wanted to go with it. And that's it! One meeting, over and done. My association with *Freddy vs Jason* was just a fun, quick thing back in '85 and then again in the '90s. Looking at the actual movie that came out years later, I think I would've done it very differently than they did it. I would've tried to put that third element into it about the effect of horror movies on certain people and let that become its own kind of reality.

DM: You're into some deep psychological territory with that premise.

TM: Yeah, I thought so. Psychological would be the right word to use, but it's definitely the wrong word to put into the heads of the people you're trying to sell this pitch to. To me, those are the best kinds of horror movies. *The Exorcist, The Others*, we could go down the whole list. Give the audience a chance to figure out the movie in their own heads. That's how you get great cinema. You don't have to spell everything out for people.

DM: That direction is so, so dark. I don't see much room for laughs in that.

TM: No, I would think there would be relatively few laughs in that version of the movie. But that's just where I was at the time. Look at the progression of my body of work. My monsters went from being Freddy, Jason, and Stephen King creations in the early days to AIDS, global warming, serial killers, degradation, alcoholism, and mental illness later on. As my career progressed, the monsters in my movies became very real. I even began to research them. I would have shocking phone conversations with people on death row who had mass murdered or shot children. Their sociopathic way of thinking was that it was all for a very good reason. They would say those terrible things they did were meant to happen. They either felt justified or would claim it didn't happen and have no idea what you're talking about. That's so different from how I grew up, which was to believe that if you did something bad, you would lay awake at night dealing with the guilt from it. For me now as an adult, those people on death row were what scary had become.

I did a film called *Murder of Innocence* with Valerie Bertinelli about this young woman who had literally walked into a school and shot kids. It was a true story. After the incident occurred, there were a number of copycats that happened as a result of that. So then it became a question of when you put that stuff out there, are you giving people the idea to go ahead and do that? I remember after Columbine, anything that even came close to something that might could incite a young person to violence was banned. There was this great film, *Battle Royale*. It's one of my favorites. They completely botched its release because of it.

DM: I'm intrigued by your pitch. It sounds like you would've given a frightening new edge to these slashers.

TM: Well, thanks. I would like to have explored it more. My intention would have been to pull in some of the monsters from society that had been created or fed by these movies. Again, not that these movies cause people to commit violence. I'm not saying that at all. What I am saying is that if you've got a bad flame in you, these movies could be gasoline to that bad flame. It's not something that hasn't been examined in other ways. Look at Wes Craven with *New Nightmare*. He was approaching that territory, but that sequel ultimately went in another direction. Wes was a very smart filmmaker. I wouldn't be trying to copy what he did. I would mostly want to draw influence from my own experiences in looking at art versus real life.

DM: So who wins in your *Freddy vs Jason*? Or do they both lose?

TM: Who wins? I really cannot remember how I had the outcome. I'm thinking that somehow the monsters lived on, but the people that embodied them did not. To me, it would only work if you could challenge the audience to say '*Do you really believe this?*' not unlike a good ghost story.

DM: You did *Jason Lives* first and later on you also directed an episode of *Freddy's Nightmares*. Some might say that uniquely qualifies you to take on *Freddy vs Jason*. You've already worked in both worlds!

TM: Yes, I enjoyed having those bragging rights for a few years. I was one of the only directors to do a Jason piece and a Freddy piece, but I didn't do them just to do them. If I get hired onto something, I want to actually contribute to it and not just make the material as is. I want to process it and put my passion for the genre into it. At any point, *Freddy vs Jason* could have just been two monsters battling it out. You could have done that easily. But I think you'd do better by trying to make something interesting and different, something with a lot of thought behind it.

DM: You mentioned having seen the 2003 film. What was that like for you?

TM: I did go see it when it came out. I went with a bunch of friends, all horror fans. We go out every other month to see these kinds of movies, sort of like our own horror club. With *Freddy vs Jason*, it was hard for me to be objective while watching it because of my history and involvement with these characters. The rest of the guys I went with really enjoyed it just because someone had finally made a Freddy/Jason movie. To them, the big fight sequences were all that really mattered. The audience I saw it with clearly had fun with it.

Honestly, I thought they did a really good job with it. I thought much of it worked, though some of it didn't. I've worked on too many movies to just sit back and go, '*Well that all sucked.*' I can't do that. I know how hard it is to get something like this made. You may start out with a really solid concept, but as it moves forward it becomes an entire committee making the movie and not just you. By the time it winds up on screen, you don't know who made what choices that got into the final product. I will say that it was completely different than what I would've done with it. Still, I think it worked for a lot of people. To me, that's the bottom line. People walked away satisfied. It wasn't as satisfying for me as what I would've loved to have done with it, but I didn't get that opportunity. I can't be bitter about it and I'm not.

INTERVIEW: Adam Marcus
Screenwriter/Director, *Jason Goes to Hell: The Final Friday*

DUSTIN MCNEILL: Right off the bat, I've got to ask how you managed to score *Jason Goes to Hell* as your first writing and directing gig. I really enjoyed that sequel and have always thought it got an unfair shake from critics and fans.

ADAM MARCUS: Thank you for saying that. *Jason Goes to Hell* came about because of a script I'd written with Dean Lorey called *Johnny Zombie*. We had been working on it for years and had full storyboards for it, an entire package. It was the movie I wanted to start my directorial career with. We had written a crazy, over-the-top, super bloody horror film. We even had musical numbers worked into it. We got Sean involved and he immediately wanted a re-write, which we did. We re-wrote it into something we were really proud of and Sean loved it.

Next thing you know, *Johnny Zombie* gets sold to Disney. They love the script, but the problem is… they want us to get rid of the zombies. That's a really big part of the movie! I mean, it's called *Johnny Zombie*! Then they wanted to know if Johnny could seem less dead and more, like, tired. I swear to God, that was a note we got. Immediately, I went to Sean and said *'I'm thrilled to be a producer on this thing, but I'm not directing it. It'll be the beginning and end of my career. They're making it into an early '90s Disney film and it's going to be PG-13. They're neutering it!'* And I think Sean totally understood. He then said to me, *'Look. Paramount is selling the Jason rights to New Line. If you can figure out a way to get that goddamn hockey mask out of it, I'll let you write and direct the next Jason movie instead.'* And that was the beginning of it.

I was twenty-two when that offer came in and I jumped at it. I wrote the first treatment in about seventy-two hours, which was a much darker movie than we ended up making. I went for a creepy, evil, hard-to-watch kind of movie. The original title was *Friday the 13th: Heart of Darkness*, which I know is an incredibly pretentious title. My whole thing was that I was going to be twenty-three when I directed this and Orson Welles was twenty-three when he tried to direct his first feature, which was supposed to be *Heart of Darkness*. And because my movie was about the black heart of Jason Voorhees, I thought it would be a cool title to use.

DM: What caused the tonal shift from your original treatment to the movie you made?

AM: That came out of the process of developing it into a full script and also from studio notes. New Line was awesome throughout the development process, just terrific to work with. My two executives on the picture were Mike De Luca and Mark Ordesky and I've never met more supportive guys in our industry. Through that development process, the movie became *Jason Goes to Hell* as we know it.

DM: Was it a struggle figuring out what to do with Jason after the last film?

AM: By the end of *Jason Takes Manhattan*, we had almost gone full Toxic Avenger with Jason in the sewers. Then he turns into Baby Jason like it's *2001: A Space Odyssey* or something. I still don't know what the hell is going on in that movie. The fans were also told Jason would take Manhattan and he took a boat ride instead. He showed up in Vancouver for fifteen minutes of the

26

movie and then one shot in Times Square, which was a glorious shot. Overall, it was a let down. My thought was that Jason is a character with eight movies on him. By now, the fans are bored. I was bored. *Jason Lives*, to this day, is still my favorite of them all by a landslide. I just think it's incredibly clever and funny as hell. The problem was that Jason then fought Carrie in *New Blood* and went up against the baddest city on the planet in *Takes Manhattan*. Where the hell do you go next? I know there was talk of *Jason Takes Los Angeles*, but I was like no, no, no. *Please no.*

DM: So it's safe to say you're a fan of these movies.

AM: I am an uber-fan of the *Friday* movies. I saw every single one of them in the theater, some of them multiple times. When it came to *Jason Goes to Hell*, I wanted it to be fresh and original. I wanted to treat the fans with the utmost respect. The problem was the only fans who were really left by then were the hardcore Jason freaks. It wasn't a casual horror audience anymore, people that wanted a good scary movie. It was people who really loved Jason Voorhees. I then made a Jason Voorhees movie without a lot of Jason Voorhees in it. Yes, he's technically in it the whole way through in that it's still his black heart going from person to person, but because the hockey mask wasn't in every third scene, suddenly there was a huge problem.

The really funny thing is that when you add up the time that Jason has the hockey mask in my film, it's actually longer than his screen time in most of the other *Friday the 13th* films. That's the real irony. The couple of sequences in my movie where Jason is fully present are actually really long. The ending battle scene? That's a ton of Jason. Plus, I felt that when he finally came back at the end of the film it would be this explosive exciting moment for the audience, that they could cheer his return.

DM: It was that moment, though. That's exactly how it played for me.

AM: That was the idea. But because the people who saw that movie on opening night were mostly hardcore Jason fanatics, they were pissed. It's really a shame because a lot of people thought I was pissing on the franchise. I was doing anything but that! I thought the people who loved this series deserved a different movie. We'd been down those roads before.

DM: It seems to me that, despite its initial reception, *Jason Goes to Hell* has aged really well, not unlike *Halloween III*. I've seen a handful of articles in recent years that suggest people may be coming around to it.

AM: Well, thank you. That's very cool to hear. I've seen those too. Honestly, I'm very proud of *Jason Goes to Hell*. It's unfortunate that I've had more people want to fight me over it than anything else in my life. One guy actually told me I had raped his teen years! And the only response I could think of was, '*You're welcome?*' What do you even say to that? '*I'm sorry I did that, I guess?*' The intention was to embrace the character and give him some mythology, not screw anyone over. Certainly not to rape anyone.

DM: How did you manage to keep your sanity given that kind of feedback?

AM: The good part about *Jason Goes to Hell* was that the internet back then was not what it is now, not by a long shot. So I didn't have to deal with a lot of the hatred live in that moment. If I had to deal with it now with social media, I'd probably have to move to a remote island somewhere. I did go to a lot of conventions that year and it was a completely split thing. There were a ton of people thanking me for the movie. The fact that my movie had more kills than the other ones helped a ton. Greg Nicotero, Bob Kurtzman, and Howard Berger did an unbelievable job on the effects for that film, just extraordinary work. Then also at these conventions, there would be big dudes literally threatening me over the movie. So the response was a mix.

DM: In your mind, was this really going to be *The Final Friday*?

AM: Yeah, in my mind. There was not a lot of talk about *Freddy vs Jason* on our set. There's legend out there that we did have it in mind because of my film's ending, but it's just not true. It's funny. Later on, I actually had to testify in court about the ending where Freddy's glove comes up and grabs Jason's mask. There was a guy suing New Line claiming they stole that idea from his screenplay and gave it to me for *Jason Goes to Hell*. Believe me, nothing could be further from the truth.

I had to show up in court and tell a judge how I came up with that. I was sitting around my apartment one day with my roommates, who were all getting stoned out of their mind, thinking up all of the different in-jokes we could possibly sneak into the film. We came up with the Necronomicon from *Army of Darkness* and the crate from *Creepshow*. And suddenly in the middle of the conversation, I said, '*Wait, doesn't New Line own Freddy outright?*' and my friend is like '*Yeah.*' I said, '*Okay, they've killed Freddy already. He's gone. He would be in hell. If Jason is getting dragged to hell, what better person to do it than Freddy?*' I knew we couldn't afford Robert Englund for the film, but maybe we could still pull it off. I called Ordesky and De Luca and asked them if I could borrow the Freddy glove for the end of the movie. And there was a long pause and they go, '*Why?*' They were very protective of the character. I told them what I wanted to do and they could not have said yes any faster. They were so excited for it.

I specifically remember the moment that ending first screened with a live audience. They leapt to their feet cheering. Both of my executives high-fived right next to me. It was the most '*Oh my God, this is really going to happen,*' moment ever. I knew then that Freddy and Jason would absolutely be in a movie together. I still felt like I had made *The Final Friday*, however, because that movie was going to be *Freddy vs Jason*, not an actual *Friday the 13th*. Plus, I knew that Sean was not a fan of these movies. He's made a lot of money pretending to be a fan, but he's not. He loves the first movie, God bless it, and I totally get why. You have to understand that Sean made an indie potboiler that eventually became a zombie wrestling movie, which is just not who Sean is. It's not. He's very excited for the success of the franchise, but I think he was ready for it to end. I also think he was excited for *Freddy vs Jason* because he was interested in taking the material to a new place and doing new things with the character. Ultimately, I think Sean wants to make movies that are more about characters, mystery, and suspense, not about slaughtering people in increasingly gory ways.

DM: What were your earliest impressions of *Freddy vs Jason*?

AM: The development hell on that project was unbelievable. You've just never seen a slave of so many masters. Dean Lorey and I both looked at possibly doing it, but we immediately saw that it was being developed to death, which is why it took a decade to come out. New Line took so long with it that they risked losing the rights to Jason if they didn't make another movie, which is how *Jason X* came about. I was approached for *Freddy vs Jason*, but New Line was in a very tricky place at that time. Ted Turner had just bought the studio right after *Jason Goes to Hell*. I was in the middle of a deal for *Freddy vs Jason* and it all fell apart because Ted Turner didn't want New Line to do horror anymore. He tried to crush it out of the company and suddenly they were making war epics like *Gettysburg*. It was a weird period for the studio.

I will say that I was interested in doing *Freddy vs Jason*. Dean Lorey and I had talked a lot about what it might look like. Dean had a take on it and I had a different take. But I was lucky not to have gotten involved with it. When you saw the amount of red tape and all the people overdeveloping it, you got weary. It made you step back and go, '*Life's a little too short for this kind of shit.*' And it made you want to move on.

DM: What would have been your direction on the film?

AM: For my money, I wanted the first scene to be Freddy in his environment. Jason shows up and fucks up that environment, much like there's a scene in the movie where that happens. Then suddenly, the floor splits between them and you realize they're in hell. The idea was that both of these guys were hell's assassins. For me, the idea of hell having an assassin that kills teenagers when they've sinned so they go straight to hell was interesting. My movie would've started with hell spitting them both back up to Earth where it becomes a contest between them. I would've brought in Nancy Thompson and Tommy Jarvis as the main characters. I would've also brought back Creighton Duke, who would have survived *Jason Goes to Hell*.

DM: Nancy, Tommy, and Creighton? Sign me up!

AM: Yeah! And the movie is Creighton Duke protecting the two of them from Freddy and Jason. Whoever kills Nancy and Tommy wins the contest and gets to stay on Earth as hell's permanent assassin. The loser of the contest goes straight back to hell. For me, that's a movie the fans would love because we've got both the heroes and the villains of the franchises back. Steven Williams is so fuckin' badass as Creighton Duke. I would've loved to see him team up with Heather Langenkamp and Corey Feldman. The other cool thing is that anytime Freddy or Jason got close to killing Nancy or Tommy, the other killer has to stop them from doing it because they want the kill.

DM: I don't think anyone would've wanted to fight you over that story. That's a really interesting premise.

AM: I would hope not! It would've been a total love letter to the fans. That's what is so frustrating with *Jason Goes to Hell* because it was for the fans by the fans. And I meant it. Had I been involved in *Freddy vs Jason,* that would've been the same deal. I wanted to see the heroes of *Elm Street* and *Friday the 13th* have go up against the maniacs.

Chapter Two
The Abernathy/Schow Drafts

1993

THE SCREENWRITER

The first screenwriter to tackle *Freddy vs Jason* is a subject as interesting as the project itself. The film's foremost scribe was Lewis Abernathy, a man of many talents and interests. Who is Lewis Abernathy? For starters, he is variously an actor, writer, script doctor, director, effects maker, private investigator, surveillance expert, treasure hunter, armorer, weapons manufacturer, and deep ocean explorer. We know him best as the mind behind the unrealized *Nightmare 13: Freddy Meets Jason* screenplay, which he wrote in 1993 following the release of *Jason Goes to Hell*. His work as an uncredited script doctor on that sequel led filmmakers to name James Gleason's SWAT character after him (Agent Abernathy). This nod is particularly fitting since it was the screenwriter's own prop-weapons company, Reel Guns Inc., that armed the cast to kill Jason in that film's opening raid on Camp Crystal Lake.

Within the world of horror, Abernathy's work has mostly been on projects involving Sean Cunningham in some capacity. He co-wrote the Cunningham-directed *DeepStar Six* before writing and directing *House IV*, which featured Kane Hodder in an uncredited role as a talking anchovy pizza. (If you're unfamiliar with this franchise, that should be all the recommendation you need.) He would later pen the Cunningham-directed *Terminal Invasion* starring Bruce Campbell. Even if you somehow missed those films, chances are good that you have still seen Abernathy's work and simply not realized it. He is recognized as having turned in the first draft of *Titanic* for longtime pal James Cameron. Although not a credited writer on the final film, Abernathy was given a featured role by Cameron. He played the part of Lewis Bodine, the bearded researcher on Bill Paxton's team that co-interviews Gloria Stuart's Old Rose throughout the film. You may more specifically recall him asking "So what happened next?" immediately following Rose's nude portrait session with Jack.

But wait, it gets even weirder! Abernathy is *also* officially acknowledged as having inspired several parts of cult-favorite *The Big Lebowski,* not the least of which was John Goodman's character. According to the book, *I'm a Lebowski, You're a Lebowski*, Abernathy was one third of the inspiration for Goodman's Walter Sobchak. Scenes involving Jeff Bridges' The Dude and Walter tracking down a high school student from homework left behind in a stolen car were lifted wholesale from Abernathy's actual life. He was also once struck by a police officer with a coffee mug during his private investigator days. Friend and filmmaker Peter Exline shared these stories with the Cohen Brothers, who then adapted them into their film unbeknownst to Abernathy himself.

Getting back to *Nightmare 13*, Abernathy originally sought to direct the crossover sequel from his own script. But with only one feature credit to his name, even he recognized himself as an unlikely candidate for the job. To his credit, the screenwriter's bid to direct the sequel was endorsed by James Cameron, who reportedly met with Michael De Luca at New Line on his friend's behalf. Even so, this impressive endorsement failed to secure Abernathy the gig.

THE PLOT

Nightmare 13 begins with a psychotic cult of Freddy worshippers setting out to resurrect their idol. The cult's plan involves kidnapping and impregnating a virgin bride through whom their master can be reborn. When thirteen-year-old Lizzie is abducted for this purpose, getting her back safely falls to big sister Meagan and her friends. This leads them to an incarcerated ex-cult member who suggests they resurrect the fearless Jason Voorhees to defeat Freddy and his cult. Meanwhile, a deranged state trooper trails closely behind both groups. All parties eventually converge upon a televangelism studio for an explosive showdown between Freddy, Jason, the teenaged heroes, the state police, and the cultists.

With regard to *Freddy vs Jason*'s development history, the importance of this first stab cannot be overstated. Although New Line would ultimately reject Abernathy's take, his script would go on to influence many of the drafts that would follow after it. Curiously, that influence would extend just short of the final script draft that became the 2003 film. Abernathy's vision for *Freddy vs Jason* represents ground zero for the project, meaning the ideas in his script are entirely his own. As we will see, few drafts throughout the crossover's development were this original, often recycling one or more elements from previous iterations.

Taking into consideration the writer's background and interests, *Nightmare 13* plays out exactly as you might expect it to. Abernathy's story is chock full of dark humor and explosive action. His script seems to be keenly aware of its own absurdity and, as a result, never takes itself too seriously. That *Nightmare 13* is the most comedic take on *Freddy vs Jason* likely owes to the fact that it was written before *Wes Craven's New Nightmare* reoriented Freddy back to dark and scary. Here the character continues on in the campy tradition of *Dream Child* and *Freddy's Dead*.

In Abernathy's take, the true winner is neither Freddy nor Jason, but rather the visual effects teams. The writer's penchant for such effects is most evident in his writing. If realized, this draft would have given visual artists ample opportunity to wreak all kinds of gory havoc. Equally evident is the screenwriter's affection for high-powered weaponry. His script begins and ends with massive firefights between the cultists and law enforcement. Such an approach seems to reason that a horror movie with twice the monsters ought to have twice the blood, bullets, and bodies and this script certainly does.

Nightmare 13's efforts to intertwine *Elm Street* and *Friday the 13th* begin on its very first page. The opening nightmare sequence turns up the familiar Freddy chant, which dissolves into Harry Manfredini's equally familiar "Ki, Ki, Ki, Ma, Ma, Ma." The 2003 film would combine these iconic themes even sooner than the first script page, blending them before the opening New Line Cinema logo faded to black.

THE HUMANS

This story's rebellious teenage heroine is Meagan, who we learn has been suffering from Freddy nightmares. She feels protective of her developmentally disabled younger sister, Lizzie, whom the cult kidnaps for their nefarious purposes. Meagan's boyfriend is Jesse ("There is no Jesse!" anyone?), who faithfully aids in her rescue mission. Also along for the ride is her best friend and nonconformist oddball, Stormie, whose latest phase is man-hating militant feminist. ("What's it fuckin' to ya?")

In order to defeat Freddy and the cult, Meagan's group springs ex-member Erwin Kelper from prison. Haunted and hyper-paranoid, he is well aware that his unceremonious exit from the cult constitutes a major betrayal, setting up an unpleasant reunion with his former master later on. ("Well, well, well… if it isn't my ol' pal, Erwin!") He becomes instrumental to the group's mission, divulging cult secrets and masterminding a plan to resurrect Jason to fight Freddy.

The *Friday* and *Elm Street* franchises have historically been light on secondary villains. Sure, the goals of authority figures such as parents, teachers, and law enforcement have sometimes been counter to those of our protagonists, but there have been few actual secondary nasties. *Nightmare 13* introduces additional threats on both sides of the titular conflict.

On the *Elm Street* side, we have the Freddy worshippers (more commonly known as the Fred-heads, though Abernathy's script does not call them this), intent on resurrecting their master. This plot turn was barely a year shy of *Halloween*'s masked maniac getting his own cult storyline in the Daniel Farrands-scripted *Halloween: The Curse of Michael Myers*. Not to be left out of the fun, Jason would later slash through his own cult in Scott Phillips' novel, *Friday the 13th: Church of the Divine Psychopath*. Visually, the cultists appear about as you would expect. Dirty-looking red/green sweaters and brown fedoras cover their burn-scarred flesh. In a bit of science-fiction, Abernathy writes that the cult keeps in constant contact with Freddy through the use of narcotics ("dream dope") and what appear to be light-up sunglasses. The red flashing lenses simulate a "sustained ocular input that causes your brain to resonate at approximately the same frequency" as the dream state. In what may have been an effort to keep the cult from competing with Freddy's screen presence, the script does not specify a leader or hierarchy as later *Freddy vs Jason* scripts would.

The cult's plan, as revealed in a blood-scrawled note to reporters, is to impregnate a virgin bride from which a soulless child will be born - a vessel for Freddy's return. This seems to mark their end of their scheme. From there, "Freddy will rise and rule the darkness forever," seemingly imbued with his dream powers in the real world. Thinking ahead, you have to wonder if he would emerge from the womb an infant and take two decades to mature into an adult or if he would pop out five-foot-ten and fully dressed à la Jason at the end of *Goes to Hell*. If the answer was the former, the protagonists might have had several years to find the cultists and kill baby-Freddy before he was even potty-trained. Sequel, anyone?

On the *Friday* side of things, we have a deranged state trooper rumored to be the only law enforcement officer to ever survive a Jason encounter. Harsh judge, swift jury, and eager executioner, Captain Renton Murdoch has no qualms about killing anyone he deems a "punk," even if that someone is a child. The script tells that he was not always this way, rather that his fateful encounter cost him more than half his brain. A metal plate is all that keeps his remaining mind-matter from dripping out. Ever since the incident, he has been a merciless proponent of lethal injustice and, as the script notes, he went from voting Democrat to straight-ticket Republican. (Might equating brain trauma with voting Republican constitute a political statement?)

These secondary threats affect our perceptions of Freddy and Jason differently. The cultists are aligned with Freddy and therefore serve to enhance his overall threat. Captain Murdoch, however, is out to kill practically everyone. This results in some audience sympathies going toward Jason despite him having made this new madman.

THE TITANS: JASON VOORHEES

Abernathy's story finds a heartless Jason resting in pieces at Eternal Peace Cemetery. You may wonder how he went from being dragged into hell to being buried in his old resting spot, but reconsider the events of *Jason Goes to Hell*. Yes, we did see him pulled into the underworld, but that was the reborn Jason. What of the earlier Jason that got blown apart by the SWAT team? His exploded remains were taken to the coroner's office where his heart was devoured by a morgue attendant. Presumably, this dismembered corpse would have been buried following autopsy. Since *Nightmare 13* finds the titan in pieces and without a heart, it stands to reason that Abernathy's Jason is not the regenerated slasher from the ending of *Goes to Hell*, but rather the classic version as obliterated in that film's opening moments. How's that for precision continuity?

Nightmare 13 puts forth a reinvention of the titan for its storytelling purposes. This depiction is decidedly different from both the cold, silent slasher of the Paramount sequels and the body-hopping snake demon of *Goes to Hell*. Instead, Jason is presented as a misunderstood anti-hero. Like most screenwriters that would follow after, Abernathy charges that, while Jason is indeed evil, he is arguably *less evil* than Freddy and therefore someone the audience can root for. One of this draft's biggest changes to the slasher involves modifying his tragic roots so as to establish a new motive for all those years of killing. As Erwin tells it, Jason is "looking for revenge on the camp counselor that murdered him as a child," and going about that by "hacking through every teenager he finds until he gets the right one." So, whereas we previously thought Jason drowned as a child, we now know he was actually murdered. But by whom? Can you guess?

As for why the heroes should want to resurrect him in the first place, Erwin explains that Jason will ultimately succeed against Freddy where others can only fail. He argues that Jason is someone without fear, making him "the perfect dream warrior." Since Freddy's power is derived from the fear of the dreamer, he will - in theory - have no advantage over Jason. Not all *Freddy vs Jason* scripts would characterize the hockey-masked titan as being without fear. The script that would become the 2003 film, for example, gave the character a childhood-rooted fear of drowning, but that's a complicated controversy for another chapter.

Visually, the Jason of *Nightmare 13* is overhauled for what may be his most grotesque appearance yet. The heroes reassemble his corpse using "barbed wire and fishing line," reinforcing limbs with steel braces. As the script notes, "Jason looks nineties and butch." Yet there is still the matter of his missing heart. To this end, Meagan breaks into the Springwood City Morgue to locate her recently slain boyfriend. She personally retrieves his heart to use in reviving Jason, no doubt risking her own sanity in the process of this surgical errand. The heroes electrocute the titan back to life in a wonderfully *Frankenstein-*esque sequence. Like the Fred-heads, the concept of Jason's revival-via-dead-character's-ticker would resurface throughout subsequent drafts.

Once on his feet, Jason chases the heroes around the dilapidated campgrounds. Meagan yells for the titan to stop his attack, which - surprisingly - he does. She then briskly argues that he should spare them since it was they who revived him. Taking this a beat further, she proposes a deal with the hulking butcher: if he helps them kill Freddy Krueger, they will then help him find his own killer so that he may finally exact a long overdue revenge (two birds with one stone, though they don't yet know this). Jason extends his hand to shake on the agreement and a bizarre alliance is formed. Going forward, the titan is squarely on their side. He offers them protection, communicates nonverbally and even chauffeurs Erwin around in a stolen ambulance. (Who taught Jason to drive, you ask? Likely the same patient soul who taught Michael Myers in *Halloween*.)

Truth be told, the biggest issue concerning Jason in *Nightmare 13* is not in his modified characterization or driving ability, but rather in how pitifully little screentime he receives as a title character. The titan is revived on page seventy-one and dead again in less than forty pages. He is essentially resurrected at the second act's conclusion only to drive straight to the televangelism studio for the finale. In Abernathy's defense, his script is incredibly lean and tightly paced, though *Friday* fans would surely have wanted more than this.

THE TITANS: FREDDY KRUEGER

According to Abernathy's script, the ending of *Freddy's Dead* would not have totally destroyed the titan, only badly weakened him. As this story begins, Freddy can still haunt dreams, but is incapable of affecting any real harm upon the dreamer. Erwin reveals he will remain powerless until reunited with the dream demons that left him at the end of the last sequel. Unfortunately for the heroes, this revelation occurs one scene prior to said reunion. To bring back Freddy, the cultists pour the demons into his charred skull, which they have exhumed from Springwood Auto Yard. In a fantastic sequence that begs for stop-motion attention, the scene direction reads: "Close on Freddy's remains as the dream demons swim around inside his skull. His bones start to bleed, blood becoming arteries and veins, vessels becoming muscle, muscle growing scarred flesh."

After a flash of light, a fully-realized Freddy leaps from the pit to greet his followers. His first line upon resurrection is "Smokin'!" which channels Jim Carrey's *The Mask*. Oddly enough, *Mask* scribe Mark Verheiden would later pen his own take on *Freddy vs Jason* as we will examine in Chapter Eight. In another note of trivia, the 1994 fantasy-comedy was helmed by filmmaker Chuck Russell, whose directorial debut was none other than *A Nightmare on Elm Street 3: Dream Warriors*.

You might expect a screenwriter with such close ties to *Friday the 13th* to favor Jason, but this is not the case. The dream slasher and his followers actually take up a lion's share of the screenplay. Whereas Abernathy creates new mythology for Jason, he mostly sticks to existing lore for Freddy. The same old dream rules apply and he remains the most vile soul you could ever imagine. The script does clarify Freddy's relationship with the dream demons via Erwin's insider knowledge: "Freddy made a pact with Satan when he died, so Satan bestowed upon him the dream demons. They're the source of Freddy's power to manipulate our reality. Without them, he's nothing more than a bad dream."

The standard power dynamics still apply in *Nightmare 13* - Freddy is strongest in the dream world and most vulnerable in the real world. The notion that you can only kill a bad dream when it is no longer a dream remains in play, meaning Freddy must be pulled out of the dreamscape in order to be hurt. Yet as we have seen time and time again, this merely vanquishes him back into the dream world. Erwin does suggest a possible way to kill Freddy *for good*, though he is unsure of its effectiveness. Per the rumor, you can permanently destroy Freddy if you shoot him with silver bullets blessed by a priest. Before you roll your eyes, note Erwin's defense: "Hey, they're not my rules. Somebody else wrote 'em."

HALLOWED GROUND

Nightmare 13 would have assuredly pleased fans of both franchises with its pilgrimage back to classic locations we have long known. The only catch is that the script obliterates the two most iconic venues from each story. We are talking *Amityville 3-D/Halloween Resurrection* levels of fiery landmark destruction here. Make no mistake, *Nightmare 13* is playing for keeps.

Following Meagan's opening nightmare, the script travels to a rundown 1428 Elm Street where Freddy's followers have barricaded themselves inside. As a SWAT team storms the house, the cultists set fire to the ground floor with molotov cocktails. A moment later, they detonate a bomb in the basement, causing the burning structure to then explode. Fortunately for the cult, the remaining membership escape through a secret subterranean passageway beneath the house (speaking of *Halloween Resurrection*). This early scene marks the first and only appearance of Elm Street in this version of the crossover. At scene's end, the house at 1428 is still ablaze.

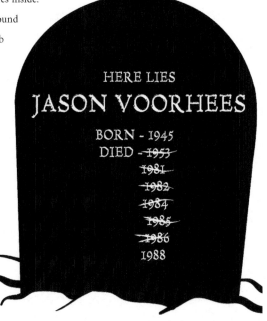

Abernathy's script also makes a return trip to an abandoned Camp Crystal Lake, which is where the heroes transport Jason's blown-apart remains to be reassembled and reanimated. The hockey-masked titan spends little time here, however, as Captain Murdoch calls in an airstrike on the area. More specifically, he orders a military jet to drop a laser-guided napalm bomb on the campgrounds.

Nightmare 13 also ventures back to Eternal Peace Cemetery, which fans should recognize from *Jason Lives* as where Tommy Jarvis accidentally resurrects his tormentor. In a fun gag, Jason's headstone has one "Born" date but lists an unfortunate series of "Died" dates, all but one scratched through for the many times he has required reburial. Naturally, these dates correspond with the release years of the *Friday the 13th* films excepting the original. Continuity sticklers would have surely wondered why 1985 is listed since Jason is assumed dead and buried between the events of 1984's *The Final Chapter* and 1986's *Jason Lives*, but this is still a nice touch.

DREAMS/NIGHTMARES

The overall tone of any given *Elm Street* outing is often dictated by its nightmare scenes. Such sequences are also responsible for defining Freddy's threat from film to film. In the Abernathy draft, the nightmares start out fairly dark but grow increasingly outlandish with each new dream. By script's end, they are dripping with camp and slapstick. The same is true of Freddy.

The script begins with a nightmare set inside a creepy dreamscape version of 1428 Elm Street. As Meagan approaches, she spots the familiar Elm Street Quartet jumping rope out front to their favorite tune. With each new verse, scenes from the corresponding *Nightmare* films flash onscreen, meaning "3, 4, better lock your door," conjures images from *Dream Warriors, Dream Master,* and so on. For a crossover script not overly concerned with what has come before, this is a fun hat-tip to the previous films. Inside, Meagan finds a "Nightmare Chapel" where she is to be wed to Freddy, who is decked out in his best tuxedo. The scene is macabre; the bridal party in bodybags and the pews full of decaying witnesses. She flees into Jesse's arms, who turns out to be Jason. This foreshadows Meagan using her dead boyfriend's heart to resurrect ol' hockey mask after Freddy kills her beau.

The kookiest dreams are reserved for those closest to Meagan - Jesse and Stormie. The former dreams he is a sheriff in the old west about to pistol-duel Freddy, who resembles the famed outlaw Black Bart. Quivering with fear, Jesse quickdraws, emptying a sidearm into his opponent. In return, Freddy pulls out "the biggest goddamn gun you ever saw" before quipping, "Go ahead. Make my dream!" He fires on Jesse, killing him instantly. ("This nightmare ain't big enough for the two of us!")

Stormie confronts Freddy with much greater confidence. She warns him that countless hours of watching television violence have made her incapable of being grossed out, daring Freddy to try his worst. He counter-dares her to punch him in the nose, which she does. The titan snorts as her punch connects, inhaling a micro-sized Stormie into his nostril cavern. Here she encounters the obnoxious "Boogerman," whom the script notes appears like a disgusting green version of Jabba the Hutt. They battle, though Freddy soon tires of this back-and-forth and sneezes, splattering Stormie's corpse across a wall.

Much of the criticism levelled at *Nightmare 13* has focused upon Abernathy's depiction of Freddy and the resulting nightmares. While these do far more evoke the punster who hosted MTV rather than the boogeyman who terrorized Nancy Thompson, we ought not entirely fault the screenwriter for this. Let us not pretend, even for a moment, that Abernathy took the *Elm Street* series into some weird, unfamiliar place with these campy kills; he did not. The character spoofing Clint Eastwood here is certainly no worse than him donning drag as the Wicked Witch in the last sequel.

This material might have felt like a natural progression coming off of *Dream Child* and *Freddy's Dead*. Looking back at *Nightmare 13* through the lens of *Wes Craven's New Nightmare* makes for a different perspective. If we are being honest with ourselves, Freddy's slow descent from nightmare figure to pop culture clown began around the time of *Dream Warriors*.

One sequel later he was hosting music video marathons and promoting his own 1-900 number. Any subsequent team of filmmakers could have steered the franchise back toward scary, but none opted to. This is how we wound up with Freddy stealing from the Wile E. Coyote playbook in *Final Nightmare* by rolling a giant bed of spikes onto a roadway.

Keep in mind that Abernathy was the only screenwriter in *Freddy vs Jason* history to draft his version prior to the existence of *New Nightmare*. That entry effectively reversed four movies of gradually increasing camp, returning the titan to his more straight-faced horror roots. One could argue that Craven's meta-sequel paved the way for future writers to re-envision the character as they saw fit, campy, frightening, or somewhere inbetween. Judging by this script, we can see that Abernathy simply embraced Freddy where he was at the time.

BLENDING BACKSTORIES

Nightmare 13 expands upon the mythologies of Freddy and Jason by intertwining their backstories, reshaping long revered story material in the process. This was arguably Abernathy's riskiest move. At best, it would have upped the stakes of the current conflict. At worst, it would have seriously alienated longtime fans. Curiously, the next eight drafts of *Freddy vs Jason* would also attempt to combine backstories, though in varying ways. Abernathy's biggest twist is the revelation that young Jason's infamous drowning at Crystal Lake was not accidental, but an intentional act of murder. As the heroes zap the titan back to life, he remembers the details of his death. This vision ends with a distorted look at whomever is forcing him underwater, the killer's identity unknown. Later on during the final battle, Freddy tries to drown Jason in much the same way, triggering another flashback. This time, Jason is able to identify his killer... who is none other than thirteen-year-old Freddy!

In stark contrast to the wacky dream sequences, the initial flashback to Jason's childhood stands as the darkest material in the script, finally showing what other *Friday's* have only tiptoed around. As you might expect, we are shown that Jason's upbringing was an ugly one. The scene finds Mrs. Voorhees interrupting her husband as he prepares to rape their son in what appears to be a disgusting tradition. Handing her son a jar of money, she instructs him to hurry along to the nearby summer camp. Furious, Mr. Voorhees turns his anger upon his wife. No longer a victim, she brutally stabs him to death within earshot of her fleeing son. *Nightmare 13* profoundly deepens the tragedy of Jason's childhood death by setting up Camp Crystal Lake as a safe haven for the boy. The other kids may have been there for a fun summer experience, but Jason was simply escaping the hell of an abusive homelife. This further strengthens the case for Pamela Voorhees' descent into madness following her son's drowning. In a desperate attempt to save her only child, she unwittingly sent him away to his death.

Abernathy was not the first writer to consider incorporating Jason's father into the mythology, only the most recent. Named Elias, he initially featured into the script of *Jason Lives,* though he was ultimately cut from the film. In a deleted ending, a well-dressed and formidable Elias shows up to visit Jason's grave at Eternal Peace, only to find it empty. The character was briefly mentioned in *Jason Goes to Hell*, nearly appearing in that sequel as portrayed by Kane Hodder. *Nightmare 13* takes an alternate approach to the Voorhees patriarch as a vile, drunken hillbilly who abuses and sodomizes Jason, challenging Freddy for the title of sickest character in the story. Elias would next appear in the 1995 Topps Comics series *Jason vs Leatherface* in a depiction consistent with Abernathy's. Here he again abuses young Jason and here again Pamela (erroneously named Doris) stops him with a machete to the skull. One slight concern with Abernathy's backstory is that Pamela is in no way implied to be the camp cook, instead referencing it to Jason as "that camp up the road."

The Abernathy draft also suggests a new origin for Jason's iconic hockey mask, previously introduced as a random acquisition in *Friday the 13th: Part III*. This new story contextualizes it as something young Jason was forced to wear by his father ("What did I teach you, boy? Don't ever take your mask off out in public. I don't want nobody to see that ugly mug of yours.") This does not negate the mask's re-introduction in *Part III* and may actually lend some motive as to why Jason would take it in the first place, be it instinct or bizarre nostalgia.

The backstory of Freddy attending Camp Crystal Lake is not overtly contradictory to the character's origins. It is entirely possible that Mr. Underwood, his adoptive father and abuser from *Freddy's Dead*, may have wanted to be free of his son for a spell or that Freddy was able to scrounge up enough money to escape his adopted father for the summer.

CALLBACKS

For longtime Freddy and Jason fans, the Abernathy draft packs a few winks and nods that serve nicely as connective tissue to the past. In the absence of returning characters, such callbacks are welcome. On the *Elm Street* side, the script opens with a double nightmare fake-out just as *Dream Warriors* did previously. The chest-of-souls gag from *Dream Master* also appears in the opening while the original *Nightmare*'s tongue-through-the-phone gag shows up for the final scene. Meagan's mother is later shown to have a drinking problem that recalls Marge Thompson's alcoholism from Craven's original film.

As previously mentioned, *Nightmare 13* opts to include a more recent addition to Freddy's mythology, one that most crossover scripts would rather sidestep - the dream demons from *Freddy's Dead*. Although arguably one of the hokier elements from that film, the demons are made more tolerable here by Abernathy's decision to render them mute. They also don't free-float through space or pop out in 3-D, which further helps their appearance.

The screenwriter tips his hat to early *Friday* outings with *Nightmare 13*'s own prophet of doom, conjuring memories of Crazy Ralph from the first two *Friday the 13th* movies. Abernathy calls this character "Crazy Coot," though his function remains the same - to ominously warn those who would dare mess around in Jason country. We can safely assume the naming of Deputy Miller, subordinate to Captain Murdoch, was no coincidence, but a tribute to *Friday* co-creator Victor Miller.

THE NIGHTMARE ARENA

Near script's end, the cultists take over televangelism studio WGOD where they plan to live broadcast an unholy marriage ceremony uniting Freddy with a now brainwashed Lizzie. The studio is soon converged upon by Jason, the teenage heroes and the state police for a violent showdown. Seeing Jason in action, a spooked Freddy hastily retreats into the dreamscape with Meagan and Lizzie, closing the portal behind him. Thinking fast, Erwin double-injects Jason with dream dope so that he can follow after them. The titan stumbles forward before literally *falling* asleep, landing in what the script calls the "Nightmare Arena." Had *Nightmare 13* been realized, this would have been the sequence still being talked about today.

Abernathy describes the Nightmare Arena as a boxing ring from hell with ropes made of entrails and corner-posts topped by severed heads. Demons, monsters, and zombies comprise the uproarious crowd. Real-life serial killer Ted Bundy steps forward as the announcer, dubbing this the "fight of the century." The crowd cheers Freddy's entrance, but boos Jason. Bundy declares that the winner will get Meagan and Lizzie, who hang caged above the ring. Among the spectators are infamous figures from history such as Lee Harvey Oswald, Adolf Hitler, Eva Braun, and Benito Mussolini.

The match begins with Freddy easily overpowering Jason, who is unable to connect a single punch. One missed blow decapitates Bundy, whose head goes flying off into the audience who then devour it. Jason eventually gets the upperhand at which time Freddy downs a rotten can of spinach (a hearty blend of worms and maggots) in a foul parody of Popeye. His arms and chest rapidly expand. Freddy then pulverizes his opponent, driving him into the ring floor, even beneath it. With his head forced under the mat, Jason begins to drown in the dark abyss. He once again flashes back to his adolescent death and suddenly realizes his killer then and now are one and the same. The titan explodes up through the mat, grabbing Freddy by the throat. Their tremendous upward momentum propels them through the arena ceiling and back to reality inside the WGOD studio.

THE ENDING

Back in reality, Jason immediately throws his opponent to the ground. Freddy only manages two words ("Oh shit.") before Jason stomps a boot onto his face, "squashing it like a tomato." The dream demons crawl out from their host's open skull. Outside, the cultists are engaged in a shootout with state police. With Freddy's defeat, their heads implode and they fall dead to the ground. The demons slither into an open media cable, which causes Freddy's laughing visage to fill every studio monitor. Erwin figures that he is attempting to uplink himself to a broadcast satellite, the ramifications of which would apparently be disastrous. The heroes manage to re-direct the satellite dish toward the sun at the last moment, causing the beam to disintegrate from the intense heat. For now, Freddy appears defeated.

This might have been a happier ending had the cult's demise not cleared the way for Captain Murdoch to charge the studio. Finding Jason and the heroes inside, he opens fire, killing Erwin instantly. Just before Murdoch shoots Meagan, Jason grabs the deranged trooper by the pants, lifting him off the ground. (The script calls this a "Jason-wedgy.") The titan then "jerks the shotgun from Murdoch's hand and jams it up his ass, right through the seat of his pants. Murdoch's cheeks bulge out as the muzzle slams into the roof of his mouth. Jason cocks the shotgun and...BOOM!" An over-the-top death for a larger-than-life villain.

As the SWAT team storms WGOD, Jason is obliterated in a hailstorm of bullets. Falling back, he reaches into his wounded chest cavity and tears out his newly transplanted heart, handing it to Meagan. As he dies, she begins to weep. Jason has now exacted revenge upon the one responsible for setting his entire wretched existence into motion. Maybe now he can truly rest in peace, his own reign of terror ended. Except... *Freddy lives!* The next scene finds Meagan and Lizzie back home safely. The phone rings and a familiar tongue slithers out. ("I'll be seeing you in your dreams!") As she hangs up, we see Erwin's silver-bullet-loaded-pistol under her pillow. She smiles. The phone rings again and cut to black. Roll credits.

In a weird way, *Nightmare 13* ends almost exactly where it begins. Jason is once again dead and Freddy is still haunting Meagan's dreams. Is she able to shoot him in the dreamscape? Does Erwin's theory hold up? We have no idea. How then are we to judge the winner of this battle royal? Sure, Jason manages to stop the dream slasher from enacting his evil plan, but only one titan lives on as the credits roll - Freddy. And does that fact negate Jason's newfound peace? Or did this one-time smackdown serve as justice for Freddy's crime against Jason? In this writer's opinion, Krueger wins.

CONCEPT ART: THE NIGHTMARE-MOBILE

One of the wilder moments in *Nightmare 13* involves an attack on the heroes by both Freddy and Jason in a sequence that doubles as a high-speed car chase. The scene unfolds as the teens are en route to Crystal Lake with Jason's bagged remains in the back. The dream slasher pulls up behind them in "The Nightmare-mobile," which is everything you might expect from a Freddy-inspired roadster. With circular-saws and "big chrome pipes belching hellfire," the Nightmare-mobile launches an all-out assault on Jesse's car. ("Shouldn't dream and drive.") The teens are so busy warding off Freddy's attack that they fail to notice Jason's severed limbs coming to life in the backseat. His parts then start their own attack, choking and kicking the heroes. Jason's entrails even snake around Erwin and Stormie, trapping them. As Jason's boot floors the gas pedal, Freddy manages to pop Jesse's tire, sending their car careening into a tree, ending the nightmare. The heroes wake badly injured.

As seen below and across the next two pages, Abernathy sketched out several designs for the Nightmare-mobile, basing its look off a 1957 Cadillac Eldorado Biarritz. The vehicle's interior includes a ghastly mash-up of bone, teeth, and skin. In an amusing touch, the writer depicts four severed heads atop the car's light-rack. From the artwork, we can see that these heads belong to Robert Shaye, Michael De Luca, Sean Cunningham, and Abernathy himself.

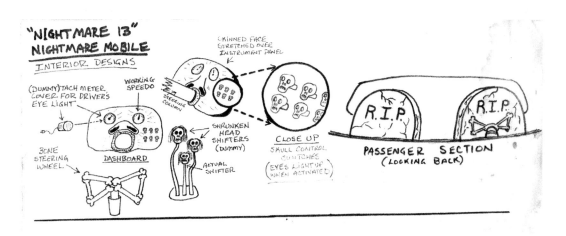

(Artwork courtesy Lewis Abernathy)

1957 CADILLAC ELDORADO BIARRITZ

"NIGHTMARE 13"
NIGHTMARE MOBILE

HEADLIGHT EYELIDS NARROW

ALTERNATING RED/AMBER LIGHTS

TEETH IN GRILL MOVE UP & DOWN

ROTATING DRILLS IN BUMPER BULLETS

SECRET PANEL REPLACE TURN SIGNAL

CHROME PIPE COVER

CHROME ELBOW

TO GAS

TRANSLUCENT INTESTINES

RUNNER LIGHTS

© 1995 LEWIS ABERNATHY

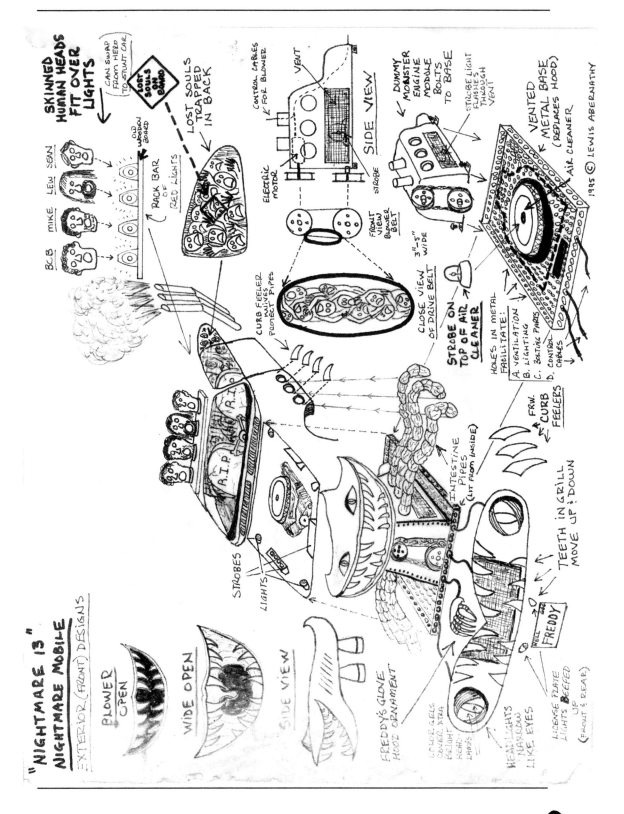

THE SCHOW RE-WRITE

Several years after passing on the Abernathy draft, New Line reconsidered some of *Nightmare 13*'s concepts by way of having famed splatterpunk author David J. Schow rewrite the script. No stranger to the world of *Elm Street*, Schow's first credited screenwriting gig was on a 1989 episode of *Freddy's Nightmares*. That same year also saw him pitch an original treatment for *Nightmare 5* called *Freddy Rules*. Although this failed to win over New Line, it did impress them enough to earn him a job polishing dialogue on the eventually selected *Nightmare 5* script titled *The Dream Child*. Unfortunately, practically none of Schow's material made it into the final film. He would follow this up with screenplays to *Leatherface: Texas Chainsaw Massacre III, Critters 3/4,* and *The Crow.*

"*Freddy vs Jason* was the easiest screenwriting job I ever got," Schow told author Peter Bracke in *Crystal Lake Memories*. "I just happened to be in New Line's offices one day, and literally I got this job with Mike De Luca looking up at me and saying, '*You want to take a crack at this?*'"

Dated February '96, Schow's rewrite was called *Freddy vs Jason: Friday the 13th: Hearts of Darkness,* which was not exactly the most marquee-friendly title. Had this version been greenlit, it would most likely have been shortened to simply *Freddy vs Jason: Hearts of Darkness* since, at the time, Paramount still held rights to the *Friday the 13th* brandname. Schow's rewrite reigned in some of the campier elements from the original script, taking Abernathy's vision in a much darker direction. The Freddy cult, now officially referred to as the Fred-heads, were also given greater prominence in this version of the story. The group was bestowed with a leader named Dominik Cochran, who served as a link to their master. Another change from *Nightmare 13* was that final girl Meagan was renamed to Michelle. Sibling Lizzie is also no longer a special needs child, though she is still captured by the cult early on for the purposes of marrying Freddy.

Jason's role was also expanded in the rewrite, though his function as a means to defeat Freddy remained the same. The teenage heroes do not find him at Eternal Peace Cemetery this time around, but instead at the bottom of Crystal Lake. After killing Michelle's boyfriend, Freddy tosses his heart into the lake where it conveniently falls into Jason's open chest cavity, reviving him. This particular plot point, along with the Dominik character, would return in future drafts.

In one exciting sequence, the heroes induce Jason into a dream state using a special drug, which triggers a flashback to the traumatic memory of Freddy drowning him as a boy. The group manages to rouse the titan with a poke from his own machete. As Jason wakes, he pulls Freddy out of the dream - *along with the entirety of Crystal Lake*, which comes flooding out of the dreamscape and into reality.

INTERVIEW: Lewis Abernathy
Screenwriter, *Nightmare 13: Freddy Meets Jason*

DUSTIN MCNEILL: How did you start out working with Sean Cunningham?

LEWIS ABERNATHY: Becka Boss was a friend of mine. I had made a low-budget picture with her and afterward she introduced me to Sean. So Sean and I then did a picture together called *DeepStar Six* from a script I'd originally written called *Deep Six*. After that, I became one of Sean's stable writers. He just kept giving me work rewriting junk. I worked on a couple of the Jason movies for him. He'd always bring me onto something that was in trouble, which is partly my claim to fame. A lot of people will hire me when their script has gone off the rails. I'm known in the industry as a script doctor or script fixer and I did a lot of that type work for Sean. We've been friends for a long time.

DM: So you did polishes on some of the Jason movies?

LA: Yeah, I did. Remember in *Jason Goes to Hell*, the opening scene where he's chasing the girl through the woods and it's actually an ambush? I wrote that. I just thought it was a great beginning to a sequel. I was also thinking, at that point, they had run the franchise straight into the ground, so I was trying to have it make fun of itself a little bit. I really felt like the time had come to turn the property on its head. Maybe audiences would get a kick out of that. I mean, my God, that was number nine, right? We've seen it all before by now. But no studio with a big franchise wants to hear you talking about using that approach with their material.

DM: And that led you into *Freddy vs Jason*?

LA: Yes. I remember first hearing about the possibility of *Freddy vs Jason* from Sean. He told me that New Line was seriously considering merging the two properties. He had originally sold the franchise off and then it came back to him. That was a huge deal. Then it went to New Line, who were known in the business as "The House that Freddy Built." Freddy was what they were primarily known for until the *Ninja Turtles* came along. Between those two, they were established as a mini-major studio.

So New Line was goofing around with the idea of merging them and I was looking to direct my second picture. I had done *House IV*, which I wasn't terribly proud of. It was my first movie and I felt like I made a lot of mistakes with it. Interestingly enough, my good friend James Cameron speaks glowingly of it. He says '*There are moments of brilliance in House IV,*' and I just don't know about that. But I tried to do some interesting things with it.

So I thought *Freddy vs Jason* might be a good second picture for me. The way to get that going would be to write the script myself and that's exactly what I did. I just wrote it on spec and figured I'd see how far it took me. I will say that I don't think New Line cared for my direction at all. My desire was to turn it into *Abbott and Costello Meet Frankenstein*. I thought the two franchises had run the gamut of straight horror and it was now time to make it a mildly amusing satire, which neither Cunningham nor the studio were particularly thrilled by. But New Line bought the script anyway, so it was a nice little payday.

I don't think I was being particularly inventive or ingenious with my approach either. That's simply what Universal had done with their classic franchises when they got a little stale. They turned them into comedies and they were wildly successful. I say if you're going to steal, steal from the best. I thought it was a good idea. Nobody at New Line liked it, especially the executive in charge. He's still around, De Luca. He really hated my take on it, but he bought the script anyway.

DM: How responsible did you feel to the continuities of the eighteen films you were merging?

LA: (laughs) Continuity! That's an interesting word because, if I recall, there was none. I mean particularly in the Jason movies. I felt like they had already come off the rails by that point. Jimmy Isaac and I got into a screaming match about that when he did *Jason X*. We almost came to blows. Sean had brought me up there to work on that one. I was saying, '*Hey, blow Jason out through the airlock and then have him go into a black hole,*' which is like a writer's dream, right? Anything can fucking happen in a black hole! So he goes out the airlock and into the black hole and then you can do anything you want. Jim came from a special effects background and I told him, '*This is right up your alley, dude. Do a 2001-type computer graphics LSD trip and then cut to Earth, Camp Crystal Lake, 1955, or whatever when this all started. Have Jason land like a meteor at Camp Crystal Lake!*' I thought I had just solved the entire continuity problem for the series right there, but it was not met well. We fought over it. Sean took me to breakfast one day after and said, '*Listen, I need you to stop saying black hole.*' (laughs) He had to step in! I'm still convinced that would've been genius, a great ending to a mediocre picture.

But getting back to your question, I remember watching all of the movies and writing everything down. I tried to keep track of a timeline that covered what transpired in what movies. I think I came to the conclusion that I could kind of do whatever I wanted. I didn't really see that there was anything that I had to stay faithful to except for the origin stories. You've got Jason, who is like your… well, Sean always called him '*untimely death.*' How Jason became a supernaturally invincible mutant from being a mental defective in a hockey mask was never fully explained, not in my mind. Freddy had the whole dreamscape thing. You could either drag Freddy out of the dream and kill him or go into the dream with super powers or some kind of psychological-type weapon and battle him there. But that's about all I felt like I had to take from the original franchises.

DM: What was your approach to Jason in the script?

LA: Somewhere along the way I said, '*I think Jason's ready to be a superhero.*' And Jason became the good guy in my script, so to speak. I wanted to have him killing child molesters and pedophiles. He would be killing people that deserved it, dammit. I thought it stuck with the whole '*He only kills bad camp counselors,*' which led me to '*What if the whole reason there's a Jason is because when Freddy was a camp counselor he killed Jason?*' Then I made Freddy another camper, I think.

DM: Tell me about the Freddy cult. That idea seemed to live on beyond your story into other drafts.

LA: It seems to me you have a problem when you're dealing with two worlds. Freddy's world is the dreamscape and Jason's world is reality. The Freddy cult was a way of extending Freddy's danger beyond '*Oh I can't fall asleep,*' because that doesn't work for me past a certain point. I think the cult was a way of getting Freddy's world to merge with reality, if that makes any sense. They were an extension of him.

As for it being used in other *Freddy vs Jason* scripts, imitation is the sincerest form of flattery, right? If they're stealing from me, great! God bless 'em. That may have been why De Luca bought my screenplay in the first place, so that he could extract what few good ideas he thought I had and give them to other writers. He may've even included those elements in his marching orders to those other writers.

DM: When did you realize your script wasn't moving forward and what was that like?

LA: I had a feeling from my one and only meeting with Michael De Luca. He just wasn't interested in my take, so I knew right away that my directing it probably wasn't gonna happen. From that meeting it was clear that he didn't care for a lot of what I was doing. In terms of the rejection, you can't be in the movie business with thin skin. It's their show, not mine. I don't own Freddy or Jason. I had just gone out there and done this thing. They could've very easily told me to go to hell, but they didn't. They bought my script, so I feel I did well off it. I'm sure I was disappointed that they bought the screenplay and didn't use it.

DM: How do you feel about the fact that your script was leaked online?

LA: Somebody sure had a lot of time on their hands, huh? *Nightmare 13* is not my best effort, but the fact that we're still talking about it and I've gotten some positive comments back is great. It certainly isn't my proudest moment, but I think I wrote that thing in three weeks. I just hammered it out. The fact that I made a pretty substantial payday off it is reward enough. That someone goes and leaks it onto the internet seven or eight years later, I don't feel one way or another about that. I just don't care. It doesn't upset me or anything. What's not on the internet? There's probably a lot worse things out there about me.

DM: Did you ever see the 2003 film?

LA: Honestly, I didn't see it. Here's where the interview comes to a screeching halt! (laughs) I didn't and I don't know why. I saw that it was coming out and I thought, '*I have to give that a look.*' It just left the theaters before I had a chance to go see it and for whatever reason, I just didn't see it. No real reason, really. I'm just into other stuff now.

DM: You inserted several real-life slashers into your story. Tell me about that.

LA: Ted Bundy was big at the time I was writing the script. I haven't heard that name in years, but he was still topical back then. Hitler was an obvious pick to include if you're using real villains because, you know, he's Hitler. Nazi's are great. You can do anything you want to Nazis. That's another old writer's trick. If you want legions of bad guys to kill, just make them all Nazis.

I also tried to get some more fictional monsters in there, ones audiences would easily recognize. I remember De Luca getting on to me about trying to include the Frankenstein monster in one draft. He said '*We'll never get the rights to put these characters in our film.*' And like a young jackass writer, I pointed out to the big studio executive that the Frankenstein monster is in the public domain. You just can't do Boris Karloff's version because Universal owns that imagery. But if you make it a big guy with bolts and scars all over his face like Hammer did, people will know who the fuck you're talking about. I also tried for Dracula, but got the same response. But again, both De Luca and Cunningham thought the whole Nightmare Arena thing was way over the top.

DM: Speaking of bad guys, tell me about how you came up with Captain Murdoch.

LA: I was trying to turn Jason into a good guy and that's a tall order, you know? I was trying to make him a sympathetic character, if you will. Murdoch was the way that I showed there are people out there worse than Jason. I always liked the *Maniac Cop* movies. So here's a thoroughly evil version of *Maniac Cop*, a guy who's just so far out of control.

This was also written at a time when there was a lot of trouble between the LAPD and particularly the black community. Certain neighborhoods were actually at war with the LAPD. I don't think that's an exaggeration either. So Murdoch was a marketing idea of mine. If you have a bad guy cop, it might appeal to the black/latino communities. The Freddy and Jason movies were very big with them - they love being scared. And so I think this was one way of maybe reaching out to them like, '*Hey I feel your pain - here's someone we can all hate - a rotten cop.*' That isn't to say I have anything against cops - I don't. I was just trying to find a character that made Jason a little more palatable.

DM: Murdoch's death was particularly brutal, though fitting for such a nasty character. Did you ever worry about the MPAA throwing a temper tantrum over that?

LA: Undoubtedly they would. That's what they're there for. It's what Sean Cunningham calls '*the magic act*.' We're always trying to top each other with gore. At some level, the best thing you can do is have the MPAA say '*We're banning this movie. This is too hardcore.*' You almost live for that. It's like ringing a dinner bell for audiences. I didn't fear the MPAA when I wrote it. But it's also how you shoot it. I cannot be the first guy nor the last guy to envision someone having a gun stuck up their butt and being killed that way. Surely that exists in a hundred movies by now, right? It's how you photograph it.

But suppose the MPAA saw your picture and came back to you with a PG-13 rating. You'd recoil in horror. '*Oh no, we need the hard-R!*' One of the things with Sean is nudity. I'm not big on nudity. It just seems to me that nudity was the way you got the hard-R. In my experience, nudity often made people uncomfortable, even more so than the gore, which says something about our society. I'm not like a prude or anything. If there's a reason for nudity, then great. I think scantily clad is sexier than nude.

I didn't have a naked chick, so it was like '*Hey, I'm gonna get to that hard-R any way I can,*' so I did the shotgun death with Murdoch. I'm less about gore now. Gore is a lot like porno. Once you've seen one porno, you've kind of seen them all. Once you've seen a guy get his head blown off or shotgun stuck up his butt, you're never going to top that. I'm now seeing where people are trying with varying degrees of success to go the Val Lewton route. You know, artistic gore.

DM: Tell me about your use of the number thirteen. It's throughout your script. Thirteen miles, thirteen bullets, and so on.

LA: I cannot remember why I did that right off hand, but it sounds like something dopey I'd do. I was probably trying to re-enforce the number thirteen as a way of connecting it back. Because we're always saying *Friday the 13th* and it makes for a logical hybrid title - *Nightmare 13*. That becomes a mantra, a rallying cry. That's the thing that keeps reappearing.

DM: A release date falling on a Friday the 13th would have been a must.

LA: Oh, sure. They loved doing that back then. They would work overtime to try and make those release dates happen.

DM: So going back to my first questions, it's safe to say that you came onto the project from the Jason side of things, right?

LA: Well, I'm from both camps. I actually worked on the first *Nightmare on Elm Street*.

DM: Wait, *what??* Why didn't you lead with that? Now you've got to tell me all about that!

LA: There's not much to tell! I worked with Tassilo Baur. A bunch of us got called in. The only thing I did on that picture was paint the stripes on the car at the end of the movie, the Freddy convertible where the top flops down onto the actors.

DM: You have got to be kidding me.

LA: No, I was with Tassilo Baur. We did special effects at USC together. I did effects with Tassilo on the original *House* too. That was my first job for Sean on *House* doing the George Wendt stuff. He was fishing in a closet and his reels plays out. He hooked a big fish or ghost and his line comes flying off his reel. I was the guy on the other end of the reel. I built a little spindle that I powered with a power drill. So I was just off-stage winding in his reel line.

I screwed it up because the line was supposed to play out and be gone. I rigged it too hard and it jerked the pole right out of George's hands, which surprised him. I thought they should've used that because his reaction was real. So yeah, I worked one day on the original *Nightmare on Elm Street* and painted red stripes on the roof of the convertible car.

DM: You kill off many of the villains in your script. Did you view your script as the final story for these characters?

LA: Freddy and Jason get killed in a movie, what does that even mean anymore? Nothing! Haven't they been killed in every damn movie ever made about them? What would be interesting to me is to try and leave a little trap door open for them to return, but I don't remember if I did. I'm surprised I didn't have a scientist come in and scoop up some of Jason's DNA or a cultist left alive that carried on Freddy's spirit or something. But killing them off means nothing. It just means you've got to be more inventive in the sequel to bring them back.

DM: Were you aware of the David Schow rewrite?

LA: I was aware of it. At some point, someone from New Line called me or it may've been someone from Sean's office. They called simply to say '*Hey, they're going back to your draft for a rewrite. Thought you'd like to know.*' And that was it. I thought it was an interesting turn of events, that maybe they had come around to my way of thinking. But I didn't get excited about it, which is good because that version didn't get off the ground either.

Chapter Three
The Braga/Moore Draft

1994

THE SCREENWRITERS

By mid-1994, New Line had officially passed on the Abernathy draft and was in search of a new direction for the project. Across the next year, they would develop two vastly different *Freddy vs Jason* screenplays. One of these continued on as a direct sequel to the parent franchises as the other tried to distance itself from such tangled continuity. The first came from the writing team of Brannon Braga and Ronald D. Moore, neither of whom had ever written a horror film.

Braga and Moore were then best known for their work in the *Star Trek* universe. This included writing and producing several seasons of *Star Trek: The Next Generation.* Their sole film credit heading into *Freddy vs Jason* was on *Star Trek: Generations,* a cinematic spinoff of their television efforts. Development lore tells that longtime Trekkie Michael De Luca hired the duo based on these credits. (The studio chief would later co-write an episode of *Star Trek: Voyager* with his latest *Freddy vs Jason* scribes.) Following their work on the crossover sequel, Braga would go on to write and produce shows like *24, Terra Nova,* and *Flashforward* while Moore would become a fixture in the *Battlestar Galactica* universe. They would both go on to win Peabody Awards for their writing, albeit for different projects.

Braga and Moore's crossover screenplay was officially titled *Jason vs Freddy,* the only in the project's history to reverse the more common ordering of *Freddy vs Jason.*

THE PLOT

Jason vs Freddy begins with the untimely murder of two realtors scouting Crystal Lake in hopes of redeveloping the area into a luxurious vacation resort. Their deaths draw the attention of local law enforcement, who succeed in finally capturing the *real* Jason Voorhees upon which the fictional *Friday the 13th* films are based. The infamous killer is tried for his crimes, but the legal proceedings are cut short when a vengeful relative shoots up the courtroom. A life-long insomniac, Jason requires powerful anesthesia for the emergency surgery to patch his bullet wounds. While asleep, he begins to dream for the first time in many years, reuniting him with a monster from his past - Freddy Krueger. The dream slasher quickly seizes upon Jason as a gateway into the real world. Once crossed over, Freddy uses his dream powers to wreak widespread havoc upon reality, slaughtering hundreds of people. The only ones with any chance of stopping his reign of terror are a defense attorney, a psychoneurologist, and Jason himself.

With the exception of 'The Bottin Trio', few *Freddy vs Jason* scripts were alike throughout its development, each with one or more unique features that separated it from the rest. What distinguished Braga and Moore's take could be immediately sensed from its very first page. You need only notice the title line - *Jason vs Freddy*. This reversal of the more

JASON VS FREDDY

common *Freddy vs Jason* moniker was not for nothing. The writers anchored their entire story on Crystal Lake's most famous son - beginning, advancing, and ending with ol' hockey mask. Their script quite often feels like a concluding chapter on the *Friday* saga, one that just happens to feature a guest villain appearance by Krueger. Considering most crossover scripts were extremely Freddy-centric, this draft makes for a refreshing change.

Braga and Moore's script was also notable for its more adult tone. Whereas any given *Nightmare* or *Friday* might center on teenagers or twenty-somethings, this match-up featured an entirely new lineup of adult characters. In doing so, the story eschewed the more familiar high schools and summer camps of previous films for courtrooms and police stations. The first two acts play out much like a horror-themed episode of *Law and Order*. Yet this new direction may have ultimately worked against the project as the Braga/Moore draft landed just prior to Wes Craven's *Scream*, which would usher in the teen slasher craze of the late 90s. Had their script been produced, it might have found awkward company alongside such postmodern horrors as *Halloween H20, I Know What You Did Last Summer, The Faculty, Disturbing Behavior,* and *Urban Legend*. (Both *Jason Goes to Hell* and *New Nightmare* also took a more adult oriented approach with mixed results.)

A POST-MODERN FREDDY VS JASON

Braga and Moore's take on the material was arguably ahead of its time, but just barely. Their script carries itself with a sharp self-awareness you might expect in a post-*Scream* slasher, except that *Jason vs Freddy* was written more than a year before the Wes Craven masterpiece. Their take is a genre-bender that is fully aware of your expectations going in. The screenwriters regularly lean into familiar tropes only to sidestep them at the last moment for something completely different. Subverting audience expectation is something Braga and Moore do well and often in *Jason vs Freddy*.

This postmodern angle owes largely to another Craven production - *New Nightmare*, which came out less than a year before this script was written. Rather than continuing in that film's "reality" timeline, *Jason vs Freddy* instead returns to the original *Nightmare*-verse where the initial six Freddy films played out. In that continuity, the *Friday the 13th* movies exist only as movies, though all loosely based on a real-life killer named Jason Voorhees whom we follow in this new story. This direction has confused more than a few fans over the years. To put it most simply, the planes of existence breakdown from most real to most fictitious like this: *Wes Craven's New Nightmare > Nightmare on Elm Street > Friday the 13th*. This reasons that the *Friday* movies are only movies within the world of *Elm Street*, but the *Elm Street*'s are only movies within the world of *New Nightmare*, which represents the top-most level of reality. *Jason vs Freddy* exists in that middle reality.

One particularly meta scene finds Jason's public defender preparing for court as a fictional sequel - *Friday the 13th Part 10: Jason's Greatest Hits and Chops* - plays on television in the background. In the movie, a young girl wanders into a dark house after hearing strange noises coming from within. The counselor cannot help but talk back to the screen, not unlike countless audiences have done before with the actual *Friday* movies. She scolds the girl for searching the house alone. Naturally, Jason emerges from the darkness to kill her. ("Yeah, yeah. You know what? You deserved it.") The screenwriters use this moment to playfully mock the established genre rules and yet also to remind you that they won't playing by them.

Jason vs Freddy not only pokes fun at the genre, but at the fringes of fandom as well. Browsing the horror aisle of a video store, this draft's scary movie expert hails *Zombie Sluts from Beyond the Grave* as being "a seminal film for having the first ever depiction of a fully nude triple impalement." He also defends Sean Cunningham's original *Friday the 13th* when

Jason's attorney dismisses it as garbage, calling it "a breakthrough picture" and "an instant classic." The public defender sighs, unimpressed by his knowledge and unconvinced of his claims. Playing up the absurdities of horror fandom may have been an attempt on the writers' part to make the crossover feel more accessible to general audiences. (Allow me to save you a disappointing Google search. *Zombie Sluts from Beyond the Grave* is not a real movie. I'm sorry.)

THE HUMANS

The main character of *Jason vs Freddy* is defense attorney Ruby Jarvis, named in tribute to Tommy Jarvis of *Friday's 4, 5,* and *6*. As the only public defender within fifty miles of Crystal Lake, Ruby is assigned to defend Jason against the long list of murder charges against him. She is immediately shown to be tough, sharp-witted and able to hold her own against the men who would dismiss her. Early in the script, Ruby outsmarts an FBI agent who tries to move Jason into federal custody. Her quick thinking manages to keep the proceedings local for the moment. This astuteness extends beyond reality and into to the dream world where she is also quick to realize when she is dreaming, making her less vulnerable to Freddy's tricks. Defending Jason is something Ruby takes seriously, though Braga and Moore hint that she may be inwardly struggling with the moral crisis that would naturally come with defending one of history's most notorious serial killers.

Ruby's assistant is Danny Kwan, a professional twenty-something with an enthusiasm for horror films. As a non-fan of the genre, she is largely dependent upon Danny's knowledge of the *Friday the 13th* films to help plan her case. Ruby's other colleague is cynical psychoneurologist Dr. Joe Sena, who aims to help her develop an insanity defense against Jason's murder charges. Dr. Sena's irreverent brand of humor plays nicely off of Ruby's stone-cold seriousness, such as when he suggests Ruby tell the court that Jason is a bed-wetter. ("I always throw that in. It makes the jury feel sorry for the defendant.")

THE TITANS: JASON VOORHEES

As previously mentioned, this script puts forth an entirely new version of Jason. This is not the same titan that battled Tommy Jarvis, got telepathically knocked around by Tina Shepard, and cruised on up to Manhattan. This film's Jason is supposed to be the *actual* Jason Voorhees upon which all those movies were loosely based. You can almost hear movie-trailer-voice-guy Don LaFontaine now: "Forget everything you thought you knew about Jason."

So who is this new guy? He most closely resembles the character that featured into the first three *Friday the 13th* sequels; a powerful, hockey-masked serial killer who stalks the abandoned grounds of Camp Crystal Lake. Although not overtly supernatural, he does remain superhuman in both strength and endurance. Visually, this script takes the character's appearance down several notches of grotesque from his depictions in *New Blood* and *Jason Goes to Hell*. In another departure from previous movies, the titan spends a significant portion of *Jason vs Freddy* in police custody and without his mask on. The script makes the following note about Jason's first unmasked appearance in the story: "This is not the hideously deformed mutant seen in the other Jason movies, but a real man. He's no less frightening, however, and he bears the scars of countless fights and wounds."

Jason retains a strong fondness for his dead mother, only she too is different this time around. *Jason vs Freddy* would have you purge all memories of Betsy Palmer's performance in the first *Friday* as that characterization no longer applies here. The real Pamela Voorhees, as it turns out, never went on a vengeful killing spree nor was she decapitated by a camp counselor. She died of ovarian cancer in 1969 and, as we will address later on, had pretty bad taste in romantic partners. The screenwriters are essentially rebooting the series years before rebooting became an industry trend. Why reboot the titan for his long-awaited tussle with Freddy? For one, this resetting lends itself much better to the story's more grounded approach to Jason, which is less unkillable-zombie-slasher-returns and more legendary-recluse-killer-caught. Secondly, in a world where there are multiple supernatural beings running around, the wild and fantastic seem much less wild and fantastic. Grounding Jason in reality intensifies the unique threat posed by Freddy as the only supernatural character in the story.

This resetting also unshackles the screenwriters (and the audience) from the monstrous web of tangled continuity that is the cinematic *Friday*-verse. With each new sequel, Jason's crimes became significantly more heinous in number and detail that he would undoubtedly be world infamous by now. You could well argue that he already was thanks to the *Friday* movies, but Braga and Moore seem to suggest these filmic depictions are greatly exaggerated from reality. And let's face it, Jason would have landed atop the FBI's Ten Most Wanted list for *Part 9*'s police station massacre alone.

The screenwriters do run into a spot of trouble with this new timeline business. As court proceedings begin, Jason's earliest documented murder is noted to have occurred on May 13, 1980. Yet later in the screenplay, a character references the original *Friday the 13th* as having been released in 1980, which it actually was. More specifically, the original *Friday* arrived in theaters on May 9, 1980, which meant the movie came out four days *before* Jason's earliest confirmed killing. That may not seem like an issue at first since it was Pamela Voorhees - not Jason - who did the killing in the first *Friday*. The problem is that this universe's Pamela passed away in 1969 without ever having killed any counselors. That means the murders that inspired the original *Friday* were committed by Jason, not his mother. The quagmire then is in how a movie based on Jason's crimes could hit theaters *before* his first confirmed crime took place! All things considered this is a minor oversight, but one that sharp-eyed horror fans would have surely caught.

Jason is again depicted as the less evil monster in the title fight, which leads him to team up with his public defender and psychoneurologist to beat Freddy. He isn't exactly high-fiving Ruby and Dr. Sena, but there does seem to be a mutual understanding that they share a common enemy.

THE TITANS: FREDDY KRUEGER

With so much attention paid to Jason's revised characterization, you might expect that Freddy would receive the same treatment. Yet Braga and Moore instead present the audience with the same Freddy they have long known, though on a level they have not seen in several sequels. Whereas the Abernathy draft continued on with the punster rapscallion of *Freddy's Dead*, this script reorients the titan back toward his darker roots. The screenwriters are slow to reveal the dream slasher, teasing him out with micro-appearances throughout the first two acts. Freddy is not fully featured until page fifty-three and does not take center stage until the third act when he crosses over into reality.

In a move that may have irked *Nightmare* purists, *Jason vs Freddy* appears to have taken a page from the *Freddy's Revenge* playbook. Recall that the second *Nightmare* was widely criticized for what many perceived as "breaking the rules." In the first film, the only way to bring Freddy into reality was by grabbing hold and waking up, pulling him out of the dreamscape. Nothing in Wes Craven's original suggested the character could cross the this boundary on his own, yet that was exactly what happened in *Freddy's Revenge*. In that first sequel, Freddy took over Jesse Walsh's body and used it to enter

reality, literally climbing through his chest. What's more, Freddy's dream powers remained intact as he ravaged a pool party of teenagers. ("You are all my children now.") In *Jason vs Freddy*, the character crosses over into reality in much the same way by crawling through the chest cavity of a slumbering Jason. And once again, his powers remain intact. For all the justified cries of rule-breaking, there is something terrifying in being Freddy's involuntary doorway between to reality.

Although this is the same Freddy we have long known, Braga and Moore do try something new with the character. In the *Nightmare* films, Freddy is consistently depicted as having confident knowledge of the rules that govern the dream world. He is keenly aware of his powers and limitations, particularly when other characters are not. This most often makes for an advantage. In this script, the titan is not all-knowing. He discovers that Jason serves as a doorway to the real world purely by accident. As he stabs his claws through Jason's chest in the dreamscape, they simultaneously emerge from Jason's chest in the real world. This marks a breach in the boundary that separates the dimensions, a revelation that stuns Freddy as much as anyone else. His surprise quickly gives way to an eagerness to capitalize on this newfound portal.

While the screenwriters keep Freddy's characterization consistent with previous films, they do make one significant change to his established origin. The first two *Nightmare*'s suggest the Springwood Slasher was employed by a local power plant at or before the time of his 1968 arrest. *Jason vs Freddy* alternately suggests Freddy was working as a janitor at Springwood Junior High when arrested, which would have allowed him better access to children.

THE OPENING SEQUENCE

Braga and Moore's opening sequence at Crystal Lake is masterfully crafted in the art of the slow reveal leading up to Jason's first appearance. The script begins with two realtors, one quite obnoxious, surveying the ruins of Camp Crystal Lake in hopes of transforming the area into high-end vacation properties. As the male realtor notes, tourism has dropped ninety-eight percent in the past decade due to most people associating Crystal Lake with "inbred psychopaths running around the hills with axes and hockey masks chopping up teenagers." Those Hollywood productions may sell movie tickets, he continues, but they do not sell vacation getaways. "That, my dear, is what we call an image problem."

After getting lost, the realtors stumble upon the ruins of what the audience quickly realizes to be the old Voorhees home. Curious at this find, they force their way inside. The pair naively stumble through sign after telltale sign that they should not be snooping here. In the kitchen, they find a pristinely sharp machete. The hallway closet is full of meathooks and chainsaws. Upstairs, the female realtor finds a weathered hockey mask and newspaper articles detailing Voorhees family tragedies. Alarmed at this last discovery, she runs downstairs to find her partner slain and "a hulking figure of a man" sitting calmly in darkness of the living room. This might have played out like Jason's countless other murders had the male realtor not been on a cell phone at his time of death. The person on the other end of the call immediately dials emergency assistance. The script then begins to ramp up with several rapid phone conversations involving a 911 operator, a sheriff dispatcher, the FBI tactical response team, and ultimately local defense attorney Ruby Jarvis.

In an interesting creative choice, the screenwriters opt to forgo showing what would have surely been a thrilling sequence; the FBI's assault on the Voorhees compound and subsequent arresting of Jason. The arguments against showing this capture do make sense. For one, the most recent *Friday* sequel already opened with a Jason-vs-the-FBI blowout and to return to this territory so soon might've felt repetitive, especially in light of what putting this onscreen would have cost. The one detail that distinguishes this from the raid in *Goes to Hell* is the FBI team's intention. Whereas in that film they sought to destroy Jason, their goal here is to take him alive. (Fun mental image: The poor chap tasked with handcuffing him.)

Another argument against showing Jason's arrest might have been that inserting such a high-caliber action sequence ten minutes into the story could have wrecked the pacing of everything that followed. Tonally, the jail and courtroom scenes might have been undermined coming after something so high-energy. As is, this material is infued with suspense and intrigue.

While the opening unfolds with a terrific energy, it poses an awfully stupid question: How did police never think to look for a notorious killer in the most obvious place imaginable - his family home? The script does provide an answer; the structure is tucked away deep in the forest and not on any local maps. Fair enough.

TRIAL OF THE CENTURY

Looking back on the previous nine *Friday's*, you might think the hockey-masked titan has been subjected to nearly every abuse imaginable: He has been stabbed, shot, run over, drowned, electrocuted, buried, blown up, set on fire, impaled, and drenched in toxic waste. Braga and Moore daringly began their screenplay by doing the one thing no one dared try with the character. Their story opened with the arrest and trial of Jason Voorhees. For a plot choice choice that may well elicit groans from skeptics, the first act centering on Jason's capture and arraignment make for an enthralling start to

Jason vs Freddy, partly because this is completely uncharted and unexpected territory. The writers go about this development in practical fashion, depicting what might happen if this occurred in the real world. Such a case would likely go beyond the skills and experience of Crystal Lake's modest law enforcement. There would be a media circus, public protests, and a dispute over whether state or federal got to prosecute, not to mention some mighty angry relatives of the deceased.

The material is not so tedious as to focus on things like pre-trial motions and jury selection, but the screenwriters do allow us to witness opening statements and hear some of the many, many charges brought against Jason. No doubt audiences would have looked on seeing this lumbering killer tried with the same jaw-dropped disbelief as those in the story itself. In both the courthouse and holding cell, Jason is dispirited and lethargic. He has been removed from his only purpose in life, to protect his homestead camp against anyone that would violate its sanctity.

At one point, Crystal Lake's district attorney insists he wants Jason's case handled perfectly as to avoid "any Miranda problems on appeal." This may well have been a reference to when Freddy was arrested for murders he committed in life as the Springwood Slasher. *Elm Street* lore tells that something was mishandled procedurally with the case, allowing Freddy to escape murder charges and prompting the vigilante mob that would burn him alive. The original *Nightmare* briefly mentioned that Freddy walked free because "someone forgot to sign the search warrant in the right place," but the pilot episode of *Freddy's Nightmares* alternately depicts the character escaping prosecution due to the arresting officer forgetting to read him his Miranda rights. Either way, Crystal Lake's district attorney is not having that today.

As to how Ruby Jarvis could possibly defend an obviously guilty Jason against such a loaded docket, she makes a valid legal point. Because of his cinematic portrayal as a brutal killer, "people have a preconceived notion of guilt." Indeed, there may be no place in America beyond the reach of the *Friday the 13th* movies. Jason would be synonymous with his on-screen depiction, accurate or not.

Not unlike the Freddy cult in Abernathy's original *Freddy vs Jason* script, this "Trial of Jason Voorhees" material is so freshly original that it could well work as the plot of a standalone *Friday the 13th* movie if they are ever in need of ideas. (The long dry spell between sequels might suggest that they are.) These scenes are rife with striking imagery of an unmasked Jason sitting in police custody, heavily shackled under armed guard. Such images evoke distant memories of Boris Karloff and Lon Chaney Jr's monsters in similar predicaments from the Universal classics *Bride of Frankenstein* and *Ghost of Frankenstein*.

HALLOWED GROUND

Given that *Jason vs Freddy* plays out in the *Elm Street*-verse, there are no shared locations with any of the *Friday* films. Yes, we have previously seen places like the Voorhees homestead and Crystal Lake Police Department, but their appearances here are supposed to be of the *actual* locations and not their filmic counterparts. The first two acts unfold throughout the small town of Crystal Lake before transitioning to Elm Street for the final act.

Upon crossing over into reality, Freddy's first measure of business is to head for Springwood, which we learn is but a quick eight mile journey from Crystal Lake by way of Interstate 77. Elm Street does make an appearance in the story, though not the 1400 residential block we have so often seen in *Nightmares* prior. Instead, Freddy travels to the Elm Street Shopping Mall where he counts on there being masses of unsuspecting teenagers hanging about.

BLENDING BACKSTORIES

Like Abernathy before them, Braga and Moore attempt to intertwine the backstories of the title characters. Their predecessor had written into *Nightmare 13* that a teenaged Freddy had actually drowned young Jason at Camp Crystal Lake. Braga and Moore have a slightly different take on that fateful encounter. As in Abernathy's version, this flashback to the past is triggered by something traumatic. In *Nightmare 13*, that something was being electrocuted back to life. In *Jason vs Freddy*, the flashback-inducer is the powerful anesthetic Jason receives in order to undergo surgery following the courtroom shooting.

This new flashback shows young Jason walking in on his mother and a pre-burn Freddy having violent sex. ("I didn't know you had a son. *I just love kids!*") A naked Freddy chases the frightened boy out of the house and onto the lakefront. Pamela is unable to follow due to Freddy having tied her to the bed. Jason jumps into a canoe and paddles out onto the water, though Freddy catches up and drowns him in what is eventually documented as a canoeing accident. Ruby speculates that Jason may even have been Freddy's first victim. Elias Voorhees is not present in the flashback nor his absence addressed. According to the story's timeline, Freddy is arrested the following year for his crimes in Springwood and slain by the vigilante mob. One year later, Jason's mother succumbs to ovarian cancer. This shared backstory makes for an interesting reunion in the dreamscape. ("It's been a while, little man. I thought you were dead.") Freddy assuming Jason died years ago makes sense considering the titan's insomnia has long kept him from sleeping and thus dreaming. Curiously, his initial dream appearance is that of his younger self. Freddy goes to slash the boy, but his claws instead land upon a hockey mask, which has suddenly materialized onto Jason's face, who then transforms into his adult form.

DREAMS/NIGHTMARES

This screenplay's first nightmare belongs to Jason's public defender as she prepares for court. Seamless is the transition between reality and the dreamscape. Yet Ruby is quick to notice the change upon being startled by a cat in her living room, just like in the fictonal *Friday the 13th* sequel she was watching. ("Wait a minute, I don't have a cat.") A moment later, the sheriff's office calls with news that Jason has escaped police custody and is headed her way. Various real-life monsters begin to appear in her apartment including Jack the Ripper, Charles Manson, Jeffrey Dahmer, and John Wayne Gacy. As the killers surround her, Jason steps forward with his machete raised. He pulls back his hockey mask to reveal... Freddy! ("Jason? Amateur.")

Jason vs Freddy puts forth a clever innovation on how the dream slasher haunts the nightmares of his victims. The premise of "your dream can kill you" is now carried over into reality where Freddy can inflict waking nightmares upon everyone around him. This may be better summarized as "your own personal hallucination can kill you." For example, you may see and experience an attack by a masked maniac, but all your friends will see are the resulting stab wounds. Freddy inflicts these waking nightmares on dozens of people at a time, resulting in bloody panic and pandemonium everywhere he goes. Dr. Sena describes this phenomenon "mass narcosis induced by transdimensional paranormal sociopathic entity." This does constitute a major expansion of Freddy's powers in the real world from what we have previously known them to be, but perhaps these powers vary based on whether he is pulled into reality or voluntarily crosses over. Both this script and *Freddy's Revenge* would suggest that voluntary passage allows him to keep some abilities whereas other *Nightmare*'s show that being pulled out of the dreamscape renders him powerless.

The first waking nightmare sequence is one in which Freddy exits the Crystal Lake Police Department having just breached reality through Jason. The screenwriters initially withhold these nightmare visions from the audience, instead showing only the reactions of the terrified. Whatever Freddy shows the first four deputies he encounters scares them so badly they immediately suicide using their own firearms. Moments later, a reporter outside the police station describes a horrific prison break, though the camera sees nothing but her being attacked by invisible assailants. Freddy then makes his way to Interstate 77 en route to Springwood. Taking over all car stereos in his path, Freddy blasts his haunting children's rhyme before slaughtering the travelers. The entire interstate suddenly grinds to a stop, the vehicles filled with mutilated occupants - an eerie image.

Fortunately for the heroes, there is one defense against these waking nightmares that renders them powerless, a medication called Neurolar. Dr. Sena describes it as a serotonin-inhibitor that suppresses the part of the brain that controls dreaming. He has limited doses available to split between himself, Ruby and Jason for the climactic end battle.

Digging through old medical records, Dr. Sena learns that Jason has, since birth, suffered from insomnolescence, a "neurological disorder affecting the hypothalamus." Essentially, the part of Jason's brain that causes sleepiness does not work, so he never gets tired and therefore never sleeps, which can cause rampant psychosis. (For what it is worth, this one part is actual medical science.) Dr. Sena suggests they sedate Jason for a sleep study to prove this theory, which would greatly bolster their proposed insanity defense against his murder charges. As the titan falls into a chemically induced REM sleep, the medical staff notice something bizarre - a second REM line appears on the sleep monitor, as though he were actually two people. For a moment, the audience might think second line represents Freddy, but this is not so. This is actually Jason's self-projection. When dreaming, Jason does not see himself as a seven-foot-tall monster, but rather a young child. When Freddy later uses Jason to escape the dream world, this dream projection escapes as well.

"The boy," as the script refers to him, exists in a state of constant terror, but is still able to speak with Ruby and Dr. Sena. Technically, this means Jason has conversational dialogue in the story, though these lines are spoken by his youthful dream projection and not mumbled from behind a hockey mask. Ruby questions the boy about his drowning, which causes him to relive its memory. A panic attack ensues and from this we learn that Jason emerged from Crystal Lake following Freddy's attack with a furious rage in his heart. Over time, this anger transformed him into the isolative serial killer he is today.

THE SHOPPING MALL SEQUENCE

In the aftermath of the police station massacre, Ruby and Dr. Sena speculate as to where Freddy will go. They both agree on Springwood, but that alone hardly narrows down his exact location. Knowing Freddy's penchant for killing youth, they rightly predict that he'll head for the Elm Street Shopping Mall. This is your average complex - multiple levels, numerous storefronts, a food court, and a cinema. Hanging about are all kinds of young people; nerds, ditzes, goths, punks, etc. Up until now, Braga and Moore have used Freddy sparingly. This climactic nightmare sequence is where he'll finally take center stage.

Freddy begins his mall-wide assault by forcing security gates down over the exits, trapping shoppers inside. From there, even the most normal things become nightmares. Pet shop puppies grow into snarling rottweilers. Lingerie mannequins reach to strangle window shoppers. Much worse terrors appear inside the dental clinic and kiddie playground area. Panic in the food court leads to a fire that quickly spreads. Freddy relishes the chaos from a vantage high on the third level. The Elm Street Shopping Mall has become one giant waking nightmare in what may be his greatest achievement yet.

Ruby and Dr. Sena arrive at the mall to find shoppers writhing in inexplicable pain, mangled by forces unseen. Self-injecting with Neurolar, they count on having ten nightmare-free minutes to find and kill Freddy. In her search, Ruby passes by the theater and notices an advertisement for another fictional sequel - *Jason: 2010* - that includes a standee of Robo-Jason, a "strange, robotic, *Terminator*-like Jason with a steel hockey mask and glowing electronic eyes." (Yes, the resemblance to *Jason X* is positively uncanny.) With Ruby's Neurolar dosage wearing off, the standee comes to life and attacks her. She is saved by the well-timed appearance of the real Jason, who managed to escape the Crystal Lake Police Department during Freddy's attack, grabbing his hockey mask and a fire axe on the way out the door. Here unfolds a brutal fight between dueling hockey-masked slashers.

Interestingly, the Jason vs Robo-Jason fight would be revisited in 2006 with a two-part comic from Avatar Press. *Friday the 13th: Jason vs Jason X* would pit the classic slasher against his upgraded self, all set against the backdrop of outer space. (In an curious creative choice, the artists depict Kane Hodder's Robo-Jason fighting against Ken Kirzinger's Jason from *Freddy vs Jason* rather than Hodder's own standard version of the titan.)

Having defeated this first waking nightmare, Jason strides through the burning mall toward Freddy, now wounded by a shotgun blast from Dr. Sena. The hockey-masked titan is stopped by the sudden appearance of fifty upright body bags surrounding him on all sides. They unzip in unison to reveal all of Jason's victims from throughout the years, now returned to attack him. ("Some old friends of yours would like to see you!") Following this attack, Freddy makes an offer to his opponent: "You're my creation, Jason. All that you are you owe to me. We're stronger together than we are apart. Join me and this world will be ours." Ever the salesman, Freddy's burned visage transforms into Pamela Voorhees to further persuade his opponent into joining forces with him.

Jason is unconvinced and slashes his mother's throat with Freddy's razor-glove. Furious, a wounded Freddy attempts to re-enter the dreamscape through Jason in order to heal. Partway through this process, Ruby injects her client with the dream-inhibitor, trapping the two killers together. In a grotesque image, Freddy's upper-body is stuck jutting out from Jason's chest. The two titans are now one monstrous entity, clawing and fighting with one another. Jason turns to Ruby and mutters in a hoarse voice: "Get out!" She flees with Dr. Sena just as the titan suicides by stabbing a propane tank, destroying Freddy along with him.

INTERVIEW: Brannon Braga & Ronald D. Moore
Screenwriters, *Jason vs Freddy*

DUSTIN MCNEILL: Given your primarily sci-fi backgrounds, how'd you both get involved with the project?

RONALD D. MOORE: Well, my memory of this - and it's going back a ways - is that we got a call through our agents from Michael De Luca, who was executive over New Line at that point. He was wanting to do *Freddy vs Jason* and wanted us to write the script. I think he was a fan of our work on *Star Trek*, so he invited us to come in and talk about it.

BRANNON BRAGA: I believe we had already written one of the *Star Trek* movies by then, so we did have some feature credibility. There was no direction for *Freddy vs Jason* at that point. We came in and pitched our concept and they liked it, so we agreed to do it. I'm a longtime horror fan and I've always wanted to do something within the horror field, so I was very excited to take this on. That's basically how it came about.

DM: Were you familiar with the franchises?

RDM: Brannon knew both franchises backwards and forwards because he's a diehard horror fan. I knew the *Elm Street* franchise pretty well. I really liked the first movie. I had seen the subsequent ones, but never thought any of them lived up to the original. I'm not sure if I had ever actually seen a Jason movie before I went on the project. I think that's when I went out and rented all the movies just so I could be familiar with the basic mythology.

DM: So Brannon, being the horror fan, which franchise were you more partial to heading into *Freddy vs Jason*?

BB: I was more partial to *Elm Street* because I thought it was the more imaginative series. The first *Friday the 13th,* and to some degree the second, had a big impact on me. I saw those years before *Elm Street* came out, but, if I had to pick one, I'd pick *Elm Street*. The *Friday the 13th* movies started to get a little repetitive for me after a while. I felt like it just became Jason killing people in increasingly violent ways. I honestly felt the Jason character was - to some degree - a rip-off of Michael Myers. You've got the mask, the indestructibility, the supernatural-esque quality. Whereas *Elm Street* was just utterly original in every way. But I thought the idea of combining the franchises was pretty unique then. I don't think anyone had really done it, not in a long, long time. So it sounded like a really cool idea.

DM: Were you guys aware that one or more scripts had already been rejected?

RDM: I think I knew that they had taken several whacks already and that none of them had panned out. I don't think we read any of those drafts. Michael might have sketched out some of the premises that they had tried and discarded along the way, but it was pretty much, '*We're not getting any traction on this, but we really think there's a movie to be made here. Do you guys have a take on it?*'

BB: I didn't know about the rejected drafts. As a matter of fact, this is the first I'm hearing about it. I don't think De Luca never mentioned that to me. I always thought we were the first writers on the project.

DM: Judging by the originality of your script, I'd say you weren't taking influence from anything that had been pitched before.

RDM: I'm pretty sure we didn't. We just tried to do something different. You'll have to remember that the OJ Simpson trial was pretty big back then, so we drew inspiration from a lot of the legal stuff that was going on with that. They were calling it the trial of the century everywhere you read. So we thought we'd show them what the trial of the century *really* looked like.

BB: Certainly the OJ Simpson trial was still echoing in people's minds. We played with the sensationalism of it all. We also wanted to postmodernize it a little bit. Instead of Crystal Lake just being this camp that people kept going back to over and over again, it was now this notorious area because of all the deaths. Like what would really happen if all the Jason stories were true? Well, first the real estate market would die off, which is why we started with these realtors who couldn't sell anything in town because of its bloody history.

DM: Your approach to the mythology was definitely postmodern. What made you want to set it in our reality?

RDM: I think that came from a discussion about what kind of world we wanted this to be in. Is this a world in which we've got two supernatural characters at war? Or is one of them grounded in reality? Do we acknowledge that there's been all these killings lately up at Crystal Lake? Or are these the first killings up in a while? There were a lot of basic questions to be addressed and I think in the course of that conversation, we went to this idea of, '*What if we say that Jason is a real-life killer and Crystal Lake is a real-life place and go from there?*' So from that, we built a new mythology that said all these movies were an exaggeration of true events involving this strange killer. But Freddy is different. He's truly a creature of the supernatural. He exists only in people's dreams and we wanted to lean into those supernatural components for him. Jason can certainly have supernatural elements to him, but we're ultimately going to ground him in the real world. He can be captured and he can be hurt. It was our way of differentiating the two antagonists.

DM: You set up this epic capture of Jason in your opening, but you don't actually show it. Did starting out with a big SWAT-raid feel too much like the opening of *Jason Goes to Hell* to include here? If not, why leave that out?

RDM: I think it did feel familiar to that, but we also wanted to shock the audience in both tone and style right from the beginning. We wanted them to see that we weren't going to do this big elaborate set piece with Jason taking on an entire SWAT team. It felt like skipping that gave us permission to treat him more like a regular criminal defendant. We wanted this to be a grounded version of his story. If he had been supernaturally strong in that opening, it would have changed the whole conversation about who and what he was. We wanted to get him in the jail cell and start treating him like a maniacal psycho-killer as soon as possible. We didn't want the human characters around him to be going, '*Why is he so strong and how can he throw people through the air like that and survive a massive hail of bullets?*' Because that would've diverted our whole storyline in a different direction.

We wanted to begin our story with what felt like a classic Jason film opening where the audience is with us going, '*Oh yeah, look at these obnoxious realtors about to get killed. This is going to be fun!*' We were going to play into that and let the audience enjoy this trope before surprising them with a SWAT team. Jason goes down. He actually gets captured and suddenly we're in a different movie. That's what we really liked about the opening.

BB: Upon reflection, yeah, it might have been cool to show the actual arrest. But I think we were trying to build to the moment that you first see Jason in the jail cell in the most unexpected way possible - unmasked and apprehended.

DM: Your script seemed to give Jason more story attention than most other drafts. Tell me about that approach.

RDM: We had a lot of discussion about what the balance should be for the movie. On a certain level, I feel like you have to ask the audience to invest in rooting for one of them. We liked the idea that Jason would be the one we start to root for. That was a fun notion for us and it allowed Freddy to be closer to the classic Freddy that we knew and loved. I think he was always much more malevolent than Jason was.

BB: For me, featuring more Jason was less about balancing the characters and more so about finding the right story so that getting these two characters together didn't feel forced.

DM: I thought the image of Jason heavily chained in the police station evoked a similar moment from *Bride of Frankenstein*. Was that an inspiration or am I reaching too far in making a connection there?

RDM: I don't remember off hand. It well could have been because Brannon is really a horror aficionado. I know he's surely going to know that reference right away. He might have written that as an homage.

BB: It's funny you mention *Bride of Frankenstein*. I don't want to say it was a direct homage to that, but I definitely was hugely influenced by *Frankenstein* and the *Bride of Frankenstein* growing up. And I definitely saw the Jason character as a tragic figure of sorts. He's a hideous serial killer, but something terrible happened to this guy. He's a monster in a monster movie and the granddaddy of monster movies is *Frankenstein*. In those first *Frankenstein's*, the monster was so tragic.

DM: You guys seem to like your Freddy on the scary side.

BB: I definitely preferred scary Freddy. In the first movie, he wasn't particularly funny. I don't remember a lot of one-liners or zingers in that one. I'm sure they were there, but he had a more macabre sense of humor then. As the movies went on he got pretty silly, although there are some very good sequels among them. I think the first time you meet a character like Freddy is probably going to be your best time. When you have a villain that iconic, it becomes really hard to do character development, even more so because he's supernatural. Beyond that, the audience doesn't want you to change him much or at all. It's not like Freddy's going to crossover into our world and suddenly become a respectable citizen. The natural evolution for these franchises is that the next set of filmmakers often feel like they need to top the last movie that was made. That doesn't work out well when you've got a character that can't grow or change.

DM: Do you guys realize you basically predicted *Jason X* with the fake movie playing at the shopping mall, *Jason 2010*? You nailed it right down to the glowing red eyes!

RDM: You're right! I guess we did! I had forgotten about that. I never connected *Jason X* back to that reference in our script. I also don't think that was handed to us. I think it was just something we thought would be funny and came up with on our own.

BB: That was our fumbling attempt to be postmodern and have some fun with it. I can't remember where we came up with that concept. It's funny to me that 2010 seemed like such a faraway time to us then and now it's years behind us.

DM: You guys had Jason deliver a line at the end of your script. Was that met with any resistance from the studio?

BB: (laughs) I think the resistance was that they didn't make our script!

RDM: I don't remember it being met with resistance at the time. I just remember us trying to find ways to surprise an audience who probably felt like they knew these characters really well. We knew we were breaking with tradition at some level, but we also felt that asking the audience to sympathize with him or understand him required more than the pantomime that we had been used to with Jason. He needed some kind of human interaction. We thought letting him speak at some point would've been really surprising and effective.

DM: I've gotta give you credit for going in a fresh direction. You definitely took it to new and interesting places.

RM: That was the mandate we gave ourselves. We decided we really wanted to be bold. Let's reinvent this and not do what everyone is expecting us to do. Let's take some chances here. That was our approach.

DM: When did you realize your script wasn't going forward?

RDM: I didn't hear much about the project after we finished our draft. Brannon and I moved onto other things. We knew it had been put into turnaround. I really didn't hear anything more until they made the movie that they did.

DM: Did you ever get much in the way of notes from Sean Cunningham or Michael De Luca?

RDM: Our talks with Michael and Sean were mostly at the story level. We did several outlines before we did our script.

BB: I never got to meet Sean Cunningham. I wish I had. Why didn't *he* direct the movie? That would have been cool!

DM: Were you guys aware that your script eventually leaked onto the internet for fans to download and pick apart?

RDM: Really? I had no idea that fans were reading it and commenting on it. That's kind-of great. We thought it was just stuck in a filing cabinet someplace, never to be seen by anyone ever again. Looking back on it, we really tried to do something bold with these characters. We were certainly proud of it, so it's great that people get to read it.

BB: I think that's very cool. Did other *Freddy vs Jason* scripts leak out? Because I love that kind of thing. It's like seeing the first pilot to a show you enjoy because they're often quite different from what you're familiar with. Take *Three's Company*, for example. You can go on YouTube and watch that now. It has John Ritter in it but two completely different girls. It was also written by Larry Gelbart of *MASH* fame, so it's a little more sophisticated than how the actual *Three's Company* later turned out. The same applies to reading a script like ours. It's like, '*Well here's what could have been.*' It's awesome, but at the same time I'm a little mortified because I'm sure my screenwriting was much more crude back then than it is today. It's been twenty years.

DM: Did you ever see the 2003 *Freddy vs Jason* movie?

RDM: No, didn't see it. I really haven't watched many of the films in either franchise beyond the beginning. I saw Wes Craven's *New Nightmare*, which reinvented the mythology and had Wes appearing as himself. That was probably the last one I saw.

BB: Strangely, I didn't go see *Freddy vs Jason* either.

"Jason doesn't stand a chance."
(Photo by Joe Delfino courtesy The Nightmare Museum)

Chapter Four
The Briggs Draft

1995

THE SCREENWRITER

After passing on the Braga/Moore draft, New Line turned to English writer Peter Briggs, who was then widely acclaimed for having scripted another franchise crossover with *The Hunt: Alien vs Predator*. Unfortunately, his work on that sequel would fall victim to changing executive leadership within 20th Century Fox. Still, *The Hunt: AVP* earned Briggs more than a few fans throughout Hollywood including Michael De Luca. Film journalist Chris Gore would later praise the unmade script in his book, *The 50 Greatest Movies Never Made*. Briggs would go on to develop numerous projects following his work on *Freddy vs Jason*, most notably co-writing 2004's *Hellboy* with director Guillermo del Toro. He is also developing *Panzer 88*, an action-fantasy that will serve as his directorial debut.

This third attempt at *Freddy vs Jason* was the first to draw major public attention. The screenwriter discussed the project in several interviews that year, even making the cover of Fangoria #144. Variety would report that New Line planned to shoot the Briggs draft in early 1996 for an August release later that year, though the script failed to secure a greenlight.

THE PLOT

This *Freddy vs Jason* opens in seventeenth-century Italy with a witch hunter attempting to vanquish a sinister necromancer. The witch hunter succeeds, though the occultist vows to return "when time reaches its close." Flash forward to late December 1999 where survivors from *Jason Goes to Hell* (Steven, Jessica, and daughter Stephanie) and *A Nightmare on Elm Street 5: The Dream Child* (Alice and son Jacob) mysteriously cross paths in Bethlehem, Virginia. Elsewhere in town, the FBI is tracking a murderous cult, who manage to resurrect Jason Voorhees from hell. Meanwhile, Freddy-related activity has been ramping up throughout the world including everything from mass suicide pacts to alarming astrological phenomena. With Jason back in action and Freddy on the way, the new millennium is beginning to look like the end of the world. That is unless Freddy, Jason, and the mysterious unseen force behind them both can be stopped.

The Briggs draft is arguably the most ambitious vision ever submitted for this project. Realizing something this epic in scope would have no doubt cost a fortune to put on screen, requiring extensive visual effects of both a physical and digital nature. Action-packed and full of intrigue, this draft is a page turner that forbids you to put it down until you have reached its conclusion if for no other reason than to find out what the hell has been going on the whole time! The screenwriter does a remarkable job of withholding that answer until his script's final shocking pages.

Briggs appears to have made a goal of surprising the audience. His story's tone is uniquely menacing, not quite *Friday* but not quite *Nightmare*. He adds to the mythologies of both slashers while closing out their stories in a very finite way. We often joke that there is nothing Freddy and Jason cannot bounce back from in the next sequel, but Briggs appears to have taken that on as a challenge. To undo the permanence of this story's ending would require nothing less than a time-traveling DeLorean. Speaking to *Fangoria*, the writer commented, "Once the ending comes, that's it. There is no way you can ever do another Freddy or Jason movie after this."

For all the thrills and chills of the Briggs draft, there is one glaring issue; this script does not service the promise of its title. The eponymous battle of *Freddy vs Jason* spans *less than three pages* at the tail end of the script. For most of this draft, the titans get along just fine with one serving as puppetmaster to the other. They even team up again following their brief quarrel! This is not a knock on the material or the writer, but rather the title. A more fitting name might have played up the armageddon angle and deemphasized the versus part.

THE OPENING SEQUENCE

Rather than open with a traditional Freddy nightmare as so many of these drafts do, Briggs opts instead for a trip into the distant past. Here we find a witch hunter, two priests, and several ill-fated soldiers as they prepare to brave a mysterious castle. Unholy terrors await them inside. So haunted is this place that the group's shadows detach and disappear into the darkness. They soon find their target within, the sinister necromancer, floating five feet above the ground. Briggs notes this man "bears more than a passing resemblance to Robert Englund."

The witch hunter unsheathes a pair of twin blades that resemble the ceremonial dagger from *Jason Goes to Hell*, which horror fans will also recognize as being the Kandarian Dagger from *Evil Dead II*. Briggs refers to them here as the "Daggers of Horvath," which are said to have been forged by Atlantian alchemists from the blade that pierced the side of Christ. They are also the only weapon strong enough to kill the necromancer. In a wonderfully spooky detail, Briggs notes that the opener plays out against an Italian version of the Freddy nursery rhyme. The witch hunter fatally stabs the blade into the necromancer. Dying, he makes a promise: "When time reaches its close and your race attains the skies, I will set my creatures to shatter this world." The crusaders then torch the castle. As it burns, the camera pushes in on a table near the necromancer. On the table, we see Da Vinci-esque plans that look an awful lot like Freddy's razor-glove and Jason's hockey-mask on a nearby table. Cue the opening titles.

As far as *Freddy vs Jason* openers go, they don't get much more unconventional than this. Briggs' opening is set neither in Springwood nor Crystal Lake, nor is it a dream, nor do Freddy or Jason appear. At scene's end, we're not even sure how this relates to the story. The screenwriter uses this as an opportunity to long range foreshadow his story's climactic twist that greater, more evil forces may be behind the titans. This would have been great fun to watch play out if not only to see Robert Englund pulling double duty as the necromancer character. Not unlike Braga and Moore's *Jason vs Freddy*, Briggs uses his opening sequence to shatter any preconceived notions you might have had about the crossover.

THE HUMANS

In another departure from most other *Freddy vs Jason*'s, the five main characters of the Briggs draft are all returning veterans from previous sequels. From *A Nightmare on Elm Street 5: The Dream Child* is the dream master herself, Alice Johnson, and her eight-year-old son, Jacob. This story finds the pair on a cross-country road trip to destination unknown. From *Jason Goes to Hell,* we have Steven and Jessica Freeman and their eight-year-old daughter Stephanie. The Freeman's now run the struggling Voorhees Motors, the services of which are called upon when Alice's vehicle breaks down. (For anyone keeping count, this would have tied Lisa Wilcox with Heather Langenkamp for most heroine appearances in the *Nightmare* series.)

As this script shows, bringing back characters from previous films can be a winning approach. In catching up with these tortured souls, we can see how they are still deeply affected by their run-ins with Freddy and Jason. The ever present trauma of those experiences make these new developments all that much more horrific for them. As survivors, their interactions are fascinating to witness, particularly between the children. In one scene, Jacob and Stephanie argue over who the "1, 2, *Someone's* comin' for you," rhyme was first written about. Jacob insists that everyone knows that song is about Freddy, but Stephanie counters that children at her school sing it about Jason with modified lyrics.

The story also features two FBI agents, Reznor and Cobain, who spend most of the script trying to figure out what the cultists are up to and whether they are tracking the real Jason Voorhees or an incredibly convincing copycat. Early in the film, Reznor fakes his superior's signature on a SWAT requisition form so that he can raid the occult bookstore from which the group operates. His willingness to forge signatures on will play a vitally important role in the script's final moments.

This draft's cult is different from those of the Abernathy and Schow drafts. They appear to be more satanic in nature with no clear allegiance to either Freddy or Jason. The group gets their kicks not from dream-enhancing drugs but from supernatural black magic. Their function in the story is limited, mostly centering on a ceremony to recover Jason from hell. Materializing inside a swirling red-and-green vortex, the furious titan immediately slaughters his resurrectors, ending the cult's involvement in the story on page twenty-eight. The script also features a return appearance by Freddy's mother, Sister Amanda Krueger, who has not been seen since *Dream Child*.

THE TITANS: JASON VOORHEES

Personality-wise, this is Jason as we have always known him, which is to say an unstoppable brute force. The Briggs draft restores the slasher's status as an angry, indiscriminate killer. He appears to grow even angrier upon reunion with Jessica and Steven Freeman for having sent him to hell in the last *Friday* outing. This Jason is incapable of aligning with anyone, not even the cultists who resurrect him. Visually, Briggs gives the titan a considerable makeover. He no longer wears the traditional white hockey mask, but a chrome facial covering with angular features, not unlike the mask seen on the theatrical poster for *Jason Goes to Hell*. This updated look, Briggs writes, makes Jason look like a "slasher Darth Vader." The titan is also more physically imposing this time around, drawing comparisons to Arnold Schwarzenegger's *Terminator* in the script.

One scene in particular conveys the full might of this Jason. Giving chase through the Voorhees Motor garage, Alice manages to drop a hydraulically raised Pontiac on her pursuer. While this might have slowed or even stopped previous Jason's, it is but a mere inconvenience to this one. The killer shreds his way up through the car's engine, sending auto-parts flying, before resuming the chase.

THE TITANS: FREDDY KRUEGER

The Briggs' draft uses Freddy sparingly throughout the script to good effect. Although the dream slasher may not be on-screen a great deal, his presence is still very much felt. The screenwriter holds back the titan's first appearance, instead teasing the audience with shadowy glimpses and nightmare visions of his razor-gloved hand. This Freddy is also far less verbose than in recent sequels and considerably less punny, not speaking his first line until page sixty-nine. When he does finally appear in full form on page eighty-eight, he is referred to as "New Freddy." This upgraded version of the character is described as having "mighty hands with scimitar blades" and an "olympian head atop a red-and-green-dressed Richard Corben superhero dream of a body." From that, you have to wonder if Kane Hodder wasn't better suited to play Freddy.

Interestingly, Briggs writes that "New Freddy" reverts to "Old Freddy" when wounded in the final battle, referencing to the character's look across the first six *Nightmare* films. Speaking to *Fangoria* in 1995, Briggs said, "*New Nightmare* sort of led towards this darker, sinister Freddy. We're taking that even further. This will be the nastiest, biggest, baddest Freddy that has ever been. It's a complete redesign of the way he looks."

CALLBACKS AND REFERENCES

As with any new *Friday* or *Nightmare* installment, you can surely count on a new offering of in-jokes for sharp viewers to pick up on. References like *Nightmare 4*'s Crave Inn Restaurant or *Friday 9*'s Cunningham County immediately come to mind. Had this version of *Freddy vs Jason* been committed to celluloid, its IMDb Trivia page would have been a mile long cataloging all the nods Briggs works into his screenplay. Some of these are standout obvious, others more subtle.

The screenplay either directly mentions or winks at horror classics like *Psycho, Halloween, Jaws, Phantasm, The Wicker Man, Hellraiser, The Hills Have Eyes, Shocker, The Omen* and *Texas Chainsaw Massacre*. In addition to *Evil Dead* props like the Kandarian Dagger and Necronomicon returning from *Jason Goes to Hell*, the cultists recite Professor Knowby's *Evil Dead II* incantation to resurrect Jason from hell. Briggs also makes several nods to *Freddy vs Jason* production personnel with characters like Signor Deluca (Michael De Luca), Pontiff Manfredini (Harry Manfredini) and Father Shaye (Robert Shaye). Beyond that, FBI Agents Reznor and Cobain are clear references to the lead singers of Nine Inch Nails and Nirvana respectively. Briggs also works in the former band's music into this draft.

At one point, the script even manages to reference itself! In a humorous exchange, Stephanie asks Jacob who he thinks might win in a battle between Spawn and the Mask (both New Line properties). Jacob responds, "I dunno. Spawn, I guess. But it'd be dumb if it was done wrong, 'cause they're from different universes and you gotta have a proper story to make it work." This is quite obviously a thinly-veiled commentary on the pitfalls of making *Freddy vs Jason* and getting it wrong.

In another scene, Briggs creates a reality-bending timeline paradox. We find Pontiff Manfredini aboard a US-bound flight bound hoping to somehow prevent the impending armageddon upon arrival. The inflight movie is none other than *Wes Craven's New Nightmare*. This comes across as hilariously retaliatory in the best sense. *New Nightmare* somewhat marginalized the original six Freddy movies as being fictional. Now this film is returning the favor by claiming such of *New Nightmare*. The cued scene is most relevant to this new story with Craven telling Heather Langenkamp: "It's old, very old. And it's taken different forms in different ages. The only thing that stays the same about it, is what it lives for. [...] Slaughtering innocence."

This writer's personal favorite in-joke? A surprise cameo from my own favorite horror franchise - *Phantasm*. While chasing Alice through hell, Freddy encounters the sinister Tall Man's silver sphere, which buries its blades in the titan's forehead. Howling in agony, he plucks the ball away and stumbles on.

BLENDING BACKSTORIES

Like the Abernathy and Braga/Moore scripts before it, the Briggs draft rewrites history in order to better serve the present conflict. In a sequence mid-way through the story, Alice finds herself inside Jason's mind. Here she witnesses a moment from the past through Jason's eyes; the parents of Elm Street debating whether or not to exact vigilante justice upon the Springwood Slasher. How could Jason, who was then just a boy, have possibly seen this? Briggs reveals that Jason was one of the original Elm Street kids!

This flashback further reveals Donald and Marge Thompson (Nancy's parents from the first *Nightmare*) debating with their fellow Elm Street parents on how to best handle Freddy. Among the concerned attendees are Pamela and Elias Voorhees, who support the group taking matters into their own hands. This marks a rare depiction of Elias in which he is not a backwoods degenerate. The scene continues with Pamela and Elias among the mob that torches Freddy in the abandoned boiler room. Afterward, they leave with young Jason and head to Crystal Lake "for a little holiday." Once there, Jason canoes out onto the lake as Alice watches on. Suddenly, the shoreline vanishes in all directions. The flashback has now changed as

Jason is remembering a nightmare. Behind his canoe, six-foot tall finger blades rise from the water in a sequence that evokes the famous bathtub scene from the original *Nightmare* (the script's own comparison). Approaching like oversized shark fins, they tear into the boat, dragging it underwater and drowning the boy. A horrified Alice watches on unable to save Jason, her calls for help reaching no one. This would mark the only time in the crossover's history where Freddy murders Jason *after* being burned to death, essentially becoming his first nightmare kill. The dream slasher would later claim credit for having created Jason as we now know him.

While this does make for an intriguing story twist, it also conflicts with details presented in the first *Friday the 13th*. In Sean Cunningham's original, Mrs. Voorhees reveals that she was employed as the camp's cook and busy preparing meals at the time of her son's drowning, which does not fit with the "holiday at Crystal Lake" narrative. With some creative shuffling, this plotline might have better fit the existing continuity.

The revelation that Freddy was behind young Jason's drowning at Crystal Lake is not exclusive to the Briggs script. How their relationship develops from then on, however, is unique to this draft. Whereas other screenplays would use this conflict to immediately pit them as enemies, Briggs instead depicts a surprisingly subservient relationship; Freddy is in complete control of Jason. ("How'd you like my little puppet? He always does everything I say!") The eventual conflict arises over who will get to kill Alice and Jessica with Jason flatly ignoring Freddy's claim to them. From this, several burning questions arise. Has Jason ever had free will apart from Freddy? Or has the entire *Friday* series now been contextualized as a spinoff of Freddy's legacy?

HALLOWED GROUND

The Briggs draft is set primarily in the town of Bethlehem, Virginia. While that exact location is fictional, there is a town called Bethlehem in *West* Virginia, though with less than three-thousand residents it likely bears little resemblance to this story's setting. The symbolic implications of playing out *Freddy vs Jason* here are rich, particularly since Bethlehem is better known as the birthplace of Jesus Christ. That Briggs positions it as ground zero for the apocalypse is deliciously ironic.

Heading out of its seventeenth-century prologue, the script travels to an occult bookstore on Elm Street. This is not the Elm Street we have long known from Springwood, but rather its counterpart in Bethlehem. (Recall what we learned in *Freddy's Dead*: "Every town has an Elm Street!") We do eventually go back to the original Elm Street, but only briefly. By way of Jason's flashback-nightmare, Briggs allows us to revisit the iconic house at 1428 and shortly thereafter Camp Crystal Lake. The script also returns to the abandoned boiler room to watch the vigilante mob burn Freddy alive. This marks the scene's third depiction after *Freddy's Nightmares* and *Freddy's Dead*. Fortunately, the screenwriter omits the moment from the sixth film where the dream demons tell Freddy to "open up" so that he can "be forever."

In a bit of a retcon, this script establishes that Springwood and Crystal Lake are located on opposite ends of Ohio. This may work for the present story, but it's a little problematic when you consider all the New Jersey license plates seen in the earlier *Friday* flicks. At first glance, this change seems to clash with Crystal Lake feeding into the ocean per *Jason Takes Manhattan*, but then again, Ohio isn't quite as landlocked as most think. The state shares a water border with Ontario, Canada through which it connects to the Atlantic via the Saint Lawrence River. Maybe New Jerseyans just really love vacationing in Ohio.

DREAMS/NIGHTMARES

The Briggs draft features several nightmares patterned in the tradition of the previous films. They are often character-based (in one scene, a smoker literally coughs up a lung), but not in a way that requires Freddy to be physically present yucking it up. This goes a long way to making the nightmares scary again. Not unlike Spielberg's use of the shark in *Jaws*, Briggs seems to understand that not seeing Freddy can be sometimes be the scarier approach to take. Although we seldom catch him in full form during these sequences, we still know he is there.

Most of the dreams in this script contain a double-take moment, something that tips off the dreamer (and the audience) that they are no longer in reality. One effective example involves a cop with a strong dislike for Christmas trees. Walking alone at night, she notices an outdoor display begin to shake violently, its colorful bulbs fading to dark. After a beat, the tree explodes with blinding light, each strand now alternating red and green. Although we cannot see Freddy, we know he is there and about to do something terrible.

One of the most significant dreams in this draft was previously discussed in the Blending Backstories section. Midway through the script, Alice happens upon Jason attacking Steven. She attempts to fight him off, but is knocked unconscious. This triggers her dream powers, which somehow transport her into Jason's mind for the slasher's flashback-nightmare combo.

There is one nightmare in this draft not induced by Freddy. In this dream, Agent Cobain finds himself in a surreal church standing opposite Amanda Krueger. She warns him of the impending "time of darkness." Unfortunately, Freddy interjects before she can impart any useful advice on how to stop the end of the world. She clutches her chest as invisible claws slash her white robe, trails of blood appearing in their wake. Her features grow skeletal as she changes into a spectral wraith and disappears. Although Amanda's appearances in this *Freddy vs Jason* are few and brief, they suggest her fate has not changed. She can have no peace in death so long as her son continues to kill. Her only purpose then is to try and warn those who find themselves in his bloody path.

BATTLE THROUGH HELL

The Abernathy draft climaxed with a boxing match in hell. The Braga/Moore draft finished with a mass-induced nightmare inside a shopping mall. The Briggs draft now concludes with an exciting chase through the underworld and the shocking reveal of who has been behind Freddy and Jason this whole time.

As Alice wakes from her terrifying trip into Jason's mind, she finds herself in the destroyed Voorhees Motors autoshop. A panicked Jessica exclaims that Steven, Stephanie, and Jacob are all missing. The two find and team up with Agent Cobain, who interrogated them as persons of interest earlier in the story. Together they head to the cult's base of operations

- Samhain Books. They enter to find Jason going into the otherworldly portal from earlier, taking a dying, withered Steven with him. The vortex then closes behind him. Alarmed that Stephanie and Jacob may be wherever Jason was headed, Alice, Jessica, and Cobain manage to re-open the portal by playing back a tape of the cult's incantations. Passing through the dimensional doorway, they suddenly find themselves in hell.

Briggs' vision of hell is wickedly detailed with seemingly endless rooms, corridors, and landscapes. One scene reveals an infinite sea of molten lava while another depicts a room full of spikes, chains and corpses. The trio quickly encounter "New Freddy," who sets after them. Jason joins in only a moment later. Now caught between two monsters, the heroes find themselves unable to escape or even fight back. A conflict arises over who will get to kill the women. Freddy quickly stakes his claim, which Jason appears to ignore. He angrily threatens his puppet, "The Master promised them to me! Don't make me hurt you again. I made you!" From this, a brutal fight breaks out between the titans. The battle is short-lived, however, due to the entrance of someone larger and more evil than them both.

A behemoth figure bursts from the ground, clasping the titans in its giant hand. This is Thanos, "Lord of the Underworld," whom the script notes is practically Satan himself. He addresses the monsters with contempt, calling them pathetic. Freddy cowers at the gargantuan demon before referencing their agreement to deliver him the souls of the innocent. With zero hour of the apocalypse at hand, their master appears to have rendered this pact null. ("Bargains forgot by hell are worth naught.") Enraged at this betrayal, Freddy and Jason attack Thanos using the Daggers of Horvath, which inflict terrible damage. Meanwhile, Alice and Jessica escape through the vortex from whence they came after having found their children. Upon returning to reality, they see that it is now January 1st, 2000, meaning they have survived into the new millennium. The end of the world is no longer at hand and - for the moment - the monsters appear to be vanquished. Or at the very least in hell.

DAYS OF FUTURE PAST

The final scene of Briggs' *Freddy vs Jason* is one that effectively slams the door shut on the past, present and future of both franchises. Returning from hell, Alice and Jessica realize that at some point they lost track of Agent Cobain. The audience will recall him stopping during the chase to notice Amanda Krueger beckoning to him from a floating window. He touches the image and is immediately sucked into it.

In its final pages, the script finds a confused Cobain in what turns out to be Springwood circa the 1960s. Wandering into the town's police station, he begins to understand why Amanda sent him here. He overhears several officers chatting about their next assignment; the arrest of the man known as the Springwood Slasher. Recalling that Freddy received a mistrial due to an unsigned search warrant, Cobain quickly locates the incomplete form on a nearby desk. Working fast, he copies an authorized signature onto the document just as the arresting team heads out. He knows what this will now mean. Freddy will be arrested, tried and executed for his crimes. Consequently, Jason will never be drowned at Crystal Lake. Future generations will now be safe from Springwood to Crystal Lake.

Cobain walks outside and looks around, taken back by how different this Springwood looks with its white-picket fences and retro-fashions. He turns to notice a group of happy schoolchildren led by Amanda Krueger, a young Jason among them. As they begin to sing the familiar Freddy rhyme, both he and the audience notice a change in lyrics. The song is now a reassurance that monsters cannot get you ("9, 10, you can sleep again."). The nightmare is truly over.

Other *Freddy vs Jason* screenwriters would try for this kind of irreversible closure on the titan's stories, but none would do it so successfully as Briggs did. This *Back to the Future*-style ending essentially erases the events of the preceding sixteen films from history. *Great scott!* New Line executive and comic-scribe Jeff Katz would later borrow this ending for use in the *Freddy vs Jason vs Ash: The Nightmare Warriors* comic miniseries.

INTERVIEW: John D. LeMay
Actor (Steven Freeman), *Jason Goes to Hell: The Final Friday*

DM: Were you surprised that Steven survived Jason Goes to Hell? Most men don't survive him and Rambo he's not.

JDL: Indeed, Steven is not Rambo. A recent article I saw about the film even referred to Steven as a bit of a nerd. Maybe it was the glasses. Was I surprised to survive Jason? Absolutely. No one survives that guy! I wear it as a badge of honor even now. I know it still drives Kane Hodder nuts!

DM: Was the possibility of reprising your role ever talked about?

JDL: I am sure the thought of a *Jason vs Freddy* was always on their mind. At least a hope. The final shot of *Jason Goes To Hell* is certainly begging for it. That is a great shot, by the way. Nevertheless, I don't remember any talk of my character coming back. If there was, I did not take it seriously. These are Jason movies after all.

DM: Were you at all aware that Steven had been incorporated into the Freddy vs Jason draft by Peter Briggs?

JDL: Adam Marcus and Dean Lorey were trying to create a coherent backstory or history for Jason. So, it would only make sense to build off of what had come before, but I was unaware of any scripts in which my character was featured.

DM: Jason eventually kills Steven in the Briggs script. Would you have returned even if it meant dying onscreen?

JDL: Sure! I remember being very jealous of all the "kills" hanging around in the KNB Effects studio. I went over to the shop for a tour during filming. Not being killed seemed so boring!

DM: Steven also returned in the comic book sequel to *Freddy vs Jason vs Ash*, where he is again killed. Had you seen that?

JDL: I had no idea they existed until you sent me that image! I just now purchased a copy of one of the comics on eBay. Seriously fun to see yourself in a graphic depiction. Love the THUNK on my head in the final Steven panel!

DM: Okay, hypothetical: Steven has beaten Jason. Literally with a shovel, as we saw it. How does he do against Freddy Krueger?

JDL: That first Freddy movie gave me recurring nightmares. What a scary premise for a horror character. Everyone has to sleep, right? Jason moves slowly…that I can handle. Freddy, on the other hand, is everywhere we are when we close our eyes. Not sure a shovel would be so helpful against Freddy.

DM: Freddy vs Jason… in your personal opinion, biases and all, who wins that battle?

JDL: I would be a fool to stick my head out and make a prediction on that one!

INTERVIEW: Peter Briggs
Screenwriter, *Freddy vs Jason '95*

DUSTIN MCNEILL: How did you first become attached to Freddy vs Jason?

PETER BRIGGS: At the time *Freddy vs Jason* swung around, I'd just come off a bruising session working on the Sylvester Stallone *Judge Dredd* movie. Actually, when I was on it, it was Tony Scott and Arnold Schwarzenegger. But I left the project, and then Tony and Schwarzenegger dropped out respectively, and it ultimately became Danny Cannon and Stallone. But *Judge Dredd* was my first incursion, my first real experience, into the development hell punchbag process, and it made me wary about a next assignment. I really didn't want to be another one of a dozen writers working on another movie that wasn't going anywhere, or being jettisoned and ending up not getting any kind of credit beyond the WGA arbitration.

Weirdly enough, right before I was approached, I was back in London. I'm a big soundtrack collector, and would find any excuse to go to the recording sessions for whatever movie was getting scored in the London studios. One crazy night, I was out with Renny Harlin, when Trevor Jones was recording the music for his Stallone movie *Cliffhanger* at CTS studios. That was an interesting evening, and he told me some stories about directing *Nightmare On Elm Street 4*.

My agent back then, this was the early 1990s, was a gentleman at William Morris called Steve Kenis. Actually, the head of the agency in London. A truly nice fellow, and he did an awful lot for me in those early days. One afternoon, I got a call from him. I'd written the infamous *Alien vs Predator* draft which sold to 20th Century Fox through Larry Gordon back in 1991.

Now, Mike De Luca was the head of New Line at that time. They'd already had several drafts of *Freddy vs Jason* at that point. Mike wanted me, simply enough, because he read my *Alien vs Predator*; loved it; figured correctly that I knew how to bolt two franchise monsters together, and wanted to hire me. So he approached William Morris, and my agent called me. And…well, I said no! I turned them down.

DM: What!? Why?

PB: I'd seen the first *Friday the 13th* and absolutely hated it. I'm not really a fan of splatter movies. I'm not squeamish or anything. I just don't "get" gore for gore's sake. Of course, that doesn't mean I haven't written those scenes myself. And I love Cronenberg's movies, and *The Thing* is one of the greatest movies ever made. But, you know, guys? Put a little grey matter into your scripts if you're going to work in that genre. And, I don't mean splattering brains across a wall, either.

On the other hand, I really liked the *Elm Street* series, to varying degrees, and had seen them all. And, Mike De Luca obviously didn't want to take "no" for an answer, and Steve called me back again and said they really wanted me for it. And so I had a great transatlantic conversation with Mike De Luca, who I liked very much, and he's a very persuasive fellow. Now, I've never made any bones about me wanting to direct. That's been my goal all along, and I'm still trying to get there. I started off as an assistant cameraman in England, getting my Union Card. And I've spent my whole career going from one studio picture to another, doing jobs people don't know I was on as you mostly don't end up with credits on rewrites and polishes. And I was pursuing directing. So, I said to Mike: '*Look. I'll do this, if you'll seriously entertain the notion of me directing this.*' And Mike, very reasonably, said they would consider it if the draft worked for them and I could make a good argument for it. And so, I was off to the races.

Now, I'd seen all of the *Elm Street*'s. In fact, they were doing *New Nightmare* at the time and Mike's assistant sent me the script. His assistant back then was a guy called Wyck Godfrey, who's now become a fairly major producer in his own right, and who I'd end up bumping into again down the line on a couple of other movies.

We'd no DVDs back in the early 1990s, so I got all the VHS tapes out from the local video shop for a refresher marathon. The *Elm Street*'s were fun. I don't like *Freddy's Revenge* or *Freddy's Dead*, but the rest are a hoot. So, I sat there with my yellow legal pad, making notes as I went through. That was a Wednesday/Thursday viewing, I remember that clearly. I remember it, because of "Black Saturday," which was the day I did the second half of the *Friday the 13th* movies. I'd started on Friday with the first few *Friday*'s. At some point in the evening I decided enough was enough and went out with some friends for a drink, and resumed again the next morning. I really struggled with them throughout the day, and by the time I got to *Jason Takes Manhattan* my brain had turned to mush and I was having a hard time going on. I genuinely couldn't see how I was going to tie the films together, and was seriously on the verge of a panic attack and thinking of calling up New Line and calling the whole thing off. But then I got to *Jason Goes To Hell*. Thank God for that movie. I don't know whether it was delirium, but a lightbulb went off, and the whole thing clicked together.

DM: Of all the unused scripts, yours had the most continuity with the parent franchises. Was that difficult to figure out?

PB: Thanks. Yeah, I saw the documentary on the *Nightmare* set with Jeff Katz from New Line where he complimented me on the continuity, so I guess I got that part right. No, I don't think it's difficult. As I said, I was going through making notes on my legal pad. I think if you're doing this for a living, it's up to you to be as diligent with your craft, whether you're writing a factually based historical biopic, or a fictional franchise flick. It's all about facts. It's all about plotting. It's structure and it's connecting the dots. That's what it is at the end of the day. Basically, my approach to script crafting is to do what I call the "Grand Unified Theory" approach. I think you owe it to yourself to immerse yourself in your chosen topic. So, I make copious notes in order to cross the t's and dot the i's. Nowadays, this is so much easier with the internet. You have to remember: there was no internet when we were doing this thing! So I was going back through musty magazines and gleaning what I could. I had the daggers from *Jason Goes To Hell*, as well as Jessica and Steven Freeman, so I knew they were my components from that. And I brought in Alice Johnson from the *Nightmare*'s, as she was obviously an extremely useful character on multiple levels.

But one of the big lightbulbs for me, was Tobe Hooper's pilot episode of that Larimar-Warner Brothers *Freddy's Nightmares* TV show. We met the Elm Street parents. We saw the botch with the Miranda Rights. And I came away from that with two thoughts. One was '*Well, supposing that the paperwork and the legal process hadn't been botched, and Fred Krueger had been jailed?*' And the other was: '*Hey!? What if Jason grew up on Elm Street before moving to Crystal Lake? What if he was an Elm Street Kid?*' And that led to the plot device of Freddy getting into Jason's head and manipulating him. If you looked at the timeline, my rationale was that it was quite possible that it was Freddy that initially pushed Jason into doing the things he did. That he manipulated him.

Now, you know. I remember seeing the DVD documentary on the making of *Freddy vs Jason*. And it was one of the two writers that were eventually credited: it was Shannon or Swift, I don't remember which one. And I remember them with a straight face saying something like '*Yeah, we were the first ones who came up with the notion of Freddy getting inside Jason's mind.*' And my script, which was almost ten years old at the point and had been scanned and pirated off onto some internet script piracy site for anyone to see. I remember yelling at the TV in indignation: '*You (expletive deleted)! I came up with that, ten years ago!*'

DM: What kind of direction, if any, did you get from New Line?

PB: Initially, not really any. Mike was very trusting. I'd given them the idea of what I wanted to do. About a week later, they came back and said '*You know...I know we didn't ask for it, but could you give us a treatment?*' I'd already signed the paperwork and was committed to just writing the script. I could have said no. But I went away and said I'd come back with something. And I gave them an outline, which was a little bit woolly, as I was still working through my index cards, and I have a fixed way I like to plot and structure, which is a little unorthodox. And because it was woolly...I also wrote for them the first thirteen pages of the script. And, yes, if you're asking me if the thirteen pages was deliberate, it was! And so they said '*Well, we're not sure where you're going with this, but we love the pages, so just keep going!*' So that was that.

DM: Numerous crossover scripts made Jason the "good slasher," so to speak. What are your thoughts on keeping Jason scary?
PB: Well, you have to. You have to be respectful to the core of what that character is. Otherwise you're fundamentally changing the nature of the villain. We know from the original movies what Jason's backstory was. To get Freddy to further manipulate him, by going into his mind, wasn't much of a jump: I'm pretty sure the credited writers of the eventual movie took that particular aspect from my draft. I spotted a couple of teensy things in the finished film that I hadn't in the arbitration, which I didn't fight, that to my knowledge weren't in any of the prior drafts. The thing I was especially happy with, also, was my wheeze that Jason was an Elm Street kid, that he'd been preyed-on by Freddy. That, to me, was a logical extension of giving him a villainous genesis. Plus, I liked those scenes from the short-lived *Nightmare On Elm Street* TV show, those scenes with the Elm Street kids parents. Why not have the Voorhees family in the mix there?

DM: Freddy and Jason exist in different realms, which many have cited as a challenge to writing this story. Did you ever think there must've been someone easier to pit against Jason? Perhaps Leatherface or Michael Myers?
PB: Have others cited that? I wasn't aware. I had no problems putting them together. Zip. It was a pleasure to write, and great fun. In fact, I even made a joke of it in the car with the kids doing their superhero "Thing vs Thing" conversation, saying that the problem with team ups was that if you do it wrong, you make a mess of it. I figured you may as well put that out there in a tongue-in-cheek fashion for the audience to get a laugh out of. Because, you know, half the fun of the original Freddy movies was laughing along with the horrific conceits.

DM: Did you read any of the previous drafts before you wrote yours? Because your script does not appear to be taking influence from any of them. It really stands on its own.
PB: Cheers. I appreciate that. No, I wasn't offered any of the prior drafts from New Line. I know I replaced Brannon Braga and Ron Moore, but I'm not sure of the chronology before them. I can't remember if I requested any of the prior drafts, or not. I might have? I've a vague recollection I might have said something to Mike De Luca, who hired me. But none of the early *Freddy vs Jason* drafts were forthcoming. When I was on the project, I didn't know how many had been written, or by whom. In fact, it wasn't until the arbitration that I saw the list of writers, and was pretty surprised at the names involved, and how many there were. I've read a few of the other drafts since, thanks to the internet. I remember sitting on the sofa with Peter Jackson in New Zealand and I happened to mention that I'd done a *Freddy vs Jason* draft: Peter surprised me by telling he'd also written his own Freddy Krueger screenplay for New Line! He seemed quite wistful about it!

New Line did send me Wes Craven's *New Nightmare* script, though. I didn't much care for it. Honestly, I thought they were nuts to make it, although I guess it was ultimately financially lucrative for the company. I felt they undid the franchise with it, a little bit. I could see how going off in a different direction was a way to keep things fresh, but…no. I didn't care for the movie.

DM: In 2005, David Goyer told the LA Times that films like *Freddy vs Jason* were "somewhat of an admission that these franchises are on their last gasp." Having written two crossover scripts, do you agree with that sentiment on any level?

PB: No, I don't. And if David thinks that, he should stop writing them and refer the executives over to me for the gig! I did bump into David at Meltdown Comics in L.A. once and had a very nice conversation with him. He's a very pleasant, very affable chap. We both commiserated on our failures to write a movie of *The Flash* for Warner Brothers; we were both briefly on that project at different times. I read that same dismissive "last gasp" comment from Joss Whedon when he started on *Alien Resurrection* and put his boot into the notion of *Alien vs Predator*.

Those kind of comments, and that mindset, harken back to, I think, memories of the various Universal Monsters movie crossovers. Now, each of those creature franchises independently had run out of steam. But, that's just because studios didn't hire talent that spins the stories off in a different direction: they just hired the first hot boy wonder to-hand with some half-baked idea percolating. Some of the crossovers succeeded. Some did not. Ironically, if you look at those Abbot And Costello movies which featured the Universal Monsters, they actually dealt with them in a pretty straight fashion….it's not like the Area 52 scene in *Looney Tunes Back In Action*. I love that scene, because it's a blast seeing the Metaluna Mutant and the crawling brains from *Fiend Without A Face* in the same scene together. But, you know, Dante did that scene for giggles, and that's the tone of it. If you came to me and said *'Can you write me a script with the Metaluna Mutant and the crawling brains in it?'*, I'd snap my heels and I'd do my best to come up with something respectful to the source material. I think when you just hire people with no awareness of the material, or the fan expectations, then it's just caveat emptor. Look: I really like most of the Freddy movies, but I have no great love for the *Friday The 13th* franchise. But I was damned if I wasn't going to treat Jason with dignity and try to have him be the baddest mofo he could be, in my draft.

DM: Tell me about Thanos. Did you have anyone in mind for that role?

PB: Originally he was called Thanatos. And I wavered back and forth between Thanatos and Thanos. And the Thanos thing worried me, because I used to read a Marvel comic book called *Adam Warlock*, and Thanos was, I don't think, really that big a deal back then for anyone who didn't know the Marvel Universe. And I thought Thanatos might be unwieldy when spoken aloud in dialogue…too many syllables…so I just truncated that back down to Thanos. Of course, he's just about to be the star nemesis of a billion dollar film franchise now, but back then that wasn't a worry!

But, to answer your question. When I write, I like to cast in my head and assign actors to the roles, as it helps you get into character and hopefully you can differentiate on the page between one character and another. But I pretty much drew a blank with casting Thanatos, myself. He was clearly going to be a guy in a massive prosthetic suit. I guess, in a way, he was the R-Rated version of Tim Curry in *Legend*. But, if he'd been realised on film, he would have had to have been the Ozzy Osbourne, Gene Simmons version of that character. He was meant to be True Evil. I honestly couldn't say, but I'm curious as to why you asked me, because it sounds like you had someone in mind!

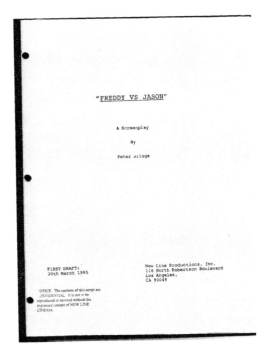

"FREDDY VS JASON"

A Screenplay

By

Peter Briggs

FIRST DRAFT:
30th March 1995

New Line Productions, Inc.
116 North Robertson Boulevard
Los Angeles,
CA 90048

NOTICE The contents of this script are
CONFIDENTIAL It is not to be
reproduced or xeroxed without the
expressed consent of NEW LINE
CINEMA

DM: I was very much thinking about Tim Curry in *Legend*! You mentioned how your script was scanned and pirated online. No doubt it's now been read by thousands. How do you feel about that? Would you have preferred it remain private?

PB: Good question. I don't know. On the one hand, you don't want your writing leaking out into the big bad world showing off ideas you've created that weren't used, because Joe Q Screenwriter out there can still plunder them for their magnum opus. But, you know: as a screenwriter you're kind of a "whore for hire." The studio paid you for your services. You've tendered them. You spent their money. You can't be too precious about it, you know? There've been a lot of scripts I've been paid for down the years that have never seen the cold light of day. Some I'm proud of. Others less so. It doesn't bother me now, especially when it's a film that already got made with another person's script. It's not like it was an original of mine.

DM: Your script was chock-full of fun references, many to pop culture, especially within the horror genre. Were these nods and winks as much fun to think up as they are to discover when others read your script?

PB: You know, I was much more of a fanboy back then. It was twenty-some years ago. You're young, you're stupid, you're goofy. Here's my position on that now: I think if you reference in-universe to other films in the franchise, then that's fine. I think if you're doing that for a "yuk-yuk" gag, you're just being a smart-ass. And I was a smart-ass back then, no question about it. You're showing off your fanboy credentials. I think when you reach the point as a writer that you stop doing that, you've matured. I had Craven in-jokes, production in-jokes: the Cobain and Reznor thing. All kinds of nonsense. I came up with the Cobain, and my brother Andy made the suggestion on the Reznor one, if I recall correctly. Or it might have been a friend of ours, Steven Horvath. He's the one that the "Daggers Of Horvath" in the script are named after, by the way.

DM: Have you ever received any feedback from fans who've come across your script?

PB: Lots. Lots and lots, and still to this day. I even had one guy who had an actual fan-page for the script, which was quite flattering. The fan response is usually the same as my *Alien vs Predator* draft: the '*Aw, man…why did they never make that* *draft? It was so cool!'* thing. It's nice when people respond well to something you've written. Conversely, there are the armchair critics — and usually they're about fifteen to nineteen years old and snarky — who think they can do better and tell you so. I remember there was one webpage that actually did a *Mystery Science Theatre* running commentary on the script. I had to admire them for their stamina. There's another webpage out there that hosts pirated screenplays — it's up there right now, you can go find it. On the page for my draft, there are whole bunch of comments calling me a hack, and laughing about the plot. It was very vicious, and I was a little hurt, right up to the point when somebody mentioned a plotpoint that had nothing to do with my story! That's when I realised that somebody had posted David Schow's version of *Freddy vs Jason*, and attributed it to me. I hope David never goes looking for that. I don't know how he'd react.

The nicest reaction was, I guess, from Jeff Katz, the former exec from New Line who went on to do some *Freddy vs Jason* comic books and tried to get the *Freddy vs Jason vs Ash* movie off the ground. On a couple of the making-of documentaries on that big *Elm Street* box set, he kept saying nice things about my draft, citing it as his favourite. I know Jeff now, but I'd never met him at the time. It did make me smile.

My favorite "out there" story, though, was around 2001, 2002. My agent sent me an email he received from the dean of a prestigious east coast university, whom I won't mention. But he forwarded a script one of his students had written, and wanted to know if we'd take a look at it and see if we recognized anything. I was curious, and gave it a once-over, and I was thunderstruck. The student in question had taken my *Freddy vs Jason* draft and performed — I dunno — I guess a three day polish on it. He changed all the character names, and tweaked references to the *Elm Street* and Jason movies so that they just felt like generic monster-killer characters instead. But I guess he didn't do enough of a job disguising his source, as his creative writer tutor had twigged something was amiss. Otherwise, just about every word was exactly the same, and this was his final graduation piece! I replied to the dean confirming that it was my draft, and asked him what would happen to the student. I guess the guy was expelled in disgrace. I had to feel for him in a way. He only did academically what a lot of lazy screenwriters out in Hollywood are getting paid to do daily, except he got called on it!

DM: Did you eventually see the 2003 film and, if so, what did you think of it?

PB: We went through a WGA arbitration right before the move was due to open, and there were about a dozen or so writers on it being judged for their contribution. The Writers Guild have you write a little document asking for your history on the project, and what you feel remains yours in the finished story, and then make their assessment on that basis. If you get a credit, well: then you get the money when the film makes a gah-zillion dollars, so it can sometimes get a bit vicious at that point. I was involved in a very nasty one on *Alien vs Predator*. There were a couple of things of my *Freddy vs Jason* in there still, but — you know — the film that was made was pretty much a straightforward teen slasher film, and quite different to mine. It was certainly better than it had any right to be. Watching it on DVD, I guess I hadn't been as diligent at the arbitration stage as I should have been, as I spotted a few more scraps of mine in there I hadn't noticed in the arbitration. But, you know. I wasn't looking for a credit on it, so it didn't bother me.

JASON VS LEATHERFACE

Long before he ever appeared on Elm Street, Jason made his way south for a bloody rendezvous with the original *Texas Chainsaw Massacre* clan. Published by Topps Comics in 1995, this three-issue miniseries was aptly titled *Jason vs Leatherface*. Written by Nancy Collins and David Imhoff, the story is outrageously fun. The comics nail the spirit of the characters, though some details are a little off such as Pamela Voorhees being called Doris and the Sawyer family living in Sawyerville, Texas, but these are minor quibbles.

The story finds Crystal Lake in bad shape. The water supply has been poisoned by toxic waste and must be drained. This frees Jason from his watery prison, who boards a train headed for Texas. (This story appears to take place following *Friday the 13th Part VI: Jason Lives*). At this journey's explosive end, he goes exploring in a forest and comes across Leatherface and Nubbins (the Hitchhiker). They initially take him for a victim before recognizing him as an equal. The pair then bring him home to meet Drayton (the Cook) and Grandpa, who still swings a mean hammer.

Nubbins continually berates and attacks Leatherface, which angers their hockey-masked guest. Witnessing this reminds him of childhood abuse he experienced the hands of his father. Jason repeatedly comes to Leatherface's defense, which results in a bizarre friendship between the silent slashers. The Sawyer family invite Jason to be their special guest at dinner, though he refuses to eat their obviously human feast. During the meal, Nubbins notices that Leatherface has left bloody fingerprints on a comic book. He goes to stab his brother as punishment, but Jason intervenes and ends up attacking Nubbins, Grandpa, and Drayton. Unable to stand by as this assault plays out, Leatherface battles Jason to save his family, resulting in their guest being knocked unconcious. The family dump his body in a nearby swamp and, upon waking, the titan travels back to Crystal Lake.

Although *Jason vs Leatherface* fits neither franchise's cinematic continuity, it does feature some intriguing writing. These issues allow the reader unique insight into Jason's thought process. In what may be a first, the titan is shown kindness, friendship, and compassion by grotesque beings not unlike himself. For a brief moment, it seems like he may even be a good fit with the Sawyer clan, dietary issues aside. As the final pages read, "Jason could have slaughtered them at any given time, but he didn't. He begins to wonder why, but loses interest halfway through the thought. He has had enough of strange people and different places. It's time to go home."

Chapter Five
The Reiff/Voris Draft

1996

THE SCREENWRITERS

Following their rejection of the Briggs draft, New Line hired screenwriters Ethan Reiff and Cyrus Voris to help steer the project back toward the framework of the Abernathy script. Studio chief Michael De Luca turned to the writing team following their work on Universal Pictures' *Tales from the Crypt: Demon Knight*, which was widely viewed as the successful launch of a planned *Crypt* trilogy. The horror hit stood as Reiff and Voris' first foray into the genre, though the notoriety it brought them led many to believe it would not be their last. Prior to *Demon Knight*, the writers had teamed on several action films including 1994's *Men of War* starring Dolph Lundgren.

Technically, this did not mark their first involvement with *Freddy vs Jason*. Two years prior, Reiff and Voris had unsuccessfully pitched New Line a more urban take on the crossover. That version saw the titans battling it out inside a housing project as Freddy sought to obtain the Holy Grail from which Christ drank. Drinking from the grail would grant him unlimited power across both the dreamscape and reality. Reiff and Voris' 1994 pitch had little in common with their 1996 screenplay, which marked a return to earlier *Freddy vs Jason* concepts. Rather than develop the script in-house, New Line paired them with Sean Cunningham for creative guidance. Submitted in late August, this first draft was officially titled *Freddy vs Jason: Millennium Massacre*. While the studio saw enough promise in their work to begin the search for a director, they still sought additional development of the material. In doing so, they reassumed control from Cunningham and began to work directly with the screenwriters.

Following their departure from the project, Reiff and Voris would go on to write screenplays for films like Paul Hunter's *Bulletproof Monk* and Ridley Scott's *Robin Hood*. They would later provide the story for *Kung Fu Panda*, the screenplay of which was written by fellow *Freddy vs Jason* writing team Jonathan Aibel and Glenn Berger.

THE PLOT

Millennium Massacre finds a powerless Freddy trapped in a space called the "Netherworld," a dark void between dream and reality. A murderous cult known as the Fred-heads look to rescue their master from this dimension so that he may unleash hell on Earth. They plan to do this by way of a prophecy set to unfold as the new millennium dawns. Per the plan, the cultists kidnap a young virgin through whom Freddy can be reborn more powerful than ever before. In order to get her back safely and prevent the apocalypse, the girl's sister and friends team up with a mysterious stranger from Freddy's past who believes

the only way to stop one monster is with another, namely Jason Voorhees. With only hours to go until New Years, this motley crew becomes humanity's only hope to avoid Freddy's dark future for the world.

Having now unsuccessfully explored three different directions for *Freddy vs Jason*, New Line brought on Reiff and Voris requesting they look to the original Abernathy draft for inspiration. As a result, *Millennium Massacre* revisits and revises several concepts that originated in *Nightmare 13*. Elements such as the murderous cult, the dream hallucinogen and the title characters' shared past all return. These ideas are not directly transposed into the new script, but rather adapted and infused with new details. The Y2K angle may owe to the Briggs draft, which was also millennium-centric. In several instances, the Reiff/Voris script contains what might be considered the strongest versions of these earlier ideas.

This *Freddy vs Jason* is much like a roller-coaster that starts at the top, which is to say it skips the slow, chain-clanking ascent leading up to the first thrilling fall. It doesn't build to tension - it starts with it. At this draft's outset, the story is already well in motion with a world writhing in chaos. A movie this fast-paced might risk losing the casual movie-goer lacking in an encyclopedic knowledge of Freddy and Jason, but Reiff and Voris implant enough exposition to keep the uninitiated up to speed. Their script more than earns the *Massacre* of its name with several blood-soaked sequences, not the least of which is a communal nightmare shared by half-a-thousand criminally insane inmates at a state hospital.

Tonally, *Millennium Massacre* is among the darker *Freddy vs Jason* screenplays. This is not a story set against the backdrop of a sleepy suburban neighborhood or quaint lakeside community. This tale unfolds on a planet that has begun to tear itself apart. The first page attributes this global panic to the rapidly approaching new millennium, which is but a scant twenty-four hours away. News broadcasts detail a harsh reality. Suicide rates have jumped seventy-five percent. Emergency rooms are beyond capacity. Places of worship are overrun with the desperate and hopeless. Mass rioting has broken out in the streets of every major country around the globe. Humanity is circling the drain.

The opening news segment contains interview material with a fictional Dr. Robert Snyder from New York University about how similar pandemonium occurred in the year 999 A.D.. The mention of NYU in *Millennium Massacre* is not particularly surprising given that both Reiff and Voris attended school there, first meeting at a graduation party thrown by a mutual friend.

THE HUMANS

The story's lead is Michelle Barrett (renamed and aged several years from Meagan in the Abernathy draft), a twenty-four-year-old registered nurse raising her fifteen-year-old sister, Lizzie (no longer a special needs teenager also per the earlier draft), in the wake of their parents' deaths. Their relationship has been strained by this loss in recent months. Michelle does have a supportive boyfriend in construction worker Jess Yastremsky.

Appearing here from the David Schow rewrite is Fred-head mastermind Dominic Necros, born Dominic Kopetnick of Queens, New York. In an attempt to resemble his idol, Necros sports third-degree burns across his entire body that have left his nerve-endings scorched. Consequently, he can feel neither pain nor pleasure, which makes him a potent adversary. As a faithful follower, he is most reverent of his wicked master ("Blessed be his unholy name.") and boundlessly dedicated to their cause. The opening news segment reports that Necros was recently arrested in connection with several child murders days before New Year's 1999. Little does anyone know that this arrest is all part of the bigger plan. On paper, saddling Freddy with a sidekick may sound like a risky move, but Reiff and Voris' show that it can be done well.

The standout character of *Millennium Massacre* is not Dominic Necros, but the mysterious Owen J. Whitaker, who shows up to assist Michelle in saving her sister from the Fred-heads. Initially reluctant to accept his help, she recognizes that he knows a great deal about Freddy, which likely explains the four elongated scars across his face. She later learns that Whitaker was the Springwood judge who forgot to sign the search warrant that allowed Freddy to walk free in 1968. Overcome with guilt, he resigned his post immediately after and has dedicated his life to learning about Freddy in an attempt to stop him. You might well think of him as *Elm Street*'s own Van Helsing.

Michelle and friends join Whitaker in his quest to stop the Fred-heads, but are alarmed to learn his plan includes resurrecting Jason Voorhees from his watery grave at Crystal Lake. Whitaker is essentially serving the same function in *Millennium Massacre* that ex-cultist Erwin served in *Nightmare 13*, that of the "timely monster expert." The difference here is that a good deal more background and motivation has been written into this new part's characterization. Another difference is that Whitaker knows to grab a fresh heart prior to arriving at Crystal Lake in order to put Jason into play, unlike in the Abernathy draft. That heart again hails the heroine's freshly dead boyfriend.

The story contains two minor characters in the first act that deliver some helpful exposition about the current cult situation. These roles are Doctor Cunningham and Detective Craven, named in marvelous tribute to Freddy and Jason's creators. In an even more fitting turn, they are both slashed to death by a Fred-head's razor glove.

RETURN OF THE FRED HEADS

Reiff and Voris are nowhere more successful with *Millennium Massacre* than in their handling of the Fred-head material, which is so strong that it serves as another reminder there is an *Elm Street* sequel begging to be made on this subject. The cult's role here is significantly expanded upon from the Abernathy draft. We learn that police suspect the cult to include anywhere from one-hundred-and-fifty to two-hundred members, with countless more copycats. True membership involves a painful initiation process. Legitimate Fred-heads scar their palms with battery acid, which serves two purposes. One, it is a visual tribute to their burned master and, two, it destroys their fingerprints, which makes them more difficult to link to the crimes they commit.

The cultists in Abernathy's *Nightmare 13* had hideous burns covering their bodies. Reiff and Voris scale back this detail to only their palms, allowing these new Fred-heads to infiltrate public spaces posing as ordinary citizens. They could be reporters, police officers, doctors - you ultimately have no way of knowing who is a Fred-head short of checking their palms. This uncertainty ratchets up the tension another level and sets up a major betrayal late in the story. The Fred-heads of the Reiff/Voris draft are also not above suiciding for their cause by way of self-immolation. Cult members are equipped with "concentrated napalm capsules" that explode when bitten.

Millennium Massacre further expands upon the "dream dope" concept as first introduced in *Nightmare 13*. As originally envisioned by Abernathy, the drug was a mild narcotic that put its users in contact with Freddy. The updated drug seen in the Reiff/Voris draft is called Tetrocaine and its effects are considerably more dangerous. A hallucinogen similar to South American tribal drugs, Tetrocaine is said to invoke shared dreams in its users. While that might be helpful in assembling an army to fight Freddy, it is put to more sinister use when Dominic Necros secretly doses the entire patient population of a state hospital for the criminally insane. The result is one huge hyper-violent nightmare.

Reiff and Voris allow the Fred-heads several chilling moments in their story, not the least of which is young Lizzie's kidnapping. While home alone, she begins to hear the faint sound of ominous singing. Flipping off the television, the voices grow louder. Somewhat alarmed, she races to the front door to find Necros and a posse of cult members chanting the Freddy children's rhyme waiting outside. The chant continues as they enter the house to abduct her.

THE TITANS: JASON VOORHEES

This draft finds the titan quite dead at the bottom of Crystal Lake with no explanation as to how he got there from the ending of *Jason Goes to Hell*. (In all fairness, that sequel did nothing to explain how he managed to walk away from *Part 8*'s toxic sewer bath.) Whitaker reasons that resurrecting Jason will require two things; tremendous power and a fresh heart. For the former, he uses a generator to electrify the waters of Crystal Lake. Beginning a chant in ancient aramaic, Whitaker tosses Jason's original hockey mask and machete into the lake, which he stole from a police locker years before. Mid-incantation, the Fred-heads appear and open fire upon the group. Whitaker overpowers one cultist and cuts a beating heart from his chest. Tossing said organ into the now bubbling waters, he finishes the incantation. Seconds later, an unsightly-looking Jason rises from the depth - masked and armed - ready to slash through the attacking Fred-heads.

With the cultists slain, the raging titan turns his attention to the heroes. Thinking fast, Michelle injects Jason with Tetrocaine, plunging him into the dreamscape where he encounters a monster from his past - Freddy. This reunion quickly gives way to a scuffle. Jason wakes mid-fight, seemingly aware of what has just transpired. He impatiently thrusts the empty hypodermic at Michelle, suggesting he wants to return to the dreamscape in order to kill Freddy. The realization that they now share a common enemy forms the basis of a frightening alliance. From this moment on, Jason works with the heroes, providing them lethal protection as they track down the dream slasher. He doesn't chauffeur them around, though he does break them out of jail when later arrested by crooked cops.

Reiff and Voris characterize their Jason as determined, unstoppable and surprisingly intelligent. He functions much like a grotesque version of the Terminator. (He's even called the "Jasonator" at one point.) His sharp perception and reasoning skills suggest a smarter version of the character than we have previously seen. This is not a Jason that would be easily fooled by Freddy impersonating his mother as in other crossover scripts. Visually, he is as imposing and rotted-out as ever with maggots seeping from his many wounds. The titan is subject to much abuse in reaching Freddy, including the loss of his right hand. Without missing a beat, he jams a machete down into the bloody stump, the blade becoming a literal extension of his arm. This then raises the question: Why has dual-machete Jason never been a thing?

One concern with the original Abernathy draft was in how little Jason appeared in it, essentially going from resurrection straight into the finale. *Millennium Massacre* avoids this same pitfall by introducing Jason much earlier in its story. Although Reiff and Voris retain Jason's function solely as a means to battle Freddy, they give him much more to do leading up to that fight. Like in many of these scripts, his desire to kill Freddy stems from a terrible secret buried deep in their pasts, which we will address shortly.

The script does contain two curious details about Jason sure to have fans scratching their heads. Before being kidnapped, Lizzie watches an investigative show called *American Blood*, which details the nation's most heinous serial killers. The host mentions Jason's body count as being at forty-nine victims, which is a bit on the low side. Going off his cinematic track record, Jason technically hit that number midway through *Friday the 13th Part VI: Jason Lives* and by this screenplay had more than doubled it. (For Jason's "official" body count, see page 179.) Similar to *Nightmare 13*, this draft notes that a makeshift grave marker has been carved into a tree at Crystal Lake. The etching lists multiple death dates that correspond to the release years of the *Friday* movies. Once again, 1985 is included despite Jason not technically appearing in *Friday the 13th Part V: A New Beginning*.

THE TITANS: FREDDY KRUEGER

Freddy's depiction in *Millennium Massacre* strikes careful balance between funny and scary. Reiff and Voris infuse their Freddy with a renewed viciousness while still allowing him to spout the same bad jokes audiences have come to expect. His nightmare appearances are also far less campy than in the Abernathy draft with the exception of a Rocky Balboa spoof near film's end. With stakes so high, *Millennium Massacre* only works if Freddy is seen as a serious threat to the entire planet. From a story perspective, the cultists greatly aid in ensuring that seriousness by allowing Freddy a chilling presence in the real world whether awake or asleep.

It stands to reason that Freddy went somewhere bad following the events of *Freddy's Dead*. To this end, Reiff and Voris introduce a winning new component of *Nightmare* mythology called the Netherworld. Described as a "black void of nothingness," Freddy floats through this negative zone unable to escape. He can still manage to pierce the fabric of dreams, but is unable to physically affect the dreamer. After harmlessly slashing at Lizzie during an early nightmare, Reiff and Voris write that Freddy is beamed back to the Netherworld "screaming with impotent rage." Dominic Necros later reveals that Freddy must be brought out of the Netherworld into the dreamscape and from there reborn into reality by way of the "dream mother."

Not unlike *Nightmare 13*, this draft makes brief inclusion of the dream demons from *Freddy's Dead*, who are again mercifully silent throughout their appearance. The specifics of their function are quite different from the Abernathy draft. They appear during the asylum's communal nightmare as the inmates begin to tear apart their own heads in a gory spectacle. An army of dream demons then emerge from their head wounds and unify in a cyclone-like funnel. From within, a familiar voice can be heard singing Freddy's trademark rhyme. As the voice calls "9, 10…", the full-figured slasher steps out from the demon-cyclone and intensely delivers: "Never sleep again!" Revitalized and no longer bound to the Netherworld, he sucks the mass of demons into his body. This all occurs within the dreamscape unlike in the previous draft where the demons appear in reality.

In a bold move, *Millennium Massacre* reinstates a trait for Freddy that was considered for the original *Nightmare*, but decided against. As first envisioned by Wes Craven, Freddy was not only a child killer, but also a child molester. This detail would have undoubtedly resulted in an even more vile and despicable monster than we received had it not been written out of the script prior to filming. It might also have significantly impeded Freddy's rise to pop culture stardom. A child killer boogeyman may get to host his own anthology show and enjoy a line of action figures, but a child molester most certainly would not. On the flip side, reinstating this for *Freddy vs Jason* might have given the character the much darker edge he had been lacking in recent sequels.

Robert Englund addressed the abandoned story point during at 2010's Spooky Empire convention: "Originally there was a hint of pedophilia. But there was a horrible scandal in Los Angeles called the McMartin case. It's been made into a phenomenal cable movie on HBO with James Woods. What really happened was a bipolar mother freaked out, went off her meds and made up this story about her son being molested being she had been neglecting him when she went off her meds, so she blamed the daycare. They wound up arresting fifteen grandmothers who had been working there since the 1940s and putting them in jail for pedophilia. It was this huge scandal while we were shooting the movie. And Wes, obviously, downplayed any hint of that. He made Freddy's crimes more a symbolic nature - child killer. It's symbolic. Freddy kills children. What are children? Children are the future. What is Freddy killing? He's killing the future. He's killing innocence."

BLENDING BACKSTORIES

Every script thus far has suggested that young Jason did not accidentally drown that fateful day at Camp Crystal Lake as we have long believed, but was actually murdered by Freddy. The Abernathy draft first charged that a thirteen-year-old Freddy intentionally drowned his fellow camper. The Braga/Moore draft then put forth that Freddy was having an affair with Pamela Voorhees and drowned Jason upon being discovered. The Briggs draft next suggested that Jason was actually an Elm Street kid and later drowned by Freddy as revenge for his parents' role in the mob that burned him alive. Like their predecessors, Reiff and Voris also attempt to merge the backstories of their title characters, but in a way that departs from these previous origins.

In this version of the story, Freddy is revealed to have been a counselor at Camp Crystal Lake. The flashback soon wades into disturbing territory as we realize that an eighteen-year-old Freddy has just finished raping young Jason. He implies that this will happen again and threatens his victim against telling anyone about what has happened here. Jason does eventually tell someone, which results in his abuser being fired from the summer camp. A furious Freddy later finds and drowns the boy for his actions. Reiff and Voris allude to this possibility earlier in their screenplay through Whitaker's research on Freddy. The former judge suspects that Jason may even have been Freddy's first victim and that Jason has been slicing through everyone ever since in a misguided attempt at revenge on his killer.

HALLOWED GROUND

Much of the story unfolds across two hospital locations, each fairly creepy for different reasons. The first is the State Hospital for the Criminally Insane where Dominic Necros induces the communal nightmare to rescue Freddy from the Netherworld. The second is the finale's abandoned Saint Lucius Hospital where Freddy was first born. Prophecy protocol dictates that Freddy must be reborn in the same place he was originally born.

As far as classic locations go, *Millennium Massacre* ventures back to both Crystal Lake and Springwood. The infamous camp of the former location is first seen in present-day ruin and later in heyday glory through a flashback sequence. The iconic house at 1428 Elm Street is also briefly featured in said flashback to the mid-1970s. Unlike in the Abernathy draft, both locations survive the story without being bombed or set on fire.

DREAMS/NIGHTMARES

Reiff and Voris' use of the dreamscape in *Millennium Massacre* is slightly different than in most *Freddy vs Jason* scripts. We do get the traditional opening nightmare in which Michelle dozes off beside a crackling campfire. As she sleeps, Freddy emerges from the flames singing an acapella version of *Disco Inferno*. He slashes at her, unable to inflict harm due to his Netherworld imprisonment. Beyond nightmare sequences, the script uses the dreamscape as Freddy's alternate-dimensional hideout. Via Tetrocaine, Necros and the cultists are able to visit their master to scheme on their next move.

In another twist, we learn that neither Freddy nor the cultists can hide in the dreamscape when Tetrocaine is involved, which links together its slumbering users. Upon re-doping, Jason is able to quickly locate his opponent. In a particularly good scene, Freddy realizes his nightmare sanctum has been breached when the familiar "Ki, Ki, Ki, Ma, Ma, Ma" reverberates throughout the dream realm. He scolds Necros for having been followed. ("Someone else is here! *Someone is sharing your dream, you idiot!*") A moment later, Jason confronts a baffled Freddy. The hulking titan lifts up his hockey mask, revealing a deformed face to Freddy (but not the audience, as the script notes), who realizes the identity and significance of the brute that now stands before him. Although Freddy and Jason's dreamscape reunion is an iconic moment, the standout nightmare sequence in *Millennium Massacre* is arguably the communal nightmare of half-a-thousand maniacs, which feels like a nod to Freddy's origin as "the bastard son of a hundred maniacs." Once freed from his cell by a fellow cultist, Necros spikes the cafeteria's lunch with Tetrocaine, essentially dosing the asylum's entire population. Several bites into the meal, the rowdy cafeteria falls eerily silent as the inmates fall asleep onto their trays. Freddy then harnesses their collective dreaming power to escape the Netherworld. To hospital guards looking in on the dining hall, the inmates appear to be sleeping. Yet the scene looks much different in the dreamscape where the prisoners are violently prying open their skulls to release the dream demons trapped within.

BATTLE THROUGH THE DREAMSCAPE

Millennium Massacre concludes with a bloody battle through the dreamscape that ultimately blends over into reality. In a surprising move, Reiff and Voris use this opportunity to revisit the outlandish Nightmare Arena sequence from the Abernathy draft. In doing so, they adjust the tone to their story and dial back much of the camp. Visually, the boxing ring appears much the same with bloody-entrail-ropes and head-topped corner posts. The audience is no longer comprised of hell's most prominent residents, but rather the Fred-heads. Necros replaces Ted Bundy as ring announcer, intoning "Let's get ready to ruuummbleee," a phrase made famous by announcer Michael Buffer (who would later help promote the 2003 *Freddy vs Jason* with a Las Vegas weigh-in ceremony). Necros announces Freddy's weight at 160 lbs while putting Jason's at an astonishing 487 lbs. (Again, for "official" stats, see page 179) Just before ringing the bell, he reveals that whoever wins the match will get Lizzie as their prize. The fight is especially brutal - Freddy rips Jason's arm off, which Jason retrieves and uses to beat his opponent positively senseless. ("Float like a butterfly, sting like a bee. The Crystal Lake Kid is no match for me!")

Just as Jason begins to overpower his opponent, the nightmare changes. Gone is the boxing ring, now morphed into a hockey arena in an audience wink on par with a certain billboard from *Jason Takes Manhattan*. Here Freddy begins to attack Jason on the ice, hitting pucks with deadly force, which pierce into Jason's body. (The script does note one hilarious detail here. Necros can be seen leisurely driving a Zamboni in the background as the titans battle it out.) Reiff and Voris use this brawl to further demonstrate their Jason's intelligence. The slasher understands that he cannot beat Freddy in the dream world. For that, he needs the homefield advantage of reality. To this end, a near-death Jason grabs Freddy's glove and slashes his own throat, sending them both crashing back into reality inside the abandoned St. Lucius Hospital.

With this, Freddy has been dragged out of the dream realm. With only minutes to go until midnight, his plan is now a wash. He is unable to be reborn in the dreamscape if he is not presently there. As Michelle notes, "Now you're just a flesh-and-blood child molesting asshole with a *really* bad complexion!" The furious titan starts after her, angrily chanting his own song. ("One, Two, I'm coming for you.") Just before finishing the final line, he raises his claw to strike... only to be surprise-attacked by Jason, who tears Freddy's claw-hand clean off before stabbing him with it. Jason then decapitates Freddy "like popping a cork on a champagne bottle." The masked titan falls back, dying from his many battle wounds. Jason turns to Michelle and, in a voice low and hoarse, finishes Freddy's song. ("We.... can sleep... again.")

Our final scene takes place at the local morgue. Michelle enters and finds two drawers labeled Krueger and Voorhees. Their disposition tags read "AUTOPSY AND PRESERVE REMAINS." She replaces them with new tags that simply read, "CREMATE." The heroine smiles, wishes them pleasant dreams, and walks away. As the credits roll, The Trammp's *Disco Inferno* begins to play, which we will remember Freddy singing during his first appearance in this script. ("Burn, baby, burn!")

INTERVIEW: Ethan Reiff & Cyrus Voris
Screenwriters, *Freddy vs Jason: Millennium Massacre*

DUSTIN MCNEILL: What are your backgrounds with these franchises?

ETHAN REIFF: Our background is we are both genre fans, but neither Cy nor myself would describe ourselves then or now as hardcore genre fans. We'd grown up loving horror movies. One of our first screenplays we worked on together was *Demon Knight*, which became the first *Tales from the Crypt* movie in 1995. That became a success and opened the door for us in our screenwriting careers and from there we did a lot of horror. We were pigeonholed as horror writers at the very beginning of our careers and, since we enjoyed horror, we embraced it.

CYRUS VORIS: As far as the *Friday* and *Nightmare* franchises, I think we were pretty old school purists in that we really liked the first movies. With *Friday* especially, it just had this great drive-in movie feel with this amazing scare at the end with Jason coming out of the water. It's ironic to me that the hockey-masked Jason that everyone knows and loves really wasn't in that first one, but it was still such an effective horror movie. I feel the same way about the first *Nightmare*.

ER: The first *Nightmare* was more creatively ambitious and of a higher qualitative level, but still had the same gut punch power.

CV: They both have these great but simple concepts behind them. Those got more convoluted and complicated as the franchises went on. Beyond the first *Nightmare,* I also really like the third one where it's like Freddy against the teenage dirty dozen band of misfits. They stumbled onto a great cast with that one too with people like Larry Fishburne and Patricia Arquette. So, we weren't huge horror guys but we liked those movies unapologetically.

ER: It was important that we didn't have any disdain or contempt for the two franchises. We could be sincere in our efforts to try and do a good job. We wanted to satisfy the audience, which we ourselves were a part of.

CV: I've never thought about it before this moment - and it's kind of absurd - but our approach to *Freddy vs Jason* is similar to how we approached *Kung Fu Panda*, which we were the first writers on. The key element we brought to *Kung Fu Panda* is that we both had a sincere respect and admiration for Chinese culture and kung fu movies. The thing about *Kung Fu Panda* is that, while it's funny, the humor is never at the cost of respect for the culture. In a way, it was the same thing on *Freddy vs Jason*. We tried to have fun with the material and squeeze out all the thrills we could but without ever being disrespectful to the owners.

ER: Right. It was important that we respect the mythology that got us to this point.

DM: Is it at all strange to you that you went from *Freddy vs Jason* to *Kung Fu Panda?* Because that is quite a jump.

CV: Oh yeah, I love it. It just goes to show you how bat shit crazy our careers have been. But with *Freddy vs Jason*, I don't think much of what we came up with wound up in the finished movie. I remember the Writer's Guild conducting an arbitration on that film, which I don't think anyone asked for. It was just automatically triggered because the movie had gone through so many different writers and drafts. I imagine the only thing that carried over from our version was probably a comma somewhere in the next draft.

DM: Who did you guys work more closely with - Michael De Luca or Sean Cunningham?

ER: Mostly Sean. New Line basically hired us and then handed us off to Sean. You have to realize that New Line was in the process of becoming a full blown Hollywood studio at the time, leaving behind their slasher roots for greater ambitions. We went through the development process with Sean for quite some time, which was actually really positive. We love Sean and had a great time with him. Working together on that culminated in one of our favorite experiences as writers, one of the highlights of our careers. Sean hosted a dinner one night at his place and afterward held a read through of our *Freddy vs Jason* script. He invited an illustrious cast of Hollywood almost big shot actors, who came as his dinner guests but were also there to read our script. That allowed us and Sean to hear it performed and make tweaks to it. It was awesome.

CV: Sean was basically our creative boss for the project. We worked on it with him for a while and, at some point, New Line took it over when they decided they didn't like the direction he was taking it in. New Line wanted to be much more hands on with our next draft.

ER: Right, but the draft we did with Sean was good enough to convince them to start looking for a director, which is when they found Rob Bottin.

CV: All I know is that Rob Bottin came onto the project with our draft and decided he wanted to take it in some other direction. By that point, Sean had been brushed aside and New Line was working just with Rob.

DM: Can you tell me a little about your first involvement with the project?

CV: I think it's a funny story. Ethan and I spent most of 1996 working on *Freddy vs Jason*, but we had actually tried for that job two years earlier, even before *Demon Knight*. Sometime in 1994, we got the chance to go into New Line and pitch our version of the movie. As I recall, it took place in a more urban setting, like a run down housing project in Cleveland.

ER: Right, but at that point there was no draft they were wanting us to work from. There was no development trail that we knew of. They were just wanting writers to come up with their own original take on how to do *Freddy vs Jason* and pitch that. I remember that our high concept hook was that Freddy needed the Holy Grail in order to come into reality.

CV: Yeah! He was after the Holy Grail because it would give him ultimate power in both the dream world and the real world. We also had a medieval cult or something. I remember at one point we had Freddy taking a piss in what he believed to be the

Holy Grail, but it wasn't really. We had a MacGuffin twist where there was this girl whose name was Holly Grail.

ER: She was something like the embodiment of the Holy Grail. I don't remember how the hell Jason got involved in all of that. I do know there was something in that pitch involving Jason that we later used in our script. At one point, Jason is struggling to kill some teenager and gets his hand shoved into a garbage disposal. They turn it on and his hand gets totally mangled and fucked up. He pulls it out and jams a machete onto the stump of his hand. And he now has a machete arm. He picks up another machete and is now wielding two at once. We later changed it in our script so that Freddy cuts off one of Jason's hands instead of the garbage disposal. We were really obsessed with this idea!

DM: When you returned to *Freddy vs Jason* two years later, were you aware of its development troubles then?

CV: We were pretty aware. When we got there, I think they had just passed on the script with the courtroom drama in it.

ER: I don't think we ever read that one, did we? The script we were given to riff from was the Lewis Abernathy draft, which I think we both liked. That one had the Freddy cult. The challenge was always how to get Jason into the dream world to fight Freddy and then get Freddy into the real world to fight Jason. Our draft wasn't really a re-write of the Abernathy script. It was more like they said, '*Here is what we like about this draft. Take it and go off with Sean to do your own thing.*'

CV: We kept asking ourselves who we should be rooting for between Freddy and Jason. Freddy obviously has the bigger personality, but he's like a child molester. There is really no way to root for Freddy. We kept thinking that, while Jason was a serial killer, he was basically a brain-damaged kid at heart. That probably made him more sympathetic to people. So from this we had two challenges facing us. One, is there any connection between Freddy and Jason that we can mine? And two, how can we craft a version of this story where you're rooting for Jason over Freddy?

DM: And you solved both of those challenges by having Freddy kill Jason at Camp Crystal Lake way back when.

ER: Exactly. I was looking through our files and found our notes from when we were brainstorming this script. I'm just going to read you what we wrote: '*One was a victim of childhood neglect and the other was a heinous child molester. Wait, doesn't that kinda make them like natural enemies? Maybe Jason was even a victim of abuse himself before he died at the camp. Maybe Springwood and Crystal Lake are right down the road from one another and maybe Freddy molested Jason as a little boy. Now Jason is out for revenge.*' And that was our a-ha moment for *Freddy vs Jason*.

DM: Tell me about your approach to incorporating humor into the script.

ER: We wrestled with what the dynamic should be between the two characters. Freddy was a child killer, but by then he had become this devilishly charming figure in pop culture. They had built a mini-industry around the character, even giving him his own anthology show. Also, the later sequels had become these campy romps, which were not at all our style or sensibility. That wasn't what we wanted for *Freddy vs Jason*, nor was it what Sean wanted. So it then became our goal to make Freddy terrifying again. Looking back, I don't know that our version rose to that challenge and managed to avoid the pitfalls of too much camp, but we certainly thought it did at the time.

CV: You still have to keep Freddy's sense of humor, though. We did have some humor. It was just darker.

DM: How did you guys come up with your story's ending?

ER: Didn't we have Jason kill Freddy with his own claw? I liked that just as I liked cutting between the real world and the dream world for the last half-hour of the movie. Jason trying to fight Freddy in the dream world is a lost cause because Freddy is basically a dream master. In ours, he didn't really stand a chance until he was fighting in the real world. We were trying to not go too campy with those scenes, but, ultimately, you just have to lean into it and stage the biggest fight you can because the audience has been waiting and waiting and waiting for this moment.

CV: I liked how they wound up in a hockey rink fighting each other. That's where you would expect Jason to have the advantage, right? But then we took it into this post-apocalyptic *Mad Max*-landscape, which is what the world was going to look like once Freddy crossed over with his powers intact. It would've been great to see Robert Englund in that setting with red and green armor with hydraulic claws. In a way, I think that scene was servicing where the *Nightmare on Elm Street* movies had gone. By that point, they were all about special effects-driven dreams and lots of crazy humor. And then we finally brought it back to the real world where, in the final moments, Jason gets the upperhand. In the real world, Freddy is just a scrawny dude with burned skin. Jason is still a big, hulky maniac with a machete.

DM: Ideally, who would you have cast as Dominic Necros?

CV: I don't think we had an actual actor in mind when we were writing it. We were picturing Trent Reznor from Nine Inch Nails or maybe Marilyn Manson, someone who dressed in black all the time. Dominic was one of the elements they wanted us to keep from the earlier draft. At one point, he took off all his clothes and revealed that his entire body was covered in burn scars in honor of Freddy. That's what made him so hard to stop because he couldn't really feel pain. All of his nerve endings had been destroyed. We tried to make him as cool a villain as possible, though he was clearly second tier behind Freddy and Jason.

DM: Did you guys feel like New Line might actually go ahead with your version?

ER: When we came on board, we could tell this project was important to New Line, but it was secondary to the big studio movies they were starting to set their sights on. Cy used to always describe *Freddy vs Jason* as being like, if you were broke or homeless, it was the one dollar in your back pocket you would always have, no matter what. So you would never spend it or get rid of it because you always knew it was there. No matter how good or bad or uncertain things were, you always had that dollar to fall back on someday down the line. So... no. I don't think there any great pressure to do it right then.

DM: What happened when you submitted your draft?

ER: Initially, New Line handed us off to Sean and we had a very positive experience working with him in developing the script. There was some creative tension between us, but I think it only ended up helping the project. New Line was completely out of the loop while we were doing that draft. When we finally submitted it to them, they seemed happy with it. We were certainly happy with it and so was Sean. New Line even began showing it around trying to get a director for it. But then they came back deciding that they wanted to make some changes, changes that Sean really disagreed with. So they got into it and we found ourselves caught between the big producer and the studio. It wasn't a situation we were really comfortable being in.

CV: And at that point, New Line just decided to keep the movie in development. It was the dollar in their back pocket. They knew that whenever they decided to make the movie, it was going to make a shitload of money. So they could afford to keep it in development until they really felt like making it. That seemed to be their attitude. There were so many versions of that project written over the years. I think there are probably multiple good versions of it that could have been made and turned out great. I don't think it was an issue where they got to the last screenplay and finally said, '*Wow, this is it. This is clearly the best version of this movie.*' I think they literally looked ahead to the next year and decided they needed a guaranteed hit in the third financial quarter and just greenlit it.

INTERVIEW: David Imhoff
Senior Vice President, *New Line Worldwide Licensing & Merchandising*
Writer, *Jason vs Leatherface (comic book)*

DUSTIN MCNEILL: First, I must give you my compliments on *Jason vs Leatherface*. Those comics were great, crazy fun.
DAVID IMHOFF: Thanks! That was an idea I had on how to get these two characters together in a classic match-up that wouldn't be too silly. That was the most important part. It didn't make any sense to do if it was going to feel contrived. When I came up with the general plot, I took it to Topps to see what they thought about it. At the time, they were working on *Bram Stoker's Dracula* with Mike Mignola, so they were open to doing something else in the horror genre. I also thought Nancy Collins might be someone good to bring onto it because I wasn't a comic book writer per se. Topps liked the idea and they brought a fantastic artist onboard. It was a fun project and I think the fans enjoyed it.

DM: Fun, absolutely. Was there ever any talk of making that into a film? Because you had already cracked a good story that worked unlike on *Freddy vs Jason*, which was fumbling through draft after draft at that point.
DI: No, but it's funny. I think, for most part, that comic book went under the radar if you look at it from the standpoint of the corporation that New Line was. They just saw it as a comic book out there on its own that didn't really cause any problems for the movie side and that was it! I do appreciate you saying that. I get the sense that you are a big fan of these properties and to hear you say you like the comic book is very meaningful to me.

DM: Tell me how you came onto New Line.

DI: I came to New Line in February of 1990. I basically set up their global merchandising division. At that time, if someone was going to describe New Line Cinema in the trades they were going to say '*The house that Freddy built.*' That was a common thread that ran through all the articles because the *Nightmare on Elm Street* series had been so successful. Unfortunately, I came on right after Reverend Don Wildmon had launched a campaign to rid the marketplace of all horror and violent toys. At the time I joined, we had a pretty significant amount of licenses placed to a third party agents. I would basically walk around toy fairs and showrooms where people would come up to me and say '*I'm so sorry. I know you're new to New Line but we will not be continuing with the Freddy Krueger license.*' From LJN to Matchbox to Mattel, it went right across the board. I thought, '*Wow! This is going to be an interesting job here.*' Everything that exists now is going to be gone, meaning I'm going to have to rebuild this from scratch. I think we did a pretty good job of doing that over the eighteen years or so I was there. It didn't hurt that I am a true horror fan and have been ever since I was a little kid. I love the horror genre. I am pretty knowledgable about it and I like the characters. I think I brought a passion to my job and I looked for a similar passion in the people I would hire. And I think it showed in a lot of merchandise we put out.

DM: That's so crazy to hear you say. I know it was a different time then, but that kind of negative thinking is just throwing away good money. It boggles the mind.

DI: (laughs) Yeah. I'm going out of order here, but when I first heard there was a possibility that New Line may be getting the rights to Jason Voorhees, I got extremely excited. I was pretty aware that there had been very, very little in the way of merchandising for that property. I think there was a model kit from Screamin' Products and some novelizations. That was virtually all they had done! And I remember thinking what a missed opportunity if not only for Halloween. Jason is a character people would love to dress up as, right?

When we got the rights, I contacted Paramount's merchandising department and said, '*I just have to ask why you never did any Halloween costumes for Jason?*' And the answer they gave stunned me. They said, '*Well, first, he wears a hockey mask. Anyone can wear a hockey mask and pretend to be him. They do it all the time.*' They also had a corporate nervousness that if they were to license a Jason Voorhees costume that someone would wear it

and rob a bank or something. I remember laughing when they first said that. I told them that could happen at any point, costume or not. You can't stop it. If you only see your character as a guy with a knife and a hockey mask, then that kind of bank robbery could happen anytime. And with any costume or any character, not just Jason.

After that conversation, I went around to all the big Halloween mask and costume companies and got the same kind of response. They said, '*We don't need a license from you. We've been selling hockey masks for years and we've been doing very well, thank you.*' One of the companies I met with was Rubie's and they've become one of the biggest. I met with Howard Beige, their head of licensing. I managed to convince him that Jason was so much more than a hockey mask and a knife. He is a monster, a supernatural creature and both his mask and face change from film to film. I finally convinced him that it was in their interest to develop a Jason product line. One of the things I came up with was you have a hockey mask that you could remove and see what Jason looked like underneath. That began a very successful range of product. It also confirmed my feeling that there was untapped demand for product. We went on to do toylines, collectibles and everything else.

DM: I never thought about it before, but you're so right. Prior to New Line, *Friday the 13th* was largely untapped.

DI: It was fun to do. I did a similar thing with *Texas Chainsaw Massacre*. I continue to represent that brand today. New Line didn't actually have those merchandising rights at that time. They had done the *Leatherface* movie and the rights had reverted back to the owners. I just felt that if we were doing Freddy and Jason, why not also have Leatherface? Later on, we branded what we were doing as New Line Cinema's House of Horrors and took it to another level.

DM: I remember when the first wave of Movie Maniacs figures hit with Freddy and Jason. That was a blast.

DI: That was absolutely where everything kicked off. We owe a lot of credit to Todd McFarlane and Terry Fitzgerald as well. They did an amazing job. Around the same time, I was also working with Todd on *Austin Powers*. It was so weird to be doing Movie Maniacs one day and the next be doing life-size replicas of Mini-Me. But we're pretty off-topic now to how we started this. When did they start developing *Freddy vs Jason*?

DM: Around '93. That's when the first official script hit.

DI: I'm not sure if you're familiar with The Licensing Expo, but it's an annual trade show where all of the major intellectual property holders present their brands for licensing. Each year, having read whatever latest draft of *Freddy vs Jason* was available, I would make presentations to all the major retail accounts that went like this: '*Okay, guys. This is the year that Freddy vs Jason is going to happen!*' And then I'd come back the following year and go, '*Okay, it's going to happen for real this time. Get ready. It's coming!*' And again the next year. It became a running joke to all the retail buyers. They would go, '*Get out of here, Dave. You aren't really going to try and sell us Freddy vs Jason again, are ya?*' I was like the boy who cried wolf. By the time they did ultimately greenlight the film, no one would believe me that it was actually happening!

DM: In your opinion, why did it take New Line so long to find a script they were comfortable greenlighting?

DI: I think it was real basic. There were two factors. One was getting the balance right. Some scripts were like a standard

Freddy movie with a brief appearance from Jason or vice versa. That was one factor. The other was that it had to deliver on the title in a way that wasn't silly. Same as in the tradition of the other great monster stories. You needed a script where at the end you could say, '*Yeah, that really was a Freddy vs Jason movie.*'

DM: Tell me about your working with David Bergantino.

DI: We had been trying to pitch a *Freddy vs Jason* video game on our own unsuccessfully for a while. David and I got connected through a literary agent I was working with and we hit it off. He was as much a writer as anything else, but he also knew gaming very well. He said, '*Let me go out there and pitch a Freddy vs Jason game. If I can get someone interested, I'll bring you to the table.*' That made sense to me, so I let him do it. I remember thinking how perfect it was that he already had the skill set needed to come up with a good video game. It's a shame that never happened.

DM: Did you intentionally hold off on *Freddy vs Jason* merchandise until the film was finally released?

DI: Yes, our thought was that any *Freddy vs Jason* product would have to follow the film. We didn't want to do anything that would either conflict with or, even worse, spoil this very, very important project for the company. The only problem we ran into was that we were constantly thinking it was about to happen and it wasn't. It was actually several years away. People came on board to work on *Freddy vs Jason* products with the expectation that it was happening that year and then it wouldn't happen. Thankfully, the movie did eventually get released and everybody benefitted from that.

DM: So the movie finally came out in 2003. Had the toy market fully rebounded from their purge by then?

DI: Yes, but not quite like it is now. It was still growing then. Today it's huge. After McFarlane, we worked with NECA and we also had a relationship with Sideshow. It was a crazy time when *Freddy vs Jason* hit because we were already in the throes of *Lord of the Rings,* which was massive. But we continued doing stuff with *Freddy vs Jason*. A lot of that product line goes out at the end of the year for Halloween, which is basically a celebration for all horror fans. The whole world goes dark. It's great.

DM: One trend I've noticed develop is that we no longer see basic Freddy and Jason figures. We now see a range of film-specific figures with tremendous attention to detail, which is fantastic.

DI: I'm glad you brought that up because it was always a point of contention between me and my licensees. Take NECA, for example, whom I respect and really like. When we first did our deal with them, they were putting out very basic figures. I had the strong feeling that much, much more could be done. When it came time to renew, they said they wanted to extend their license. I said, '*Okay, that's great, but you really need to commit to going deeper with these movies. Do different versions of the characters because they're not the same in each movie.*' They wound up not being able to do that because of everything else they had going on, so the rights came back to New Line. We then sold them to Mezco, who put out a whole range of things from the films. They did toys for the individual movies and they were fantastic.

DM: I see how that might not be obvious to someone unfamiliar with the brands or fanbase, but what a great idea.

DI: Right? That approach has been very successful. I think it's a bit ironic today that NECA is the home of Freddy and Jason once again. And they are just now doing the products that I pitched them back when they ultimately ended up losing the license to Mezco. I work with NECA now on *Texas Chainsaw Massacre*. I can honestly say that Randy Falk is one of the most talented people in the toy business today. He's also a big horror fan, which is great.

DM When you guys would license out Freddy or Jason for a comic or novel, how much control did you exert over the final product? Did you place certain stipulations on what could and couldn't be done in those stories?

DI: That answer is yes. We did have rules but there was nothing that was really written down to spell out what you could and couldn't do. For the most part, we were more concerned about getting to know the publishers we were working with. It was all about knowing what their creative approach was going to be, knowing what they might do. We could then listen to their ideas and offer suggestions to guide their creative process. It was also important that we knew who the writers and artists were going to be. When you got to know those people, you would then be able to trust that they wouldn't try to do something that was out of character for Freddy and Jason. Every single thing that came out with those characters, every panel and every word, was run across my desk first. I approved all of it. I thought we did some pretty cool things, especially early on with Innovation's Freddy comics and then the young adult novels also.

Chapter Six
The Goyer/Robinson Draft

1997

THE FIRST TEASER TRAILER

To say that 1997 was a bizarre twelve months for the monster mash-up is an understatement on par with *'Freddy isn't good with kids.'* The project's advancements this year would ultimately prove premature, setting it even further back into development hell. Heading into January, New Line was still moving forward with the latest script by Ethan Reiff and Cyrus Voris. Although the studio had initially paired Reiff and Voris with Sean Cunningham to develop their first draft, they had since re-assumed control in order to exert more influence over its direction.

Enthusiasm began to build for *Freddy vs Jason* in early March at ShoWest '97, an industry convention for theater owners held annually in Las Vegas. Film distributors also attend this event to tease their upcoming slates with lavish presentations. The '97 ShoWest was attended by New Line bigwigs Robert Shaye, Michael Lynne and Michael De Luca. The studio's biggest push this year was for *Austin Powers: International Man of Mystery*, which saw stars Mike Myers and Elizabeth Hurley appear onstage in-character. Beyond *Austin Powers*, New Line also screened teaser trailers for *Spawn, Dark City, Money Talks* and - in the surprise reveal of the week - *Freddy vs Jason!*

Variety wrote that New Line's *Freddy vs Jason* teaser garnered the biggest reaction of their entire presentation. Theater owners "applauded and howled" at the preview's conclusion, which gave the impression that the project was right around the corner. Little did they know that *Freddy vs Jason* had not yet begun filming. Nor did it have a director or cast. Nor did it even have a finalized script! The brief forty-five second teaser had been assembled using rapid-fire clips from *A Nightmare on Elm Street 4: The Dream Master, Wes Craven's New Nightmare* and *Jason Goes to Hell: The Final Friday*. To the casual viewer, these were not recycled clips from existing sequels but new images from the upcoming crossover. The video opened with an American flag waving slowly in the wind. The sound of a cheering crowd can be heard as narration begins:

> *"They are the two greatest champions the world has ever seen. All who witness their power fear them. All who try to stop them fail. Now at last they will face each other in the fight of the century, in the showdown of the millennium. Freddy vs Jason!"* (Author's note to the curious: If your Google-Fu is strong, you can find this rare teaser online.)

A ROB BOTTIN FILM
FREDDY VS JASON

One problem with the ShoWest teaser was that theater owners weren't the only ones taken by surprise. New Line had cut together the video in secret with little notice to Cunningham Productions. To some, the move to go public with was seen as a way to pressure Cunningham into finally signing off on a screenplay. That this perceived strong-arming followed New Line shutting out the *Friday* filmmaker from further developing the Reiff/Voris draft did nothing to strengthen their partnership on the crossover.

FINDING A DIRECTOR

In an effort to generate a momentum that might propel *Freddy vs Jason* out of development hell, the studio began to consider directorial candidates shortly after the ShoWest presentation. This happened despite the fact that the Reiff/Voris draft had yet to be jointly okayed by both Sean Cunningham and Michael De Luca as required by the licensing agreement. That small detail did not stop New Line from using this latest draft, finalized or not, to attract prospective filmmakers. The project was offered to a handful of directors during this time including Peter Jackson and Guillermo Del Toro, who were looked on favorably despite the lackluster performance of their most recent projects (*The Frighteners* and *Mimic*, respectively).

New Line's search led them to Oscar-winning special makeup effects man Rob Bottin, who was then perhaps best known for his stunning work on *John Carpenter's The Thing*. Bottin began his career as an apprentice to fellow Oscar-winner Rick Baker before going on to provide memorable makeups for modern classics like *The Fog, Total Recall, Robocop,* and *Fight Club*. Hiring the effects maker to direct a slasher sequel was seen by some as a risky move, though this had worked out well enough with John Carl Buechler on *Friday the 13th Part VII: The New Blood*. The only difference was that Buechler had years of directing experience prior to helming his own *Friday* and Bottin was a first-timer about to cut his directorial teeth on one of the most anticipated horror films of all time. Only one thing seemed certain. With Bottin in the director's chair, *Freddy vs Jason* was guaranteed to boast some killer makeup effects.

New Line publicly announced Bottin as director in mid-August. In a press release, the filmmaker said, "Rather than revisit old territory, my intention is to celebrate these characters by way of reinvention, elevating them both to a completely new level of horror using state-of-the-art techniques. They will be reborn in a bigger-than-life way."

At this point, *Freddy vs Jason* seemed to be shaping up nicely. The project had been formally announced, a director had been hired and the Reiff/Voris screenplay was closer to being greenlit than any prior draft before it. Then came the bombshell. Although Bottin had signed on to direct the *Millennium Massacre* script, he was not particularly impressed by it. He instead volunteered a thirty-page treatment detailing how he would like to see the crossover play out. Not wanting to lose their director, New Line agreed to ditch *yet another* script in order to let Bottin develop his own vision for the movie. This was dandy except that he had never written a screenplay before, nor did he particularly want to start writing one now. To this end, Bottin had New Line contract a new writing team of his own choosing. Screenwriter David Goyer was enlisted, who subsequently brought onboard then writing partner James Dale Robinson. Their task was to transform Bottin's treatment into a feature-length screenplay.

THE SCREENWRITERS

Blockbuster scribe David Goyer got his start in Hollywood under cult-horror filmmaker Charles Band writing films like *Demonic Toys* and *Arcade*. Soon after, he moved up to bigger studio projects like *The Crow: City of Angels* and *Dark City*. His first big break came with New Line's *Blade*. He has since gone on to write and produce major event films including the *Dark Knight* and *Blade* trilogies. Goyer would also pen Zack Snyder's *Man of Steel* and its crossover sequel, *Batman v Superman: Dawn of Justice*. He would return to *Freddy vs Jason* in 2003 to provide a last minute script polish just before the Shannon/Swift draft went into production.

Goyer has never been coy about the fact that he had little interest in writing *Freddy vs Jason*, essentially coming on as a personal favor to Bottin. This was somewhat of a convenient favor since he was already under contract to New Line. Although he has since had a change of heart, Goyer once looked down on such crossover movies. Speaking to the *Los Angeles Times* in 2005, he said, "*Batman vs Superman* is where you go when you admit to yourself that you've exhausted all possibilities. It's like *Frankenstein Meets the Wolfman* or *Freddy vs Jason*. It's somewhat of an admission that a franchise is on its last gasp."

His partner on this draft was prolific comic book writer James Dale Robinson, who may be best known for co-creating the DC Comics character Starman. His career has spanned a multitude of iconic titles from both Marvel and DC including a critically acclaimed stint on *Justice Society of America*. He would walk away from a seven-issue run on Marvel's *Cable* in order to focus on scripting *Freddy vs Jason* with Goyer. Prior to this, he had but one screenwriting credit to his name with 1995's *Cyber Bandits*. Reportedly, Robinson's passion for the slashers was on par with Goyer's.

(A note of trivia: Goyer wrote the original *Blade*, which was directed by Stephen Norrington, who has long been erroneously attached to *Freddy vs Jason*'s development. Norrington would later direct another comic book adaptation with *The League of Extraordinary Gentleman,* which was penned by none other than James Dale Robinson.)

THE SCRIPT

This take on *Freddy vs Jason* marked the first of what we might as well call 'The Bottin Trio;' three screenplays all developed from the would-be director's original thirty-page treatment. Although each of these three works covered the same major plot points, they differed greatly in the details. The Goyer/Robinson draft stands as one of the more elusive iterations of the project, even today in extremely limited circulation behind the scenes. What we do know about this version is that it was one of the darkest takes on the material, bleeding out whatever humor still remained by the Reiff/Voris draft.

Goyer and Robinson establish early on in their script that Freddy and Jason are but fictional characters from the *Nightmare* and *Friday* film franchises. From here you might expect the story to venture in one of two previously formulated directions. Things might have gone the *New Nightmare* route in which the titans supernaturally cross over from celluloid into reality. The second path, as seen previously in the Braga/Moore draft, could have involved the *real* Freddy and Jason upon which the slasher movies were all loosely based. Surprisingly, Goyer and Robinson go in neither of these directions. Their script instead suggests that the slashers are somehow *both* fictional and real-life beings. They only manage to make sense of this confusing continuity in the script's final pages via a plot twist.

The story focuses on a group of teenagers who travel out to Crystal Lake for a weekend of wild partying. Their drug of choice is a sketchy new sleep-aid called Somnambulene, a side effect of which enables its users to dream-share. Like so many sedatives, its bottle aggressively warns against mixing with alcohol, which the characters all do. The main teenager is Samantha (renamed from Lizzie in Bottin's treatment), a seventeen-year-old with psychic powers who recently helped police catch Dominic Necros, a murderous Freddy-copycat. Her boyfriend is named - ironically enough - Jason. The tripping teenagers spend the weekend pranking each other while dressed as Freddy and Jason, which makes for a dangerous game when a fugitive Necros shows up to exact revenge on Samantha. As the drug's effects intensify, she loses the ability to differentiate between reality, apparition, and dream. Is she being terrorized by the real Freddy and Jason or are they only her mischievous friends? The action climaxes into a fever pitch before transitioning... to actual reality. In a final twist, the entire film is revealed to have been but a bad dream brought on by the Somnambulene. When you think about it, this ending makes for an even stronger anti-drug message than Johnny Depp's egg-frying cameo in *Freddy's Dead*.

Watching this play out on the big screen for the first time would surely have been a disorienting experience, which seems exactly the point. Goyer and Robinson work to distort the boundaries of reality from one scene to the next. The nightmare sequences do not unfold not in faraway places created by the mind, but at Crystal Lake intertwining with present reality. This poses a challenge to the characters (and the audience) whenever someone appears to wake up. Were recent events real or only imagined? Or in some instances - both? Such is the surreal tone that permeates most of this *Freddy vs Jason*.

Addressing his screenplay to *Fangoria* in 1998, Goyer said, "I don't know if this was the correct way to go or not, but we tried to be as highbrow as possible. [...] It was sort of like Wes Craven's *New Nightmare*: Freddy and Jason don't exist in the world in which our screenplay took place, but the films do. So it was about a young woman who feels that they're real, though everyone is saying, '*No, they're just movies; you're crazy*.' It kind of dealt with that artifice."

One criticism leveled at earlier *Freddy vs Jason* scripts was that their scopes were simply too big, either involving the apocalypse or world domination. The same cannot be said of the Goyer/Robinson draft, whose scope is remarkably small. Nearly seventy percent of the story unfolds across several hours at Crystal Lake. The timeline is so compressed that the film ought to have been appended with *Friday the 13th*'s original title, *Long Night at Camp Blood*. The story's scope is further narrowed by the fact that Freddy has no grand scheme this time around, no great ambition to cross over into reality or be reborn anew. This is traditional Freddy terrorizing unsuspecting teenagers as he always has, plain and simple.

Per the Bottin treatment, the Goyer/Robinson screenplay borrows a handful of elements from previous iterations. Dominic Necros returns in this draft, though the murderous cult does not. Instead, Necros is written as an obsessed Freddy fan who has begun to imitate his idol in the most bloody way imaginable. Dream-sharing drug Tetrocaine also makes a return, now renamed to Somnambulene. The Reiff/Voris draft previously saw Whitaker resurrect Jason by tossing a fresh heart into Crystal Lake where the slasher lay dead. This version sees Necros murder Lizzie's boyfriend, cut out his heart, and unwittingly toss it into the waters of Crystal Lake where it resurrects Jason. (That means Jason's heart resurrects Jason, which *surely* wouldn't have confused anyone, right?) Further drawing from Reiff and Voris, Goyer and Robinson recycle the backstory of Freddy being a camp counselor who raped and murdered young Jason.

THINGS FALL APART

Goyer and Robinson submitted the first draft of their screenplay to Bottin and New Line in late 1997, which the studio forwarded on to Cunningham Productions for consideration. In what may have been a first in the project's history, everyone was in agreement. This was simply not a version of *Freddy vs Jason* anyone wanted to make, Bottin included. The effectsman-turned-director in particular did not feel the screenplay accurately reflected his treatment. The draft's problems were such that Cunningham Productions did not even supply notes on it. This *Freddy vs Jason* was certifiably dead on arrival. Goyer and Robinson departed the project for other ventures, neither particularly heartbroken over the rejection of their work.

Had the rejected Goyer/Robinson draft been the only problem on *Freddy vs Jason* heading into 1998, things might not have been so bad, but reports indicated that New Line and Bottin were clashing over what the budget ought be. The treatment's tall order of elaborate makeups would have required New Line spend more on *Freddy vs Jason*'s effects than they did on the entirety of *Jason Goes to Hell*. To make matters worse for the filmmaker, the studio had chosen to rollover five years of project planning costs into his film's budget. This now meant several million dollars that could have gone into casting, set building, and visual effects would be diverted to pay for work that occurred prior to Bottin's arrival. That he had just led New Line to spend even *more* money on *yet another* unused draft was a reminder of the project's troubled development.

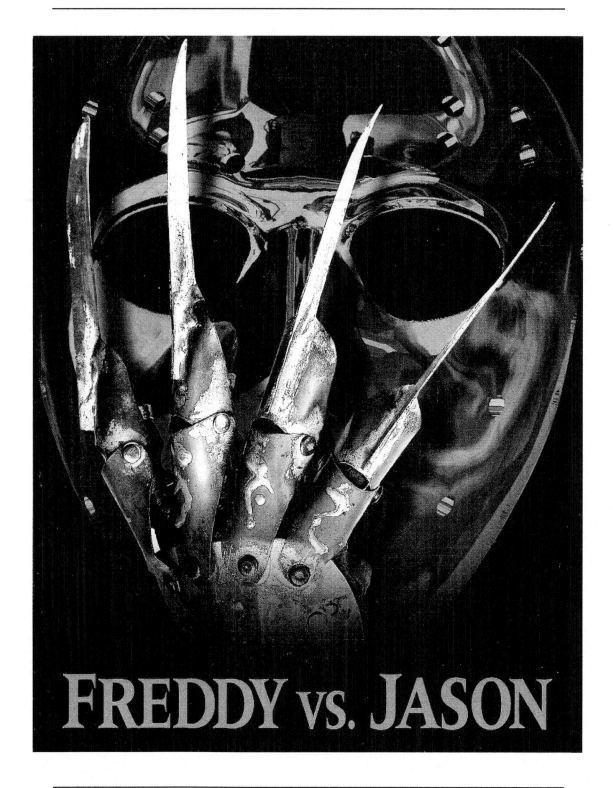

FREDDY vs. JASON

Two of the most malevolent and wildly popular horror characters in cinematic history return for the ultimate showdown, taking us to the very depths of hell and back!

NEW LINE CINEMA

888 Seventh Avenue, New York, New York 10106
For Licensing & Agent Information, Please Contact:
David Imhoff, Senior Vice President
Worldwide Licensing and Merchandising
Telephone 212 649-4944 Fax 212 956-1941

Opposite/Above: Original *Freddy vs Jason* sales art from the 1997 Licensing Expo.

(Images courtesy Charles Mineo)

To recap an altogether fumbled year; 1997 began with an almost greenlit draft by Reiff and Voris. An eager New Line prematurely stoked enthusiasm with a surprise teaser trailer in March. Bottin is announced as director in August, promptly rejecting the Reiff/Voris script. He hires Goyer and Robinson to draft a new script from his original treatment, which is summarily rejected by all parties. The year ends with *Freddy vs Jason* in worse shape than when it began with no active draft on the table going forward.

INTERVIEW: David Goyer
Screenwriter, *Freddy vs Jason '97*
Script Polisher, *Freddy vs Jason (The 2003 Film)*

DUSTIN MCNEILL: Some of your earliest screenwriting work was with Charles Band's Full Moon Pictures, notably the marvelously fun *Demonic Toys*. Could I assume then that you're a horror fan?

DAVID GOYER: I would definitely say I'm a horror fan, but not really much of a slasher fan. I was more a fan of *Elm Street* than I was of *Friday the 13th*. I thought the *Elm Street* movies - particularly the first and third ones - were trippier since they dealt with perceptions of reality. They weren't only focused on the slasher boogeyman angle.

DM: Did you know Rob Bottin prior to coming on board *Freddy vs Jason?*

DG: I did. I had gotten to know Rob through a mutual friend, Stuart Cornfeld, who had produced films like *The Fly*. Stuart, Rob, and I were all involved in a stillborn remake of *Curse of the Demon*, which Rob was planning on directing. I was going to write and also produce, so from that we all became friends. Honestly, I thought that Rob would have been a really inspired choice to direct *Freddy vs Jason*. I think his version, had it ever been made, would have probably been the most interesting take on the material. Certainly it would have been the most visually interesting. I was doing a lot of work for New Line at the time, which together with my friendship with Rob, is how I got roped into doing *Freddy vs Jason*.

I will go ahead and share an observation I had at the time, which I did voice to the studio. I was telling people, '*You're really overthinking this to death.*' By that time, *Freddy vs Jason* had already become a deeply troubled project. I just felt that when you go into something like this, you have to first ask yourself '*What is the promise of a movie like this?*' Well, it's *Freddy vs Jason*, so you need to make sure you hit the key Freddy moments and also the key Jason moments. Beyond that, you need to make sure it's a rollicking good time and that's it. Don't over think it.

Look at how many screenwriters had worked on the project, even before Rob became attached to it. They had been developing it for forever. I even said to New Line that I usually get suspicious when you have something in development that long. Was the problem really the scripts they were getting in? Really? Or was it something else? Surely one or more of those earlier drafts was worth making. And by the way, I don't think the movie that was eventually made was particularly good, either.

DM: How did James Dale Robinson come on board as your co-writer?

DG: I brought him on. At that point, we were good friends and co-writing things together. I suggested him because he was a great comic book writer having worked on *Starman*, which was a comic I liked a lot. From there I introduced him to the screenwriting world and we collaborated on a couple of projects. *Freddy vs Jason* was one of those.

DM: How much direction did you get from Rob?

DG: Initially, we got a lot of direction from Rob. I thought he was tremendously talented, but it was tough because he had never written or directed anything before, nor had he gone through a development process like this. We've all heard of development hell, but there are sometimes perfectly good reasons why certain things are developed in that way. Being a relative newbie to this, Rob was trying to reinvent the wheel, in my opinion. He had a lot of incredible ideas for the characters, but James and I felt they had to be incorporated into a story structure that worked for the movie. You need that in place before anything else could happen. So James and I were trying to thread a needle between Rob's ideas and our own Aristotelian narrative structure where we wanted a clear beginning, middle, and end. That also put us between Rob on one side and New Line on the other side, which was not a great place to be. The movie that was eventually made may have had a much more classic story structure, but it was so much less interesting than some of the earlier directions that were put forth. Honestly, it was mundane by comparison.

DM: You've worked with some truly iconic characters throughout your career. Whether it's Freddy and Jason or Batman and Superman, how do you approach using such established characters?

DG: My personal thought when you're working with pre-existing characters or well-known material is to remember that there are core DNA aspects that you need to be true to. Some of these characters have existed for a long time across multiple mediums - novels, comics, shows, and films. So my approach is to ask '*What are the essential elements that make this character who they are? What actions would be in-character and also out-of-character?*' I look at all of the different versions that have come before and try to decide what things have worked best. I try to come up with a holistic list of those things in order to do it justice because if you're not being true to the character, your movie is going to fail.

When I came onto this project, it was important for me to stop and ask myself, '*What makes Freddy, Freddy? And what makes Jason, Jason?*' You have to be careful you don't break the rules with your take on them.

DM: What are your thoughts on striking a tonal balance between two existing properties?

DG: It's always hard when you're combining two properties that were not innately born together. I faced challenges with that even on *Batman v Superman*. Even though those guys come from the same universe, coexistence was not part of the genesis of those characters. You have to admit to yourself that you're kind of mashing them together. They're having this same problem right now with the Universal Monsters cinematic universe they're trying to get started. They want to have a cohesive franchise with all of these diverse monsters and that's a challenging thing to pull off. Those are all discreet mythologies in and of themselves that individually generated many, many movies back in the day. It's a big task.

In combining two properties, you can easily fall into traps where you get too campy. You're lucky if you can have the audience pick a side. I was able to do that with *Freddy vs Jason*. I advocated for the audience to pick a side and that side was Jason. I was unable to do that on *Batman v Superman* because they're both heroes, which makes it way harder to write.

DM: Was there a time when you began to realize Bottin's involvement wasn't going to work out?

DG: We came to realize that sooner than we probably should have. We started to get a sense of things not going well even while we were writing it. Rob started squabbling with the studio and becoming more and more frustrated. There may also have been a change in the ranks of the executives at that point. I had really only come on board as a favor to Rob, so I had no desire to continue on with the project once he parted ways with New Line. But you know that was not the end of my involvement with *Freddy vs Jason*. The way that I got involved again was that I was dating the executive at New Line who became involved with the project, Stokely Chaffin. She felt that the script needed some help in the eleventh hour. So I came in to do some script doctoring on it and later on went into the cutting room and gave some notes on the editing. I came back to the project about a month before production was supposed to begin as a personal favor to her.

DM: Do you think it benefits a project like this to bring onboard a non-slasher fan such as yourself for a new perspective, sort of an outsider? Or can that hinder things?

DG: I think it definitely can help so long as you're being respectful of the characters. You can't look down your nose at it and still do it justice. Being in the business as long as I have, I tried to approach it from a craftsman point of view. I may not be the biggest Jason fan in the world, but that doesn't mean that I'm going to do something that doesn't make sense for Jason. I can still look at it objectively from a story structure point of view.

One thing I was pushing for from the beginning was that Freddy and Jason were not equally bad in this clash of the titans. I wanted you to feel sorry for Jason to a certain extent. He was someone that had been tormented and manipulated. So we decided that our story would show that Jason was being used and abused by Freddy and had been for a long time. That would have generated some audience sympathy going towards him.

DM: I think it's interesting that a lot of writers gravitated to that approach.

DG: You know, I'm not surprised by that. Doesn't it just seem like the obvious way to go with it? Freddy is the more intelligent one of the two. He was also clearly tormented, but Freddy seemed way too consciously aware of what he was doing whereas Jason came off almost like pure anger.

DM: You've voiced some distaste for the 2003 *Freddy vs Jason*. What did you like about the movie?

DG: Not much! (laughs) To be honest, I'm just not a fan of it. Not to take anything away from the screenwriters - Shannon and Swift. I just know the project suffered badly from having been overdeveloped at New Line for so long. I think the executives started to suffer what I call story fatigue. They eventually got so sick of it that they just wanted to get it made - no matter what. I think Shannon and Swift did as good a job as anyone could under not ideal circumstances.

INTERVIEW: Brian Witten
Senior Vice President, *New Line Cinema ('95 to '00)*

DUSTIN MCNEILL: How did you wind up at New Line?

BRIAN WITTEN: I was partners with this comic book guy, do you know Rob Liefeld? I had worked for Joel Silver and met Rob there. At the time, he was the hottest comic book artist in the world. Later on, I became Rob's producing partner. I was running his film and television stuff and also writing comic books for him as well, which I love. Around that time, one of my friends, a manager named Lloyd Segan who has become a very successful producer, called me and said, '*Hey, Michael De Luca at New Line is looking for an executive that likes comic books, sci-fi, and horror. You like all that stuff. You should go meet him.*' My experience working for Joel Silver taught me that the studio wasn't your friend. They were more like your enemy. So going to work for a studio was not something I was interested in. I was doing quite well financially with Rob, so why bother, right? But because Lloyd was pushing for this, I went to go do it.

I met with De Luca and the entire interview was us talking about comic books! We specifically talked about the *Amazing Spider-man* issues where Gwen Stacy and the Green Goblin die. We were talking about how different it was back then. When those characters first died, they stayed dead. They didn't come back a couple weeks later or anything. So my entire hour interview was talking about that and also *Spawn*, which New Line was wanting to make a movie out of. At the end of the meeting, De Luca told me, '*You've got the job. I want you to read through some scripts and we'll go from there.*' I was like '*Oh my God, I love this guy. I have to work here!*' I was the director of development when I started.

DM: Sounds better than any job interview I've ever had! How soon until the subject of *Freddy vs Jason* came up?

BW: That came up immediately. He gave me a few projects to develop right away, things like *Mortal Kombat 2*, *Spawn* and *Freddy vs Jason*, which was amazing to me as a fan-boy. I can remember in 1980 when *Friday the 13th* came out. It was summertime and my mom dropped my friend and me off for a matinée. We were like fourteen or fifteen. You had to be seventeen for those movies, but back in the day if your parent walked up to the theater and bought the tickets for you, they didn't care if you were underage. Your parents bought the tickets, so you were good. So I saw it. *Friday the 13th* scared the fucking shit out of me.

I vividly remember the scene at the end where the girl goes out in the canoe and wakes up and her hand is drifting in the water as the police are pulling up to the shore. I'm covering my eyes because I think I know what's going to happen. I tell my friend, '*Jason is going to jump up out of the water!*' and he goes '*Why would that happen?*' And I tell him, '*It's a horror movie. Jason has to jump out of the water!*' But the police pull up and they're waving at her and I start to think it's not going to happen. I sit up in my seat, uncover my eyes and just stare the screen. Then Jason leaps out of the water and grabs her! I am not making this up; I jumped so high that I fell back over my seat. I can even remember there were three people behind me because I saw the whites of their teeth reflected from the screen because everyone was screaming. So that's my *Friday the 13th* story.

DM: That is just too perfect, especially considering you went on to produce the *Friday the 13th* remake.

BW: Totally. Then later on, I was at NYU studying film and I went to go see *A Nightmare on Elm Street* and I fucking loved that too. Everyone knew you couldn't get hurt in your dreams since they obviously weren't real, but *Elm Street* turned that upside down and it was scary as hell. I had the poster in my bedroom at the time. While I was in college, I even found out that Wes Craven might be directing a movie at a company called Highgate Pictures in New York, so I got an internship there just so I could read what he was doing. He was going to be doing it from a book all about fears of childhood that later become real. The first thing I did when I graduated from NYU was option that book. It's now twenty years later but I still continue to option it. I haven't cracked the story yet - it's very difficult. Anyway, I'm getting long winded. When De Luca handed me *Freddy vs Jason*, I was psyched.

DM: At what point did you realize that the project was in development hell?

BW: Right away. De Luca handed me a bunch of scripts to read. He really liked the one that Brannon Braga and Ronald Moore had done, but that wasn't the direction they were going in anymore. I also remember reading an early David J. Schow script that was written before I got involved. There were lots of them, even one by Peter Jackson.

DM: Peter Jackson? Seriously? I thought that was a rumor!

BW: No, he definitely did an early version of *Freddy vs Jason*. His script didn't go anywhere, though, which is why you probably haven't heard much about it. It wasn't ever seriously considered, but he did do one. Who even knows where that is now? In the chronology of it, I think his was before Braga and Moore, but I can confirm that he did write a draft. Mark Ordesky was an executive at Fine Line Features and I believe Peter wrote it in his apartment in LA.

DM: So you went through everything that had come before, all the rejected material. What was your first move on the project?

BW: By the time I came on, De Luca had already reapproached David Schow about his draft, I believe. So I met with Sean Cunningham about further developing the Schow draft, but that didn't go anywhere. It had some interesting elements, but it wasn't what we were looking for. Then I happened to be friends with these writers, Ethan Reiff and Cy Voris, who had written *Tales from the Crypt: Demon Knight*, which I had set up when I was working for Joel Silver. And they loved the idea of doing *Freddy vs Jason*, so they read some of the different drafts and did their own. We didn't send them the Braga/Moore one because we didn't want to go in that direction again. So Cy and Ethan came up with their own take.

DM: How did you like their version?

BW: I liked their direction a lot. Sean had a very definite opinion as to where their direction should go and it didn't really align with what De Luca and I thought. So Cy and Ethan got caught up in trying to please too many bosses, if you will. Again, we weren't all on the same page with it. They knew me because we were friends, so they had De Luca and me on one side and Sean Cunningham on the other. But they had the best draft out of anyone, by far. Then around that time, I am trying to remember the chronology, you have the chronology, right? Who came next?

DM: Next I have David Goyer and James Robinson for Rob Bottin.

BW: Right. So before Bottin, there was this huge writer we were talking to, a guy named David Self. Since then he has written *Hulk* and *Road to Perdition* and other things. De Luca and I met with him and he goes, '*Oh my God. Freddy and Jason are two of my favorite characters ever! I love those movies! I want to write this!*' And De Luca and I couldn't believe it. We were like, '*Holy shit. David Self wants to write Freddy vs Jason!*' At the time, I think David was working with Steven Spielberg on some projects. So we had a bunch of meetings talking to David about his story and where he might go with it. And he eventually said to us that he wanted to write it, but that he would only do it if we would also let him direct it as his first project. We brought in his agent to talk about it and we were just about to make a deal for him to write and direct when it fell apart.

I remember we got a call from David and he said, '*I can't do it.*' And we were like, '*What do you mean you can't do it!?*' And he said that he had told Spielberg about what he was going to do, which led to a half-hour conversation about it. Apparently, Spielberg kept asking him over and over again if he *really* wanted his directorial debut to be *Freddy vs Jason* of all things. So he went along with Steven and walked away from us on it. And ironically, I don't think David has ever directed a movie since. So that was our brief flirt with David Self.

DM: Ha, I guess it wasn't a prestigious enough gig?

BW: I guess not. There was someone else that came in between Reiff/Voris and Rob Bottin. Sean Cunningham brought us a young director named Jim Isaac because Jim had done *The Horror Show* for him years before, which I was actually a production assistant on back in the day. He came in with an original approach for *Freddy vs Jason*, but honestly, we didn't like it. I can't remember what it was, but we didn't like it and never considered going with it.

DM: Really? That's interesting considering he later directed *Jason X*.

BW: Right? So next I was doing *Dark City* with Alex Proyas and David Goyer. I had also hired Goyer for several other movies at New Line. We were buddies and I loved his work. He was also friends with Rob Bottin, of all people. They were great friends. Somehow, Rob said he wanted to read the *Freddy vs Jason* scripts for fun, so I let him. Then he came and said, '*I want to direct this.*' So De Luca and I went along with it. Rob went off and came up with his own story where these kids all go out to Crystal Lake and one of the girls was taking something for sleep, the dream equivalent of Ambien. All of a sudden, we find out her boyfriend has spiked everyone's drinks with this drug, which gets everyone fucked up. So now they don't know if what's going on is real or not. Reality starts mixing in with their dreams. That brings Freddy to them.

And that tied into how De Luca thought of Freddy. He always likened Freddy to a great white shark. If you put chum in the water, the shark will find it and come to you. So we thought of the campers at Crystal Lake doing this drug as sort of like the chum. They bring Freddy into the ether. Their energy wills him into being and attracts him to where they are. And De Luca and I loved that about Rob's approach.

So he gave us that story and he said, '*I want my buddy David Goyer to write this for me.*' And we thought that was a great idea. Our experience working with Goyer was that he was a phenomenal writer. So he and Robinson came on to do it and they go off to write the screenplay, the Rob Bottin draft of *Freddy vs Jason* as we'd call it. But that still left us needing to make a deal with Rob to direct and do effects. And Rob, at that point, was the most expensive special makeup effects artist in the world. I don't recall what his supervisory fee was, but it was some astronomical amount of money. Don't get me wrong, he was well worth it and deserved it. For this project, Rob agreed to reduce all of that to bare bones, virtually nothing, because he would also be making money from the writing and directing of it.

DM: With an effects master like Rob Bottin behind the camera, I imagine Freddy and Jason would never have looked better, right?

BW: Oh yeah. One thing Rob wanted to do early on was get a research and development budget so he could redesign Freddy and Jason, which we agreed to let him do. We never did that at New Line while the script was still being written, but we did it for him. We spent a lot of money on Rob researching and developing these characters because he wanted them to look totally different. With Freddy, he came up with this notion that the clothing was very distressed, almost burned into his skin. Imagine if the flesh had evolved over Freddy's clothing. He gave Jason a similarly distressed look. He wanted to make Jason more of a deformed child rather than a lumbering guy with a hockey mask as we had previously seen in the series. To do that he spent a lot of time looking into what mongoloids and deformed children really looked like.

DM: So you've got him working on the visuals and then you get the Goyer and Robinson script. What was everyone's reaction to that draft?

BW: It was all very exciting until the script came in. I don't remember specifically why, but Rob felt that Goyer and Robinson didn't adhere to his original approach that they had agreed upon. They in turn felt like Rob had changed his opinion on what he originally wanted. So that creative partnership didn't work out, nor did Bottin work out.

DM: That must have been a huge letdown considering the anticipation you would have with someone like Bottin.

BW: Oh dude, it was. I'm not shitting you that his redesigns were so cool. Those alone could've made for a pretty amazing *Freddy vs Jason*, but we were so stuck on the script. In hindsight now that I'm far away from it, I can see that Mike and I were such fanboys about *Freddy vs Jason* in that we were overthinking it the whole time. We were trying to stay so true to each of the movies rather than just letting it be its own thing. But look what they did with the finished movie that got made, which I had nothing to do with. They just made it into a fun, fucking rompy thing and it worked! You could tell they were not overthinking it and it totally worked.

So when Bottin left, we had a bunch of scripts that contained elements we liked, but not one script that we wanted to completely get behind. We liked certain things from Goyer and Robinson, but also things from Reiff and Voris and also from the Schow one. Then one day De Luca called me and said, '*I have this meeting with Mark Protosevich, and he loves the idea of doing Freddy vs Jason. He wants to come up with a whole new approach to it.*' And that's how we got to Mark.

DM: Right, which I think was the most psychological approach to the material. Is that how you guys saw it?

BW: That's exactly how we saw it. We both loved what he came up with, but at the same time, it was really too psychological. This is Freddy and Jason after all. Mark is obviously a phenomenal writer. We loved *The Cell* because it was a smart movie. But we were worried that what he came up with was too far astray from what people would expect when they came into the theater to see two monsters fighting. At least that's my recollection of it anyway.

DM: I've talked to a lot of Cunningham's people and their impression was that New Line would have much preferred to be making this movie strictly in-house, that they didn't want to have to get Sean's or anyone else's approval. Was that your impression of the working relationship?

BW: I don't know that it was us not wanting him involved. You have to realize that his empire was built on *Friday the 13th*, which is a brilliant film. When I left New Line for Paramount, the first thing I did was go to Toby Emmerich and say, '*Let's reboot Friday the 13th because this brand has been lost.*' So I really loved Sean's work and Sean as a person, but we did not see eye to eye on *Freddy vs Jason*. And Sean's point of view is that he is an artist. Sure, he might also have been a director and a producer, but he created Jason and the world in which Jason lives. That's big. He was understandably stuck on that point of view. De Luca and I were not. We were trying to make a commercial product. We were like, '*Okay, let's do this and let's build on the mythology of these characters.*' We weren't beholden to anything because we hadn't created any of it.

DM: I talked to Sean yesterday and I'm impressed at how mellow he was about the whole thing. Ten years of development would frustrate me to hell. But he pretty much said what you just did. You guys weren't enemies, you just didn't see eye to eye.

BW: Right! And that's exactly how it was. Just remember that Sean was the creator of this amazing character and he had a vision for it. We were a studio trying to make something commercial. That put us at odds, but we didn't hate each other.

DM: You left New Line in August of 2000 just before *Freddy vs Jason* came together. What prompted your exit?

BW: Well, I had been there for five years. I'd had a great time and loved everyone, but I was being pursued as an executive vice president at Paramount. I was a senior vice president at New Line and felt like I had done all I could there. Paramount offered me *Vanilla Sky* with Tom Cruise and Cameron Crowe, who are two of my idols. They told me I was going to become the executive on all of Tom Cruise's movies, which I did. I also oversaw *War of the Worlds* and *Mission Impossible 3*. Paramount made me a great offer to basically continue doing the same things I was doing at New Line, so I gave it a try. I moved on up to the big studio.

DM: What did you think of the *Freddy vs Jason* that New Line eventually went with and released?

BW: I totally loved it. I don't know if I went opening weekend, but I went early on and had so much fun with it. I remember thinking, '*They did it. They finally did it!*' This was exactly what it was supposed to be. It was fun and it worked.

DM: You have a very humble way of looking at it considering how much time you spent trying to get it made.

BW: Well, they figured it out. I have to admit that, which is fine. They got it and I didn't. I would have kept going darker with it had I stayed at New Line. I would have gone darker and not taken the WWE heavyweight fight approach they went with, which was the right way to go with it. I'm not sure I've made enough sense in this conversation about how I thought De Luca and I had a pattern of overthinking this project. I'd like to say that I think the individual scripts that were getting turned in were good. They worked, but we were such big dorks of this genre. We wanted *Freddy vs Jason* to be this big, badass, amazing movie that does all these interesting things with the mythologies and complexity, when really the audience just wanted a fun *Freddy vs Jason*. That's all they wanted. Fun.

Opposite: One of many Freddy glove replicas.

(Photo by Joe Delfino courtesy The Nightmare Museum)

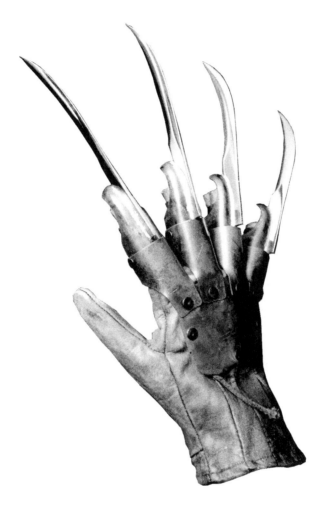

Chapter Seven
The Aibel/Berger Draft

1998

THE SCREENWRITERS

Robert Englund has maintained he was not kept abreast of *Freddy vs Jason*'s progress throughout its lengthy development. More often than not, he received news on the project as irregularly as the fanbase did through filmmaker interviews and studio announcements. *Elm Street* lore has it that Englund once got a surprise update from a fellow traveler during a transatlantic flight. He and his wife were seated next to a story editor from television's *King of the Hill*, of which Englund was a fan. After discussing the animated sitcom, the writer revealed that he had recently co-written a draft of *Freddy vs Jason*, much to the actor's surprise. This was Glenn Berger, who, along with writing partner Jonathan Aibel would script the '98 draft.

Although New Line had passed on the Goyer/Robinson draft, they had not yet given up on director Rob Bottin or his treatment. The studio had already spent a considerable amount of money on story development and special effects planning, not to mention having already widely announced Bottin as director. They would allow him to once again bring onboard a new writing team to adapt his treatment into a feature-length screenplay. This time he would pick Aibel and Berger, neither of whom had ever written a horror film before. Or any film for that matter. This meant the hotly-anticipated crossover of the two biggest modern horror franchises was set to be helmed by a first-time director from a script written by first-time screenwriters. *Take a moment and think about that.*

"The weird thing was that we had never worked in film before," Berger told *Collider.com*. "We were television writers. We had done *King of the Hill* for many years and Rob Bottin was a fan of *King of the Hill*. We had never written a film script, never even done a spec script. We still have never done a spec script. Rob plucked us out of obscurity and *Freddy vs Jason* became our first gig. It's crazy because we've also never done another movie like that - a crazy, sex abuse horror comedy."

In retrospect, it seems beyond bizarre that New Line was willing to put *Freddy vs Jason* in the hands of three people who had never written a film before, particularly when no less than eight accomplished screenwriters had already tried and failed to produce a satisfactory draft. That Bottin was able to convince the studio to hire such unqualified candidates speaks to their enormous faith in his own also unproven ability as a director. Unfortunately, this collective inexperience would result in the most narratively incoherent version of *Freddy vs Jason* yet. New Line would attempt to salvage it across three drafts, none of which would gain any semblance of internal logic. To quote Mark Haslett, then vice president of development for Cunningham Productions: "The Aibel/Berger draft was dead at our doorstep. There was just nothing we liked about it."

A ROB BOTTIN FILM

Not to worry for the sake of the writers. Aibel and Berger appear to have rebounded *just fine* since the rejection of their *Freddy vs Jason* script, both going on to wildly successful careers writing and producing animated blockbusters. They rank as the most successful screenwriting veterans of this project behind Goyer, scripting eight animated features in as many years with a combined worldwide gross of over $3.5 billion. Coincidentally, they would later provide the screenplay for *Kung Fu Panda* based on a story by fellow *Freddy vs Jason* scribes Ethan Reiff and Cyrus Voris. Aibel and Berger's other prominent credits include *Kung Fu Panda 2 & 3, The SpongeBob Movie: Sponge Out of Water,* and *Trolls.*

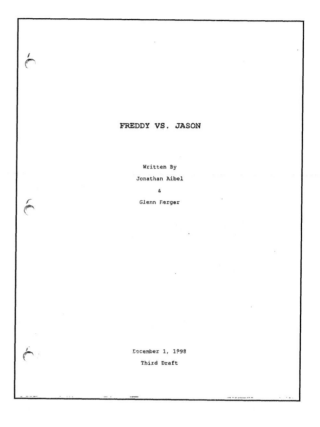

THE PLOT

This *Freddy vs Jason*, the second in the 'Bottin Trio,' again unfolds in a world where the titans are not real, but instead fictional slashers from the *Friday* and *Nightmare* movie franchises. After being terrorized by a Freddy-obsessed copycat killer named Dominic Necros, a young woman begins to dream of Freddy. She is prescribed Somnambulene, a powerful new sleep-aid with a peculiar side effect that allows its users to share dreams. With Necros in police custody, the young woman's friends seek to distract her from recent events with a relaxing weekend at Crystal Lake. Things go badly when their drinks are spiked with Somnambulene, the label of which strongly advises against mixing with alcohol. As the boundary separating dream from reality begins to disappear, the group must figure out whether or not they are being terrorized by Freddy, Jason, and Necros… or if this is all just a terrifying side effect of the drug.

Not surprisingly, the Aibel/Berger *Freddy vs Jason* is strikingly similar to the Goyer/Robinson draft since both were adapted from the Bottin treatment. The two approaches share an almost identical framework, yet differ in many of the scene-by-scene details. This new version is much lighter in tone and quick to self-reference in the style of *Scream*. Fans who enjoy a heavy dose of meta-humor with their horror might have chuckled at characters mistaking Jason as "the guy from *Halloween*." The expendable teenagers also have different names and personalities this time around.

The previous draft put forth a confusing continuity regarding Freddy and Jason, which Goyer and Robinson only got away with by framing their story as a bad dream in the final pages. Dreams, after all, do not have to make sense. Aibel and Berger go for the same postmodern approach but without the dream scapegoat. The result is a massive narrative blunder that sinks the entire draft. How can Freddy and Jason physically exist in the reality of the teenagers and yet still be fictional movie characters? The writers never resolve the issue. This draft seems unable to decide whether it wants to be a traditional sequel or something set outside the film continuity à la *New Nightmare*. There is one line that halfway attempts to rationalize Jason's appearance ("Hey, wait a minute. I remember someone telling me that *Friday the 13th* was based on a true story!"), but even this falls short of connecting all the continuity dots.

Fortunately, the Aibel/Berger draft benefits from a fun roster of misbehaving teenagers and a particularly strong female lead. This story's heroine reads like a more bad-ass version of Monica Keena's Lori from the 2003 *Freddy vs Jason*. Following in the proud tradition of Nancy Thompson, Kristen Parker, and Alice Johnson, this new final girl spends much of the script being terrorized until she reaches a breaking point, after which she flips the script to become the terrorizer. As far as 'final girl' story arcs go, this would have been a great one.

THE HUMANS

Our main character is seventeen-year-old Lizzie Daniels (renamed from Samantha in the last draft), whom the script describes as your average but beautiful girl-next-door. This iteration makes no mention of the psychic powers she possessed in the Goyer/Robinson take. Recall that Lizzie was first introduced in Abernathy's '93 draft as the thirteen-year-old developmentally challenged sibling of the main character. Now seventeen in this '98 draft, she appears to have aged in real-time.

Her boyfriend is seventeen-year-old Jason Lucas (yes, again with a second Jason character), a generally good-natured football jock. Their mischievous, slasher-fodder friends are Marnie, Todd, and Sam, the latter two of whom spend the weekend dressing up like Freddy and Jason as part of an ongoing prank war. Todd's Freddy costume is especially convincing since he stole it from the police station shortly after Necros' arrest. The brazen insensitivity of pranking a traumatized Lizzie with the claw-glove that nearly killed her in the film's opening is apparently lost on Todd. Not surprisingly, he is also the one who spikes everyone's drinks with Somnambulene.

The other major human character is the sinister Dominic Necros, making his fourth appearance in a *Freddy vs Jason* script. His depiction is consistent with the previous draft in that he is now operating solo, no longer the influential head of a murderous cult. He remains as chilling as ever. Unlike earlier stories, this script never sees Freddy acknowledge or support Necros' actions, making him a lone wolf. Compare that to the Reiff/Voris draft in which we saw Freddy and his underling scheming together on their plan for world obliteration. With regard to the character's physical appearance, Aibel and Berger write that Necros has "a cadaverous face, sinewy body, and malevolent leer. He is a vision of pure evil."

THE OPENING SEQUENCE

Aibel and Berger's opening sequence is so thrilling that you almost wish it would lead not to *Freddy vs Jason*, but to a new *Elm Street* sequel. As Lizzie and Jason settle in for a romantic evening, a figure emerges from the darkness in "a burst of cold, icy blue flame." This appears to be Freddy, though the script notes that something isn't right about this. He chases her throughout the house, brandishing a flaming skull and an extendable claw-arm. A security guard responds to the chaos and is quickly overpowered. Lizzie aims the guard's gun at her attacker, but is too terrified to pull the trigger, resulting in Freddy slashing the guard to death. The police soon respond and apprehend him, revealing this to be Necros in disguise. The tools of his elaborate charade include a mini-propane tank, spring-actuated razor glove, and an incredibly convincing Freddy mask.

The thought of an *Elm Street* fan so obsessed with Freddy Krueger that he begins to imitate him was an idea only hinted at in *Wes Craven's New Nightmare.* The Necros of the Aibel/Berger draft appears to be impersonating Freddy so that Lizzie's resultant fear will somehow attract his idol to her. The idea that fear of a fictional character can somehow will them into existence seems positively daffy at first, except that is exactly what happens. If only this *Freddy vs Jason* had explored that serviceable concept *within* the film-universe and not from reality, we might have a much stronger and coherent story. Instead, this draft's bewildering continuity betrays what might have been a decent idea.

This draft's opening is effective at establishing Necros as a deadly adversary not to be underestimated. The initial thought of a Freddy copycat may not sound like the greatest idea ever, but introducing him in this way gives the character considerable power. The revelation that this terror has been caused by an imposter makes it no less scary. The writers also depict him as having a psychotic confidence that far exceeds his abilities. Necros may not be immortal, but he seems oblivious to that fact, continuing to slash the guard's neck even with Lizzie pointing a loaded gun at his head. ("You can't kill Freddy. You can't kill fear!")

THE TITANS: JASON VOORHEES

The Aibel/Berger draft finds Jason resting peacefully at the bottom of Crystal Lake. That doesn't exactly align with the ending of *Jason Goes to Hell,* but being that this story exists outside the film universe, it doesn't have to align. This still raises nagging questions for anyone who has been playing along. How does Jason as we know him exist outside the films? Why is he at the bottom of Crystal Lake? And where is his heart? And how long has he been there? While searching a nearby cabin, the teenagers find his machete stabbed into a maggot-infested skull. Maggots only exist where there is rotted flesh, so they would not be present inside an empty skull with nothing to subsist on. Their presence then suggests a *newly* decapitated head. Are we to assume Jason slayed someone recently? If so, then how did he get into the lake without a heart? Or are we not meant to think about it this much?

In the grander scheme of things, this story's Jason ranks among the less intelligent iterations of the character. That isn't a criticism of Aibel and Berger's work, but a literal observation. This Jason is nowhere near as perceptive or intuitive as, say, the Reiff/Voris Jason. Certainly this isn't an unrealistic approach to suggest that a non-speaking, isolative, mutant hulk would possess limited intelligence. This Jason is easily fooled, not unlike the hooded-killer of *Friday the 13th Part 2* that mistakes the heroine for his dead mother.

One thing this draft does more successfully than any other *Freddy vs Jason* script is to show how Jason sees the world rather than simply theorize on it. Aibel and Berger are not the first to suggest the slasher's legendary killing spree has all been a misguided stab at revenge against Freddy, but they are the first to so perfectly depict it. This draft would have actually allowed the audience to go behind the hockey mask and see through Jason's distorted eye. We would have realized that Jason sees not the scared faces of panicked teens, but Freddy's cackling visage on every victim. This has been the ongoing source of his rage.

This screenplay goes for the same "*Jason sides with the teenagers,*" plot turn we have already seen several times before, but with much less emphasis placed upon it. The agreement between Lizzie and the titan constitutes a mutual understanding only in the loosest sense. Jason does not shake anyone's hand nor does he chauffeur the heroes around in a stolen ambulance. In fact, he still slaughters most of Lizzie's friends.

Several moments in the Aibel/Berger draft distinctly recall Kane Hodder's performance as Jason. Keep in mind that in 1998 many assumed Hodder's return was a sure thing. One such scene occurs at Crystal Lake when a confused Jason decapitates Todd dressed as Freddy. Catching the Freddy head mid-fall, the slasher notices something not quite right about this kill. A bloody head then drops out from the rubber mask. Furious, Jason rips the Freddy mask in half before punting Todd's severed head far into the woods. If that isn't a certifiable Hodder moment, I don't know what is.

THE TITANS: FREDDY KRUEGER

Like with Jason, there is no attempt here to connect with the ending of *Freddy's Dead*. The dream slasher simply begins this story alive-ish and well. *Elm Street* fans who prefer their Freddy darker would have found much to like in this deadly serious characterization, which gives the character *minimal* dialogue. This actually marks the slasher's most humorless depiction to date with nary a wisecrack or pun to be found. You can easily discern from this draft what the writers thought of the later *Elm Street* films. Whenever the teenagers impersonate the dream slasher, the script notes they come off sounding like "Bad Sequel Freddy," with cringe worthy lines like, "Freddy or not, here I come!"

With Dominic Necros anchoring much of the first act, the screenwriters are able to withhold Freddy's first appearance much longer here than in other *Freddy vs Jason*'s, which builds up a certain tension. The titan does not appear in full form until page twenty-six before vanishing for another twenty pages. Aibel and Berger's notes on his appearance match up with Bottin's proposed redesign. Of his new look, they write the slasher "appears more nightmarishly menacing than ever before. His red and green sweater is but ancient tatters, barely covering an inhumanly cadaverous form. Twisted burn-scar flesh is stretched tight over misshapen sinew and gnarled, elongated bone." Our first look at this draft's Freddy is truly nightmarish as the screenwriters note his face "suddenly contorts into a physically impossible ghoulish grin." (Be sure to visualize that as you lay down to sleep tonight.)

BLENDING BACKSTORIES

The Aibel/Berger script suggests the same intertwined backstory for the titans as the Goyer/Robinson draft, which itself was lifted from the Reiff/Voris draft. That is to say that Freddy was briefly a camp counselor at Crystal Lake during which time he sexually abused Jason. When his victim told others about the abuse, Freddy was fired from his job at the camp. On his way out of town, the future Springwood Slasher took revenge upon the boy by drowning him and staging it as an accident.

This backstory's appearance here (and in the next draft) make it the most prominent co-origin given for the characters in the project's history. In a unique addition to this tale, we get a brief glimpse of what teenage Freddy was like beyond murdering young Jason. This draft shows him playfully chasing after children, who appear to be delighting in his game, blissfully unaware of the danger in their midst. As he follows after them, Freddy sings a chillingly familiar tune. ("One, Two, Freddy's comin' for you,") In this context, it is a distrbing moment. Curiously, Aibel and Berger write that young Freddy is dressed in a "brand new green and red striped sweater," which seems like rather inappropriate wardrobe for a summer camp, but to each their own.

HALLOWED GROUND

In the plot description, I mentioned that Aibel and Berger's story unfolded at Crystal Lake, which may not have been entirely correct. Technically, the location is only mentioned once by name during one of Lizzie's early nightmares. Although the writers never definitively identify the gang's party spot as being Crystal Lake, evidence supporting the assumption is overwhelming. For one, the lakeside destination has a series of abandoned cabins dotting its shoreline. Two, one of those cabins contains Jason's mask, machete, and what appears to be a souvenir skull. Three, the story finds Jason himself at the bottom of said lake and we know how little he likes to travel, excepting *Takes Manhattan* of course.

That so much of this *Freddy vs Jason* plays out at Camp Crystal Lake only highlights its troubled narrative framework. The teenagers are shown to have firsthand knowledge of the *Friday the 13th* films, yet are painfully slow to notice anything odd about their lakeside destination. No one ever acknowledges that this spot looks exactly like Crystal Lake or that it may even be Crystal Lake. This brings us to another burning question: How does a fictional movie location manage to exist in this reality? There is just no story logic to support it. Either this script needs to unfold solely in the existing continuity or solely in our reality. The blurry area between those two spaces is a frustrating setting for a crossover sequel.

DREAMS/NIGHTMARES

Per the Bottin treatment, the Aibel/Berger draft weaves in and out of the dreamscape with dizzying frequency. In an interesting departure, the nightmares here are less clearly defined than we have come to expect from the *Elm Street* series. We can attribute this turn to the Somnambulene. Such a surreal state of altered reality keeps both the characters and audience on their toes as to whether present events are real, dreamt, or hallucinated.

For a script that seldom acknowledges the preceding sixteen films, this *Freddy vs Jason*'s early sleep clinic material warmly recalls the original *Nightmare*. Here Lizzie wakes up screaming during a sleep study, her arms covered with unexplainable slashes. She and the audience both know how she came by these injuries, but her parents and doctors are unconvinced. This leads to Lizzie being prescribed the Somnambulene, which is intended to "put you in the perfect dream state and keep you there all night." To someone experiencing a Freddy nightmare, that essentially translates to "traps you in your dream and dooms you to certain death." The introduction of the inescapable nightmare as a plot device is a commendably clever innovation to a franchise with seven films already under its belt.

Amusingly, one of the tripping teenagers attempts to bluff his way through his nightmare by dismissing Freddy and Jason as side effects of the Somnambulene cocktails. ("None of this is really happening. This is all a dream!") He patronizes Dominic Necros, taunts Jason, and attempts to explain away his friends' deaths as hallucinations. ("Beth, I'm glad you're sitting down. Uh, how do I put this? Sam just got his head cut off by Jason Voorhees.") The boy's theory is disproven when he pulls back Jason's hockey mask for a peek underneath. The titan's face is so frighteningly hideous that the teen can no longer remain calm. The mask partially shatters as the elastic strap rockets it back onto Jason's face. This results in a new *Phantom of the Opera* look for Jason, his grotesque mug now only halfway covered by the broken mask.

THE ENDING

By the end of this *Freddy vs Jason*, the only characters left standing are our brave heroine and the two titans. A beaten down Lizzie figures that her only hope of defeating Freddy is with Jason… and the only way for that match-up to happen is if Jason is dreaming. So she doses him with the Somnambulene before dosing herself, which plunges them both into the dreamscape. A brutal fight ensues in which Freddy's home field advantage allows him to quickly overpower his opponent. Conjuring an amorphous blob of boiler water, he begins to drown Jason just as he did so many years ago at Crystal Lake.

With her only savior on the verge of death, Lizzie experiences a sudden blast of self-empowerment straight out of *A Nightmare on Elm Street 3: Dream Warriors*. She reasons that this shared dream is as much hers as anyone else's, which entitles her to a certain level of control. Therefore, she and Jason are not powerless against the dream slasher, but perhaps even the opposite; they might be incredibly powerful if they so choose to be. In one of the most bad-ass moments of any *Freddy vs Jason* script, Lizzie declares to Freddy, "This is *my* nightmare. And in *my* nightmare, Freddy *does* feel pain. In my nightmare, Freddy bleeds! And in *my* nightmare, JASON WINS! This is where my nightmare ends and yours begins."

In that moment, all of Freddy's wounds begin to gush blood, sending him into a panic. Jason bursts from the floating watery blob, quaking with rage. He lets out a furious roar as the room begins to shake. Aibel and Berger write, "Every fiber, vein, and muscle in his body explodes horrifically. He transforms into a hulking, seething, mutated abomination. Jason has become the embodiment of Lizzie's pure and utter rage - a living nightmare!" The fight then transitions to reality with Jason now having the upper-hand. The masked titan's attacks appear to be more deadly than ever before. One machete blow accidentally connects with a tree, which explodes upon contact. In a last-ditch effort to stop his opponent, Freddy digs his claws into Jason's chest to rip out his newly-transplanted heart. With a final burst of power, Jason fatally skewers Freddy on his machete and says, "Freddy's dead!" Lightning strikes the dock where the titans lay dying, splintering it into pieces and destroying their remains. Cut to credits.

By the end of this *Freddy vs Jason*, the confusing postmodern narrative that troubled so much of the first and second acts is all but forgotten. Aibel and Berger instead focus all attention upon one of the bloodiest throwdowns of any crossover script. If you can manage to forget the continuity-challenged road that brought us here, the end fight is terrifically fun carnage. In a bold move, the writers opt to give Jason a little dialogue just as Reiff/Voris and Braga/Moore had tried previously. Interesting that despite the slasher's well documented rage, his singular line is not roared, nor yelled nor howled… but merely spoken.

If the Aibel/Berger ending has any fault, it may be that it cuts to credits a little too quickly. Of course, not every *Freddy vs Jason* story requires a post-fight tag scene, but this draft comes to a dead stop *less than half-a-page* after the titans finish battling.

BOTTIN VANISHES

As it turned out, 1998 was no better a year for *Freddy vs Jason* than 1997. Although New Line and Bottin saw promise in the Aibel/Berger draft, they were unable to develop it into a version both liked well enough to make. That is to say nothing of how little regard Cunningham Productions had for the latest draft. These ongoing script issues caused *Freddy vs Jason* to miss its announced 1998 release window, a disappointment to distributors and moviegoers alike. According to one *Fangoria* report, Bottin briefly considered rewriting the Aibel/Berger draft himself.

New Line's then director of development details what happened next: "I think the most telling part to this story is that Rob Bottin eventually just disappeared," Brian Witten says. "I mean that quite literally. He disappeared. I believe something was happening with one of his parents, whom he loved, and one day he just quit without telling anyone. We all thought he was still on board the project for a long time, but he wouldn't ever return our calls. I've reached out to him over the years since and I've never heard back. So he was gone from the project."

In retrospect, bringing a director onboard *Freddy vs Jason* prior to script finalization was a disastrous idea that would not be repeated. The years leading up to Bottin's arrival had shown that getting New Line and Cunningham Productions to agree on a screenplay was an extremely challenging task. Introducing a third party to that process with Bottin only made it that much more difficult. His departure rendered nearly two years of development useless, wasting a considerable amount in research and planning.

New Line's burning desire to finally make *Freddy vs Jason* appeared to have reached a fever pitch circa 1997/1998. In addition to screening a teaser trailer and announcing Bottin's involvement, the studio registered FreddyvsJason.com in May '98. They also contracted McFarlane Toys to produce official *Freddy vs Jason* action figures as part of their initial Movie Maniacs line. Advance advertising material from the toymaker listed the figures as being from "*Jason vs Freddy*" and showcased conceptual artwork from the project. The Freddy figure was even slated to include a miniature-Freddy "as seen in the upcoming movie." This was in reference to a scene in the already abandoned Goyer/Robinson draft. By the time the figures hit store shelves in October '98, their packaging had been modified to omit any mention of the further delayed production, instead featuring the standalone *Friday* and *Nightmare* film logos. The miniature-Freddy remained, which many assumed was a loose depiction of the Freddy-puppet from *Dream Warriors*. The smaller figure was, in fact, not from the third *Nightmare*... but looked similar enough to not raise any suspicion.

INTERVIEW: Mark Haslett
Vice President of Development, *Cunningham Productions*

DUSTIN MCNEILL: So when did you join Cunningham Productions?

MARK HASLETT: I joined the company in about 1995 or 1996 just as Cy and Ethan were coming onboard to do their script. Sean was running his shop with a pretty small crew. He had his son Noel and guys like Lewis Abernathy and Dean Lorey, who he did *Jason Goes to Hell* with. In terms of running his company, it was just Sean for a long, long time. So he brought me on as vice president of development to help push through new projects, the biggest of which was *Freddy vs Jason*, which he had wanted to do for years.

DM: How did you approach the project initially?

MH: In consulting with Sean, I looked at earlier drafts and made recommendations based on what I thought the direction should be. Of course, I was very young when I worked on this and one of the inherent pitfalls of the development process, I think, is that people who are young, creative and ambitious can be pretty arrogant when they're asked for their opinion. That was certainly me. I knew the project had existed well before me, though. Going back, you know Paramount financed and distributed the original *Friday the 13th* movies, but somehow Sean had gotten a hold of Jason. I don't have any idea how that happened, but that's one hell of a trick, isn't it? When he got the rights back, I understand, he had it in mind to get *Freddy vs Jason* made. He was very good friends with Michael Lynne, who was co-head and co-owner of New Line Cinema. Given their friendship, it was not rocket science to imagine *Freddy vs Jason* as a possibility. It's kind of like if you owned King Kong and your friend owned Godzilla. I can't tell you the exact biography of the idea, but it occurred to Sean very early on.

The problems we faced in getting *Freddy vs Jason* to become an awesome movie were legion. I don't know if I ever saw a draft that had everything come together. I even took a stab at it as a writer myself and couldn't do it. It's the kind of thing that development was almost made for. *Freddy vs Jason* sounds so awesome and you just know there's a movie in there somewhere. You have one or two pieces that really fit, so by God, you're going to figure this puzzle out! I don't honestly know if ultimately that puzzle had an awesome answer to be figured out.

But despite the challenges, *Freddy vs Jason* had enough interest in it that many, many smart people became absolutely convinced that there was a way to get it together. No doubt it could have easily been made from any one of the screenplays we had and audiences would've shown up, but we wanted more than that. We wanted to get the most of what we felt was a really potent idea.

DM: I respect that ambition, to want to make something genuinely good.

MH: That's one of the things I really admired in Sean's approach. He didn't want to make the easy version, but honestly, who even knows what the hell that would be? Sean felt there was a reason to be ambitious here and to try and figure out a screenplay that would work on a story level. The real home run would have had Freddy, Jason, and a great story. He wanted people to come out of the theater and go, '*Wow, that was a really good movie.*' Then we could all share in the accolade and share in the credit. He felt he could make a new classic here, something more than just another sequel. Once you get that idea in your head, you're into some thick woods.

I say that because you've got all the baggage of Freddy and all the baggage of Jason. How do you make a story from all that baggage? Do you have them fight until one of them wins? Or do they fight to a draw? Or, as became our obsession for a long time, are they going to become more or less orchestrated around a single goal where you can almost move one of them over to the good guy side? There were so many questions to answer.

DM: How familiar were you with the properties? Did you have to rewatch the older films?

MH: No, actually. That was something as a worker coming onto the project that I trusted was happening without me showing up to correct everyone. That's also pretty sticky because you can take any part of the past and suddenly decide to now emphasize that. It's like how continuity often works in comic books, not like you're doing a biography. It's all made up along the way. I didn't get much into that. I have a loose relationship with the canon, so to speak. Continuity wasn't my concern. Getting a story that worked was my concern. Horror is such a wonderful community of people with different opinions on how it should operate, but that was my focus and it was Sean's as well. It's like, what if we had been able to get Stephen King to write this script? And I'm not saying he would've been a good fit, but what if? I can imagine him saying, '*Well, what the hell is going on underneath these characters and in their whole story? And how can I embrace that?*' I feel like we never really did that in these scripts.

DM: How did you guys work together with New Line? Would you say shoulder to shoulder or back and forth?

MH: I'd say back and forth. Sean didn't have outright ownership of Jason, but he had enough leverage to be the creative head of this project. New Line was not very good at hiding the fact that they would have loved to have gotten rid of us and taken over completely. I don't know where they would've taken it. New Line was the wall that we'd hit tennis balls off of. We'd write something, send it over, and they'd send it right back with these enormous documents full of notes. They'd be the kind of notes you'd give if you watched a movie you really didn't like. And they'd say, "*What's this about? Why this? Can't you do this better? We think this would be better.*" Generally, their suggestions would ones that, if we did them, you'd have to undo all of these other things and the script would come undone. And maybe then they'd have said, "*Yes, undo those things too. We hate that stuff too!*" That was the kind of relationship that we had with New Line.

DM: What was most important for you in finding the right script?

MH: My background was in story structure. So the idea was that the story should have a beginning, a middle and an end of something where a main character goes through some kind of a journey. That's what I wanted and I didn't necessarily want the main character and protagonist to be the same person. Consider, for example, *To Kill a Mockingbird*. The main character is Scout the little girl, but the protagonist is Gregory Peck's Atticus the trial lawyer. The protagonist was the person pushing the goal forward but the main character was the person whose eyes we see the story from. That was what I wanted, though I understand these are pretty highfalutin ideas when you start talking about *Freddy vs Jason*.

The script drafts would come to me and I'd say '*I don't understand who the main character is or what their journey is. There is no depth or meaning here. Can we fix that?*' And it's kind of a weird place to be, but we had endless conversations about the main girl and how we could make a story around her. In some regards, it would've been smart to just embrace the '*It's only a slasher movie,*' mentality a little bit more. But instead the approach became, '*Okay, we're going to have a main character with depth and we need her to have a big projective story!*'

DM: So from that must have come the push to connect Freddy and Jason's origins?

MH: Absolutely. That was one thing we were really going for. Sure, they're two monsters fighting, but one of them is a child abuser and the other might be an abused child. It was like '*Hey, these two puzzle pieces fit!*' Okay, so maybe not really, but you could make the case for it and we were happy to make that case. I say we, but I don't think we were all on the same page with it.

The only problem with showing their backstories is that it emphasizes things the two franchises have done a good job of keeping under the radar. That's one of the things about great horror. It's usually the unspeakable taboo stuff that really gives it power. I don't know how you feel about the first *Elm Street*, but I'm of a couple minds about it. As a young person, it's a scary movie that I enjoyed, but, as I revisit it, I see that it has a huge power to it. Part of that power is the implication of Freddy's backstory rather than the actual details of it. The way that relates to *Freddy vs Jason* is that I don't know that this was the best direction to go in because it took the most powerful secrets of these characters and dragged them out into the light, which sort of ruins them in a way. When you do that, you change the characters.

I'm a big fan of comic books and I really love the idea that characters like Batman and Superman are on loan to you from the future. If you're a creative part of their story, you're really only borrowing them. You should never feel called upon to change a character just to suit your story. You should not feel called upon to introduce elements that finally reveal the secret that everyone's been wanting to know in a way that changes them forever after you're done with them. I don't think that's doing true honor to your franchise. In retrospect, I wonder if we were making a mistake by not looking at how could we protect the power of Freddy and Jason by not intertwining their histories.

DM: Wow, I like how you kind of walked around that story idea and tried to look at it from another perspective.

MH: I think there's something to it. I think you have to ask yourselves why these characters had to be rebooted after *Freddy vs Jason*. What happened to them in that film to necessitate that? I think you have to consider that question.

DM: You mentioned that you tried writing *Freddy vs Jason*. Tell me about that.

MH: I did take a stab, though I'm not too proud of it looking back. There was a point where a new draft had come in from Aibel and Berger. The Aibel/Berger draft was dead at our doorstep. There was just nothing we liked about it. At that point, I was pretty fed up with the entire process. I was feeling that *Freddy vs Jason* was never going to happen. I thought we should instead just go and do *Jason X* in the meantime. Sean finally agreed and we started work on that.

Around that time, Sean and I talked and both agreed that Cunningham Productions might not be the best place for me anymore. It was really tough going into work at that point. Plus, I really wanted to write. So I stopped going to work there every day and started writing. I started by taking all of the pieces that I liked from the previous drafts and combining them into a new story. I came up with my own take and gave it to Sean. He liked it enough to want to show it to the studio, but then they sent over an even newer draft by someone else and that put the kibosh on my take.

DM: So that makes you the eighteenth screenwriter?

MH: Well, I was never official. I did what they would call an in-house draft. I brought the cult down to one guy and had Freddy puppet mastering him to the point where he was going to bring Freddy into this world through some ritual using Jason. Some part of Jason's evil was essential to the ritual. That was just the mumbo-jumbo I used to get the pieces going. It then became a more straightforward story. I can praise it to the sky only because I can't remember much of it! But the point of it was to simplify, simplify, simplify. I'm sorry that I can't remember more. It doesn't deserve its own chapter, though!

DM: Who was keeping the Freddy cult alive? You guys or New Line?

MH: Everyone was pushing for it. I inherited the Freddy cult when I was hired on, but I never liked it. That was something I had to try and work with. When you get down to it, I don't think that anyone really thought the Freddy cult was such a great idea. I think it stuck around because no one was able to come up with a satisfying replacement for it. That was my impression. I was always shouted down anytime I suggested we get rid of the cult.

DM: In 1997, New Line surprised everyone by announcing Rob Bottin as director. How did Cunningham Productions respond to that news?

MH: We felt it came completely out of nowhere. I know that Rob must have had an ambition on his own or a conversation with someone that made it clear that our project was in absolute stillwater. So he showed up at New Line's office with a pitch they must have liked. I know Mike De Luca, at that time, was running things at the studio with a steady hand. I'm sure he thought he saw a way to solve all our problems by saying '*Look, here's a director and he's got a story!*' And then he sent that over to Sean.

We were surprised by it and not in a good way. Partnering with a studio is kind of like being friends with an elephant. They don't have to do much to shake you up and get you scared. And so when they did this, we saw it as a surprising power move on their part. In one single stroke, they were clearly telling us that they didn't like our story and didn't think we were getting anywhere. They wanted to take over completely and they were tired of playing footsie with us.

But at the same time, the scripts they were sending us were not scripts we were wanting to make. I mean no offense to anyone over there. Don't get me wrong. Aibel and Berger have both gone onto great, great things, but we viewed their *Freddy vs Jason* script as a complete failure. I remember there were a couple of scenes that took good advantage of the dream nature of these stories, but I couldn't point to one character or story element that I liked. In my recollection, everything was tailored to show off effects as much as possible. There was no regard to what we valued as storytellers.

I certainly shared New Line's frustration. If they had sent over a script that had a strong story, even with no input from us, I would've been happy to admit it. I would've been like, '*Way to go! You guys cracked it. We couldn't. Great job!*' But that never happened. Rob Bottin was a step forward in terms of having a director, but, in every other way a step back. I was pretty clear about my distaste for it and Sean didn't like it anymore than I did. His distaste was enhanced by the fact that he controlled the character.

DM: Speaking of 1997, what did you guys make of the ShoWest teaser trailer?

MH: That was another one of the power moves that New Line made. We were there basically Monday morning quarterbacking it. They didn't communicate to us what they were doing or the meaning of it. It was more along the lines of, '*Okay, here's a trailer that we've cut together. We're going to debut it at ShoWest!*' And we were like, '*Okay… there's no script yet but there is a teaser. What does this now mean?*' And their response was, '*Oh, nothing.*'

So they play the thing at ShoWest and the audience went bananas, which I think was proof of concept for what Sean had always wanted. I think Sean took it as a victory saying, '*Well, look. There you go. Let's get this thing done right,*' and New Line also took it as a victory saying, '*Well, there you go. Let's stop bickering and get a movie made!*'

DM: What can you tell me about Rob Bottin's exit from the project?

MH: I imagine Rob was treated pretty badly. We weren't in the position to drive anything, but Sean might've had the power to say '*Over my dead body!*' I don't know if he actually said that, but I do know that Rob's hiring was a dead letter at our office. I personally never knew what New Line really thought of his script. I do know that, based on their reaction to our scripts, they couldn't have loved it. At the same time, I feel safe in saying that Rob really put his heart into it and felt it was good enough to start moving forward on. There's really nothing worse than being told you're doing fine and then later being told no one ever liked your work to begin with.

DM: So how did you guys respond when New Line pulled those kinds of power moves?

MH: Things get rough in those situations, but it's all par for the course. It's inevitable that you're going to pull power moves on each other. When things aren't going your way, you start trying to figure out what kind of leverage you've got to work with. Remember that the relationship between us and New Line was not amicable at that point.

I remember once Sean coming back from a meeting with Mike De Luca. They had basically gotten to the point where they had boxed each other into corners and couldn't come out of it nicely. So Sean went in to talk face to face. This is where Sean made a smart move, I thought. They sat down in Mike's office and Sean said, '*Let's not do this here. Let's go out on the balcony or out for a walk,*' which Mike thought sounded great, so they did.

And while out walking, they were able to get all their feelings off their chest. They were able to agree on certain things and basically say, more-or-less, '*We all feel the same way. We want this to be good and we don't feel like we're there yet and we want to keep working on it. When we each say what we want out of the script, that's what the other person says they also want out of the script.*' That conversation addressed a lot of things. From there, they went down a checklist of what the goal of *Freddy vs Jason* was, who the main character should be, plot and so on. Then New Line would send over the next script over and we would go, '*Hey! None of that stuff we talked about is in here!*' In a nutshell, that was the problem we were constantly facing.

DM: Did you and Sean usually agree on the scripts that were being considered?

MH: Not always, but most of the time. I would sometimes complain that a script didn't scare me, even for a second. I wouldn't even see an opportunity to be scared. Sean would disagree and say, '*No, Mark. Look closer. Take this scene for example.*' And it would be a scene where the main girl is in the shower and the camera is moving around to find her. It turns out to be her boyfriend's point-of-view going to find her, but the audience would think it might actually be Freddy or Jason. Sean would say, '*Look, there's a way to direct that scene so that it'll scare people. You can take it to the bank. Don't worry.*' So I had to trust him on that.

I felt we needed to reconsider on a more fundamental level what was scary about the story of *Freddy vs Jason*. That's why I thought the Freddy cult failed at such a miserable level. It was a ridiculous idea that couldn't ever be scary to me. You could take it to a point where you make it incredibly violent and ruthless, I suppose. We could've gone there, but we seemed to stop halfway where they were just kind of quirky.

DM: I've heard talk of a *Freddy vs Jason* game that was being developed for a while. What can you tell me about that?

MH: That was a project led by David Bergantino, who wrote the official novelization of *Wes Craven's New Nightmare*. We brought him in to help develop a game. At the time, certain movie games were making massively more money than the movies they were even based on. I thought, '*This is a no-brainer. We have got to make a Freddy vs Jason game!*'

David was great because he had a level of commitment to these characters that I hadn't encountered before. He was an incredibly useful barometer as to whether or not the scripts under consideration were being true to the characters or not. That's one mistake I think we made for a long time. David was a professional writer, but he was also a fan. I think we went too long without getting input from someone like him, someone who had such close contact with the material. By the time the movie came out, I don't think it really captured what the fans loved about the characters, not truly. It was more an echo of what fans loved about Freddy and Jason than a real grasp of it. David made me aware of that fact a little too late in the game.

DM: Did you see the 2003 *Freddy vs Jason* and, if so, what did you think of it?

MH: Yes, I was invited to the premiere and was very grateful for that. Seeing it was a little disappointing. I was really happy that it did come together. I had many thoughts going through my head while watching it. There was a level of accomplishment that was pretty admirable. A Hollywood picture had been made out of this, but it was disappointingly uninvolving for me. All the babble we had about character and meaning and depth, the movie came up short on that. But I'm very critical. I don't think anyone associated with this movie needs to apologize for anything. Most people that see the film have no idea of what it took to make and how difficult that process really was. The impression I got is that they reached sixty or seventy percent of the potential, which is a considerable amount.

DM: The scripts varied in their depictions of Freddy. Some went for laughs, others for chills. Which did you prefer?

MH: I was firmly in the camp of '*Why can't we do him dark and scary again?*' Because my bias is just to go for depth and clown-Freddy is the antithesis of depth. That is one thing I appreciated about the Aibel/Berger draft. They found some slick ways to make Freddy scary again, especially in the dream sequences. Their version of the character was more ruthless than what we had been seeing in other scripts. I liked that.

With Cy and Ethan's draft… their version of Freddy seemed more like a guy who could easily have just stepped over into reality and started hosting music videos on MTV. I never connected with their take on the character. That's probably not fair because I think they still had him doing some rough stuff. Their Freddy had this weird relationship with the cult, which took away a lot of his menace. He's someone that can invade your dreams. That's a wonderfully scary idea! Don't ever do anything to take away that menace like having him hang out with a cult.

DM: Just as interesting is how many screenwriters felt the need to make Jason the less-evil slasher.

MH: I think that simply evolved from the inherent nature of these characters. Freddy was a horrible shitty person. Somehow through the magic of his own death, he became a horrible shitty spirit. But Jason started off as a victim, really. He's a deformed child with a vengeful spirit. Without getting too detailed, I think that's the essence of it. There's a very sympathetic tone in that backstory as opposed to Freddy. So when you compare the two, there's this weird gravity in their backstories that pushes one to the good guy side and the other one to the bad guy side.

It would've been smart in retrospect to somehow keep them both evil. That would've allowed us to make a scarier movie and perhaps a more successful movie. As to why our drafts kept going toward good guy Jason, it's just something we kept finding in that character. When it came necessary for our main character to struggle in her protagonist duties and figure out how to solve the problem, it seemed that reaching out for a little help from Jason made sense. That also resulted in the scene that we all felt was so important for so long, the reveal that Freddy had actually abused and killed young Jason.

DM: I suppose the opposite of that wouldn't really work, would it? No one was going to side with Freddy.
MH: Right. You'd need to have a pretty sick audience for them to sympathize with Freddy. The other challenge would've been to create an evil greater than Freddy and Jason that they were both threatened by. Then your sympathies go to them against this third party. We had a lot of strategies that were tossed around but not fully explored.

DM: When did you guys start to feel the urge to make a sequel other than *Freddy vs Jason*?
MH: I don't remember specifically when, but it slowly became the topic on everyone's mind that we were maybe going too long without a movie. There's no set recipe for how many is too many when it comes to years without a Jason picture. You have to realize, however, that every year you don't make a new movie is a year you didn't make money you could have made. Sean's intention in doing *Jason X* was very sensible, I thought. He's not an executive or a development person. He's the guy who makes the movies, so years going by without getting a movie made was pragmatically a rough spot to be in.

People were hesitant to make *Jason X* for a long time because they were so focused on *Freddy vs Jason*. I remember a conversation I had once with Sean's son, Noel. I was pushing for another solo-Jason and he wasn't behind the idea yet. He told me, '*Mark, these movies are great and they make money. They're always going to make money. Doing a Jason movie is like robbing a candy store. Doing a Freddy vs Jason movie is like robbing a bank!*' And I think that illustrates why everyone held off on doing another solo-Jason film for so long. We were ready to rob a bank, basically. (laughs)

Many guys will claim credit for it, but the idea for *Jason X* came out of my idea that Jason keeps dying and coming back. What if we went way into the future and he was still alive? And that was something they studied him for? It was a dumb idea. Honestly, I look back on it and I'm not that proud of it. But it's something where you take a tiny piece of the established universe and you see how far you can run with it. *Jason X* also shows you the danger of doing that.

INTERVIEW: Sean Cunningham
Director/Producer, *Friday the 13th (1980)*
Executive Producer, *Jason Goes to Hell: The Final Friday, Jason X, Freddy vs Jason*

DUSTIN MCNEILL: For starters, how did you manage to wrangle Jason away from Paramount?

SEAN CUNNINGHAM: Sometime in the early '90s, I had gotten the idea of doing *Freddy vs Jason* as a way of revitalizing the franchises. Both were kind of on wobbly legs at the time. It just struck me as being a cool thing to exploit and do like a big Las Vegas grudge match. The headlines were very strong in favor of it. So I went and pitched it to the people I was working with in Boston and they all said '*Yeah, that'd be great.*' Next I talked to Michael Lynn and Mike De Luca over a New Line and they said, '*Yeah, we'd love to do it too.*' Now we just needed to get the rights to Jason back from Paramount.

So the guys from Boston then went to Paramount to see about the rights. At that time, Paramount was cleaning house. Frank Mancuso Jr was no longer at the studio. The feeling I got was that *Friday the 13th* was kind of an embarrassment to them, to some people there. For them, it was a blue-collar horror movie that would come along every couple of years and make some money, which they could then invest in more worthy projects. That was the feeling I got. In any case, they didn't have a lot of money represented from *Friday 7* and *Friday 8*, so they were willing to let it go and they did, which is how we got Jason over to New Line.

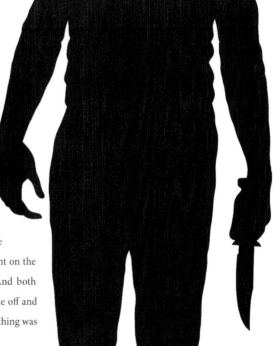

DM: Good grief, what a stupid decision on their part.

SC: Ha, yeah. They've got the rights back now, so I guess they're getting over it.

DM: So Jason arrives at New Line and you guys immediately get to work on *Jason Goes to Hell*, right?

SC: Right. We made that because I wanted to get the brand out there and keep the brand out there. I thought it was important we get something out while we figured out how to go forward with *Freddy vs Jason*. That's how *Friday 9* happened. It was meant to be something that was going to tread water until we came up with *Freddy vs Jason*. As you well know, the development on the crossover went on and on and on for years and years. And both franchises were just stalling in the meantime. Wes had gone off and made his *New Nightmare* and we had made *Friday 9*, but nothing was happening beyond those.

For years, I stood on my feet with *Freddy vs Jason* telling everyone, '*We've gotta make this movie, we've gotta do it.*' And we weren't getting anywhere. We eventually reached a compromise with New Line that said if they wouldn't greenlight *Freddy vs Jason* they would have to greenlight *Jason X*. That was a compromise.

DM: Did you ever have any desire to write or direct *Freddy vs Jason?*

SC: No, I definitely did not. I felt that you needed younger and more enthusiastic genes than mine. And I've already done my *Friday the 13th*. More importantly, there were things about both the *Friday* and *Nightmare* franchises that I honestly don't think I understood at the time. Some of those films looked so ridiculous and stupid to me, but the audiences were loving it! So not understanding what made it work, that made me a very bad candidate to direct *Freddy vs Jason*. So no, I didn't have a desire to do that. Now it's twenty years later and we're working on *Friday the 13th* the television series and that's something I'm interested in directing because it's closer to something I understand, something much closer to the original film.

DM: How was it working with De Luca on the project?

SC: I think that Mike De Luca and I discovered too late in the process that we really disagreed about the best way to structure a script for *Freddy vs Jason*. We just never could agree on that. With twenty-twenty hindsight, I think you could say we were both right. I do think it was unfortunate that we never came up with a script that incorporated what we both wanted to see in the film. Control was a huge issue.

When I first got involved, I said, '*Are you guys gonna be okay doing a movie where you share control of Freddy? This is gonna be like someone else messing in your rice bowl.*' And they assured me it was okay. '*No it's fine. It won't be a problem at all.*' And it turned out to be a really big problem because Freddy basically created that company. They had a hard time changing anything about him and so that was just one of the reasons why the feet were dragging.

DM: Most of the unused scripts tried to make Jason into a hero slasher, so-to-speak. Do you think one of them have to be less evil? Or can they both be evil?

SC: Well, I think in approaching *Freddy vs Jason* you've got to go with some dramatic basics. If you have a story, you have to have a conflict. And if you're going to have a conflict, you've got to have a conflict with opposing sides. One of those sides has to be someone the audience can get behind. Look at all the movies about World War

II. They're all about two great big superpowers shooting at each other. The audience is always on our side of it because we're fighting for truth, justice, and the American way, right? That's how movies work. You need to have someone the audience can root for. And who is that in *Freddy vs Jason*? It was really hard to figure out a way that Jason could stay Jason but still be fighting alongside the good guys. The notion was that he was a lion with a thorn in his paw. We weren't changing him into a good guy. His interests just happened to line up with the teenagers.

The alternative would be having a movie with two completely bad guys fighting each other, which doesn't work. That would be like having a World War II movie where the Nazis are fighting the Japanese. American audiences would look at that and go, '*You're both Axis of Evil, I hope you fucking kill each other.*' That's not a good movie.

DM: So then who has to win *Freddy vs Jason,* in your opinion?

SC: Jason has to win because Freddy's really a pussy. You can quote me on that! (laughs) There's really no way to answer that. They're both unkillable forces. Whoever wins, *you* win if you find a way to keep it going for more movies. I do think it's really important that you make sure you don't change them. Freddy needs to stay Freddy and Jason needs to stay Jason. You can change the circumstances around them, but you have to keep them the same. They're both boogeymen. I don't think it's appropriate or productive to kill them off at the end, to have a definitive ending. The ending that we have on the film now is kind of ambiguous, which works very well for the fans. If you're a Freddy fan, you say '*Alright!*' and if you're a Jason fan, you say '*Fuckin' A!*'

DM: Do you recall the 1997 ShoWest teaser that New Line put together?

SC: I do remember that. I thought that was a great teaser! It embodied my notion of what the promotion for should be.

DM: Wasn't that a bit premature, though? There wasn't even a finalized script yet.

SC: Of course, it was premature. That's not unusual in this business. There's often a dichotomy between the creative part of a company that makes the movies and the distribution part that sells them. Sometimes, distributors say '*What the fuck are you guys thinking? Who wants to see this movie?*' That wasn't the case at all with *Freddy vs Jason*. With us, they were saying this was something they could get behind 100%. They could easily sell this. They didn't give a shit what the movie was. They just wanted to put pressure on the creative part to make it! (laughs) That's what I think was happening.

DM: What did you think of New Line hiring Rob Bottin to direct from his own original treatment?

SC: I think our experience there proved that move to be a huge mistake. I don't think Rob had any sense of the fact that he had the tiger by the tail. Sure, he was a very talented special effects guy, but just take a second and look at the long list of accomplished screenwriters that had already worked on *Freddy vs Jason* and failed. Those were good people we had writing for us and they couldn't do it! What was Rob Bottin going to bring to it? He had nothing to offer. I wasn't against him being the director. I was always open to suggestions of outside directors because the problem was never with the director. The problem was with the script.

DM: Did you ever step back and wonder if this was a nut that could even be cracked?

SC: No, I never thought that. Hell, I thought we had already cracked the nut, but I couldn't convince New Line of that. My feelings on it were straightforward. In the world of film, there is a genre called horror, which has lots of sub-genres. Horror films are characteristically not very well written. As soon as you get a horror script that's well written, everyone starts to call it a thriller or something else (laughs). Being that this was a horror picture, we knew it had to have certain elements in it. But that didn't mean we couldn't also take rules that would apply to any other meaningful script and apply them here. We could've made a damn good film out of *Freddy vs Jason*.

I often refer to horror screenplays as affirmative action for the writing impaired. That's a joke, but it's kind of true. Horror writers often think story rules don't apply to them because they're doing a horror script. Sure, at some level, there's truth to that, but that's not how you get to the best possible product. I was obsessed with finding a story structure that would really pay off for audiences. I wanted to create something worthwhile, something that hadn't been seen before with *Freddy vs Jason* and that wasn't how other people were coming at this. They might say to me, '*Sean, wouldn't it be cool if Jason ripped someone in half, tore out their heart and ate it?*' Uh... no, I don't really think so. That might make a good scene in the gore porn sub-genre, but I was always more focused on figuring out dramatic plausibility than gore.

DM: I really respect that intention. It sounds like a tough order, though.

SC: It was tough. Just because you're doing *Freddy vs Jason* doesn't mean you're forgiven the obligation to give the audience a really good ride. Look back at the ShoWest trailer. That's a movie that anybody would want to see without regard to what it is. All that trailer said was, '*This is gonna be cool!*' My feeling was if people came out the theater and the movie was better than they expected, then you'd have something with legs that could really take off. I always felt that.

DM: Practically every unused draft of *Freddy vs Jason* tried to intertwine their backstories. How did you view that?

SC: I can't speak for Freddy, but I know that Jason has a history that contradicts itself at every other turn. I know a lot of people have done a lot of work to try and figure out some kind of continuity, but give it a rest. The last time we saw Jason before this movie, he was in outer space. I mean, what the fuck? I think you could have satisfyingly solved the challenge of combining their histories, but I would ask, why? Why do that? When you go see a movie, you don't really give a shit why the characters are doing certain things. If you care about something, it's gotta be something that's happening presently and something that is yet undecided. The backstory is only valuable to the extent that it affects the present story. To spoon out information on what Jason did when he was twelve or who was mean to him at camp, who held him underwater or what his mother thought about it is boring to me. What's this got to do with the teenagers that are running around the camp right now? We came out to see this movie to find out what's happening right now. Does that make sense? I think you'll find that fans can get caught up in digging out backstories, especially in fan fiction. And that's a lot of fun, but it's not a part of the movie experience. That's more a part of the fan experience. I think a good script has to have something happening now that keeps your attention. That's really storytelling 101. If you don't have a new story to tell, your audience is going to get bored and then you're in trouble.

DM: In 2001, Michael De Luca was suddenly fired from New Line. How did you react to that news?

SC: In my mind, I didn't know what it meant. I was really surprised by it. De Luca was a very special talent and he was really crucial in building New Line into what it later became. Even though Mike and I didn't always agree on *Freddy vs Jason*, I think there was a mutual respect there. I continue to have enormous respect for the guy. He's really talented as a producer and that's not an easy talent. So when they fired him, I thought it was bad news not just for *Freddy vs Jason*, but bad news for the company as well. It was not Mike Lynn or Bob Shaye's first choice to make De Luca go away, but they just couldn't come to an agreement as to how they were going to run their business. So they said '*My house, my rules,*' and he was gone.

They hired Toby Emmerich to run the company after Mike. Toby and I met and he said '*Look, I don't like horror movies and I don't know anything about them, but we'll put you together with a development executive that does ;ike them and we'll make this movie.*' And I thought that sounded great. Then a brand new set of production development people came onboard with a mandate from above to finally make the goddamn movie.

DM: Was the Shannon/Swift draft the one that got it all right?

SC: No, it was not, but so what? I just didn't think it was a very good story, which is what the issue will always be. I did some pretty extensive notes on their script. I don't know who read them or who did the last polish. David Goyer maybe? But they were still flailing around trying to figure out what to do at the last minute. I know that - as persuasive as I can be - there are a lot of other people out there that are equally or more persuasive that don't agree with me! So in terms of the script, I lost some of my influence on it. But after ten years, we finally decided to make the movie and see how it turned out. At some point, you've just got to hold your breath and jump in the water.

DM: From a creative standpoint, how do you judge the final film?

SC: In the end, I thought it worked. Some things in the script turned out to be pleasant surprises, some things not so much. Some scenes didn't quite unfold as they were originally meant to. They would get shot wrong, acted wrong and spliced into the movie wrong. So instead of being a scary mindfuck, those parts fell a little flat. Yet the fact that it didn't entirely work on that level probably made it easier for non-horror aficionados to watch. It wasn't as dark or grim as it could've been. But the undeniable fact is that audiences were having a really good time with it.

DM: After two weekends atop the box office, were there any calls for a sequel?

SC: With grosses like that, those calls absolutely happened. The questions were along the lines of, '*What would a sequel be like? Do we increase it to five monsters instead of just two?*' How the fuck are you gonna make that script work? We couldn't even make *this* script work all that well. Plus, one of the things that made *Freddy vs Jason* a success was its novelty. If you subtract the novelty, what are you left with? No one had answers to those questions. This movie also cost $30 million before advertising. I don't know that Toby Emmerich was eager to make that kind of investment again so soon.

Chapter Eight
The Verheiden Draft

1999

A BACKUP PLAN FROM OUTER SPACE

1999 saw *Freddy vs Jason* enter into its sixth year of development. Half-a-decade had passed since the last installments in the *Friday* and *Nightmare* franchises, which were among the lowest grossing to date. There was no denying that Freddy and Jason were no longer kings of the horror box office, which was now topped by burgeoning franchises like *Scream, Urban Legend,* and *I Know What You Did Last Summer*. This stagnation was especially frustrating for Sean Cunningham, who was more accustomed to actually making movies rather than just developing them.

This generated discussion within Cunningham Productions about the possibility of mounting a new Jason movie should a suitable script for *Freddy vs Jason* not materialize soon. Cunningham considered pitches from collaborators Todd Farmer, James Isaac, David Bergantino, Mark Haslett, and Noel Cunningham. Isaac, who himself had unsuccessfully pitched New Line on *Freddy vs Jason*, suggested a wintery sequel set amid a frozen Camp Crystal Lake. This direction was nixed over concerns it might interfere with the unwritten events of *Freddy vs Jason*. Cunningham then issued a stipulation for future pitches: the new Jason sequel must not conflict in any way with the impending crossover. In turn, the group shifted their focus to distant locales for Jason to terrorize like Los Angeles, the Arctic, and even the Middle East.

The concept for what was ultimately decided upon came together in pieces. Mark Haslett suggested a futuristic setting on the basis that the immortal Jason might still be slashing teenagers hundreds of years from present day. Todd Farmer next envisioned a story set in outer space due to mankind having rendered the earth uninhabitable due to pollution. According to Noel Cunningham, the final piece of the puzzle - a half-robot Uber-Jason - originated from the Braga/Moore draft of *Freddy vs Jason*. These elements came together to form *Jason X*, less affectionately known by its critics as *Jason in Space*.

Todd Farmer delivered his initial treatment for *Jason X* in March 1999 following the final rejection of the Aibel/Berger draft. At Cunningham's request, he soon expanded this treatment into a full screenplay. Meanwhile at New Line, Michael De Luca was in search of yet another new writer to pen *Freddy vs Jason*, which had now also lost its director. Cunningham informed the studio boss he was tired of waiting for the project to emerge from development hell. The *Friday* filmmaker's mandate was clear; either make *something* with Jason or lose rights to the character. One way or another, this titan was headed back to the big screen.

THE SCREENWRITER

Michael De Luca's search for a new screenwriter to tackle *Freddy vs Jason* would lead him to Mark Verheiden, who was well regarded within New Line for his contributions to 1994's *The Mask*. Verheiden's writing career circa 1999 was certainly respectable, but had yet to explode as it did in the new millennium. His other notable mid-90s credit was on Universal's *Timecop* starring Jean-Claude Van-Damme. Outside film and television, he had also contributed writing to numerous comic books including acclaimed issues of *Alien* and *Predator* for Dark Horse. The filmmakers behind 2004's *Alien vs Predator* would pay tribute to Verheiden's work by naming actor Tommy Flanagan's mercenary character after the writer. ("You want a piece of me, you ugly son of a bitch?") To date, he has more than one hundred comic book writing credits to his name.

Following his work on *Freddy vs Jason*, Verheiden would write and/or executive produce some of the most popular genre shows of our time. These include *Heroes, Smallville, Daredevil, Hemlock Grove,* and *Falling Skies.* Several subsequent projects have teamed him with fellow *Freddy vs Jason* scribes. Verheiden would serve as writer and executive producer on episodes of *Battlestar Galactica* with Ronald D. Moore and *Constantine* with David Goyer. In 2007, he would write and produce Bruce Campbell's self-spoofing *My Name is Bruce.* In 2008, he would adapt Sam Raimi's original *Evil Dead* into comic book form. As this book goes to print, Verheiden has been announced as the showrunner for the groovy third season of *Ash vs the Evil Dead.*

Unfortunately, *Freddy vs Jason* would not be the last time Verheiden found himself attached to a long awaited project that never took off. He would later write and produce a *Dark Shadows* revival pilot in 2004 in addition to providing unrealized screenplays for Stephen King's *Dark Tower* and DC Comics' *Teen Titans.*

THE SCRIPT

This draft marks the final entry into 'The Bottin Trio' of screenplays and was the only draft written after Bottin's departure from the project. Consequently, the Verheiden script is the most loosely adapted of the three with an entirely new first-half. Yet the same basic framework remains in place. Things go badly when a girl experiencing Freddy nightmares mixes sleep medication with booze while partying at Crystal Lake where Jason Voorhees is accidentally resurrected with a new heart. Titans fight, girl lives. Roll credits.

Verheiden's *Freddy vs Jason* begins at the Springwood Recreation Center where local teenagers have staged a serial killer-themed haunted house for Halloween. Naturally, their walkthrough attraction includes areas dedicated to both Freddy and Jason complete with masked impersonators. It's here that main character Lizzie dozes off and experiences a terrifying Freddy nightmare in which the exhibits come to life and begin attacking people. She wakes up back inside the rec-center, which is now a bloodbath littered with real dead bodies, killer unknown. Lizzie continues to dream of Freddy and Jason at home with increasing frequency. Her concerned parents get her a perscription for a powerful new sleep-aid called Somnambulene, which she refuses to take, choosing instead to join her friends for a weekend getaway to Crystal Lake. Lizzie's parents secretly dose her with the Somnambulene before the trip, which reacts badly with the alcoholic beverages she consumes. The drug winds up amplifying her nightmares so intensely that they bleed over into real-life. Her friends begin to suffer horrible deaths at the hands of Freddy and Jason or so she believes. As dream intertwines with reality, a disoriented Lizzie finds herself trapped in a battle between two horrific killers.

The first half of Verheiden's script marks a departure from the Goyer/Robinson and Aibel/Berger drafts, though it veers back into familiar territory once the teenagers reach Crystal Lake. The screenwriter takes aim at some of the more problematic elements from the previous two drafts. Most notably, he removes all traces of Bottin's postmodern framework, more comfortably placing the story back into the continuity of the prior sixteen films. He further cements this connection with nods both subtle and overt to the events of earlier *Friday* and *Nightmare* films. The most direct new reference may be to Rod Lane from Wes Craven's original *Nightmare*, whose younger brother appears here in a supporting role.

Also gone in this draft is the character of Dominic Necros. Verheiden dedicates the freed-up space to giving the titans a bigger presence earlier on in his story. The scene in which Necros cuts a teenager's beating heart from his chest remains but with Freddy now doing the slashing. The victim's heart is again unmindfully tossed into Crystal Lake where it again resurrects Jason from a watery grave. As in the previous two drafts, Lizzie's boyfriend is still named Jason, meaning that Jason's heart still resurrects Jason, which is no less weird here than when first introduced in the Goyer/Robinson draft. That a heartless Jason Voorhees is again found at the bottom of Crystal Lake in this story makes you wonder once more what events have transpired in the years since *Jason Goes to Hell*.

The backstory of camp counselor Freddy abusing and drowning young Jason remains in this draft, though Verheiden shifts it to the beginning of his screenplay. Here that reveal is part of Lizzie's initial rec-center nightmare. Placing this moment so much earlier in the story helps to generate more immediate sympathy for Jason while establishing a motive for his grudge against Freddy. This also lays earlier groundwork for Lizzie and Jason's semi-partnering against their common enemy later on. Like his predecessors, Verheiden refrains from outright teaming Jason with the teens, instead keeping him as a fearsome and deadly figure.

Although Lizzie and boyfriend Jason remain largely unchanged from the Aibel/Berger draft, their prankster friends are once again fitted with new personalities. They still essentially serve the same purpose, to fall by Freddy's glove and Jason's machete. Speaking of the dream slasher, Verheiden delivers a Freddy more in line with how we have long known him, leaving behind the dreary and humorless depiction of the last draft. His quips may be back, but there are no *Looney Tunes* gags to be found here.

Curiously, this draft marks the only story in either franchise set during Halloween, which opens up all kinds of glorious opportunities when you start to think about it. Using the holiday as an excuse for Lizzie's friends to dress up as Freddy and Jason is far more believable than having them stage a cosplay prank war per the previous drafts. Have the franchises been thus far hesitant to mine this territory due to Michael Myers' long standing claim over it? Possibly so, though it is a shame.

Reportedly, the Verheiden draft was the most well liked adaptation of Bottin material, not as dark as Goyer/Robinson or as nonsensical as Aibel/Berger, but still not favored enough for the project's overlords to jointly agree upon, particularly in light of Bottin's mysterious exit.

TWO ENDINGS

The Verheiden draft is unique from other *Freddy vs Jason* scripts in that it never had a true ending. Instead, the screenplay offered up two possible conclusions, one in which Jason prevailed and, alternatively, one in which Freddy prevailed. The original plan, as devised by Michael De Luca, was for both endings to be filmed and randomly distributed onto roughly 2,500 screens. His hope was that audiences would pay to see the film twice in order to experience both endings, upping ticket sales in the process. This gimmick, which was previously tried on 1985's *Clue* with three randomized endings, was not looked upon favorably by either Sean Cunningham or the screenwriter himself.

"I really didn't like the idea of having two endings," Cunningham says. "Fortunately, De Luca never followed through with that. It's bad and I'll tell you why it's bad. You go to a movie for a story, right? And in any story the characters are presented with a whole bunch of difficult choices to make. Those choices ultimately decide the ending. Look at a tragedy like *King Lear*. If all of a sudden you decide that the story should end with him setting up house with Cordelia and beheading the other two sisters, that story wouldn't work! That's just not what it was building towards. The ending is a critical part of any story. To have a random ending for your movie means its story doesn't have a point. If your movie has a point, it has to be pointed *at* something and that something is the ending."

The dual-ending approach also raises several questions, the answers to which we will never know. How would this have been handled on home video in the age of videocassette? Or on broadcast television? And how might such a development have complicated the timelines of future *Friday* and *Nightmare* sequels?

INTERVIEW: Mark Verheiden
Screenwriter, *Freddy vs Jason '99*

DUSTIN MCNEILL: How did you get involved with *Freddy vs Jason*?

MARK VERHEIDEN: My memory is feeble, but, as I recall, I had some fans at the studio, particularly Michael De Luca. I had done *The Mask* for New Line and another project that didn't get made. A call came through my agent that they were looking for someone to do a new pass at *Freddy vs Jason*, so he asked if I had any interest. I'm not sure if my agent knew that when I first moved to LA, my very low bar for success was that I wanted to work on a Jason movie because I loved the Jason movies. I also like the first *Elm Street*, but the *Friday the 13th* franchise just registered with me more. They're not the greatest movies ever made, but something about them I just loved seeing in theaters year after year. So that's how the job came in.

DM: Did you have to binge watch the franchises to prepare?

MV: I had watched all the *Friday the 13th*'s as they came out, so I didn't need to watch them again. I was pretty familiar with those. I had also seen all the *Nightmares* in the theater but was less familiar with them, so I bought all the tapes and rewatched them. I believe they gave me one or two scripts to look at before beginning. I don't recall reading all the drafts.

DM: Was it weird coming onto a project with this much development?

MV: It was weird in that, when you walk into a project with that much development, it makes you wonder if the people involved really know what they want. Maybe it's been difficult for them to put their finger on what they're looking for, so they're flailing around a little bit. In that situation, you feel like you're working with a bit of moving target in that you're trying to make your script fit whatever it is they're looking for. I was aware that a lot of other writers - very good writers - had been unable to get their scripts to a point where New Line felt comfortable pulling the trigger on it. I was like, '*Okay, I'm just curious. What is it they're not doing that I can now do in order to push this project into production?*' Obviously, they didn't like my take on it either, so I never found that sweet spot.

It was my goal coming in to figure out what the problems had been up until that point and then see what I could do to address those in my script. That's what my meetings with New Line focused on. I recall having meetings with De Luca and Sean Cunningham, both together and separate. I was interested to get their takes on what they liked and didn't like with the previous drafts.

DM: I assume you would've gotten along pretty well with Cunningham since you preferred Jason?

MV: I see why you would think that, but my memory of our meeting is that it was a little tense. I'm not sure if Sean wasn't frustrated at how many writers had been thrown at it, like maybe I was the latest impediment to it getting made. We only spoke together that once about it, but he seemed frustrated. I know if I were him, I'd be frustrated too.

DM: How responsible did you feel to the existing continuity?

MV: In this case, what you want to do is figure out what you can use, so the existing continuity was helpful for me. I believe the idea that Freddy was actually working at Crystal Lake and was responsible for drowning Jason, which is why Jason turned into this malignant figure, was from an earlier draft. I thought that was great. What I really looked at for my script were my favorite *Friday*'s, which were *Final Chapter* and *Jason Lives*. What I liked about *Final Chapter* was that the last half-hour built up to a chaotic, scary kind of tension. It almost felt like a *Texas Chainsaw*-type ending. Then I also liked the humor in *Jason Lives*, really the whole feel of that film. Then you've got *New Blood*, which has the best makeup. So I was constantly referring back trying to pluck anything that would help me tell a richer story. Having said that, pretty much all of my characters were new characters coming into this world.

DM: Do you recall the plot for your version?

MV: I do. Some of it was from an earlier draft, but there was a troubled teenage girl. Freddy and Jason are entering her dreams and she can't figure out why. There's also this new drug, Somnambulene, which is a hyperactive drug that puts you into a dream state. Her parents inject her with it against her will because they think she's losing her mind. So she takes off for Crystal

Lake unaware that she's been injected with this stuff and goes into a sort of fugue state. Freddy and Jason then have a war with her in the middle. Jason winds up protecting her from Freddy and, in an odd way, becomes the good guy of my script.

The other thing my draft had was two endings, one where Freddy kills Jason and one where Jason kills Freddy. The idea, as I recall, was that they would shoot both conclusions and then randomly give them out. That way you had no idea which ending you were getting when you went to the theater. They thought it would make everyone want to see it twice, that people would track down which theater had which ending and go to see it a second time. At this point, both franchises were wheezing a bit in terms of audience and box office, so they were looking for anything that would maximize people to come see it.

DM: That's a pretty bold gimmick to take with properties this big, don't you think?

MV: I'm of two minds about it. You're right in that it's a gimmick, in all the good and bad senses of that word. As a fan, I recognize that it's also kind of fun to think about. There's a nutty showmanship to the idea that I like. However, it was a little tough to write because my script clearly set up Jason as the one you'd want to win, even though he kills a lot of people. To have Freddy take him out didn't seem like a good ending to me. Freddy was so horrible. Between the two of them, he was the much worse bad guy. To see Jason win felt right. In doing multiple endings, I think you risk pissing off the audience in a big way. Suppose someone went to see *Freddy vs Jason* and didn't get the ending they felt was right? They might say '*To hell with it. I hate that movie.*'

DM: What kind of feedback did you get on your draft?

MV: I turned in my first draft and got a lot of notes back from the studio. Based on those, I did a rewrite and turned in my second pass, which was the last I ever head of it. In these kinds of situations, it's not like they give you a call to tell you they're moving on. They just do it and you eventually read about it in the trades that they hired someone new.

DM: You wrote your script around the same time as the Columbine Massacre. Did that have any effect upon your direction?

MV: Around the same time as *Freddy vs Jason*, I did a script for Dreamworks based on the video game *House of the Dead*. That was a very college-based script. Then Columbine happened and they dropped the project completely. I don't recall Columbine coming up in terms of *Freddy vs Jason*. What I do remember is that I didn't really like the Freddy cult. One of my pitch points to New Line coming in was to drop them. I said, '*You've got Freddy. You've got Jason. You don't need a charismatic cult leader who looks like Freddy on top of that.*' It felt like they were gilding the lilly a little bit. We already had bad guys in our story. We didn't need an entire cult of additional bad guys, especially ones that were mimicking Freddy. We have Freddy himself, so let's use him. Not that it was a horrible plot point. To me, that just doesn't belong in a *Freddy vs Jason* movie. It belongs in another movie, probably a *Nightmare on Elm Street* movie. The fact that New Line let me drop it probably meant they were wanting to try something different as well.

DM: Tell me about your opening with the serial killer haunted house.

MV: I thought that might be fun. It began as a regular haunted house, which then morphs into a Freddy nightmare version of a haunted house. And with Freddy now in Lizzie's head, she winds up at Crystal Lake where she sees a young boy drowning, which we learn is Jason. So in those first few pages, she is learning that Freddy may have been involved in Jason's death, which explains why Jason might not be as bad as we think. Well, obviously he's pretty bad, but maybe there's a reason for why he's bad. There's no particular reason for why Freddy is evil - he just is. We don't go back into his past, but we do go back into Jason's past. And what we learn is that Jason is really just getting revenge for what was done to him. He's wrong for what he's doing because he's basically picking a fight with people who had nothing to do with how he was abused, but there is a psychological rationale for his behavior.

I admit I haven't seen the *Nightmare*'s in a long while, but I don't think there's anything in Freddy's past to have prompted his turn to evil. I'm sure he had a troubled childhood too, but Freddy is a sadist. With Jason, you don't get the sense he's a sadist. You get the sense that he's really mad, like his brain is going, '*All these kids act like the kids that were supposed to be protecting me at Crystal Lake. That's why I'm going to kill them.*' Freddy, on the other hand, seems to take great pleasure in murdering people in the most grotesque ways. So I think that makes him more evil than Jason on the scale of why they're doing what they're doing. Both are awful individuals, though. It's just interesting when you try to make one more of a hero or understand what they're about a little more.

DM: You seem to like your Freddy on the darker, meaner side. Is that right?

MV: Definitely. I wanted the scary Freddy for my script. I really did not like how they made him into a comedian later on. I thought that diminsihed the power of the character. I wanted to go back to the Freddy that was a child killer, a sadist returned from the dead. I don't think there are a lot of jokes in my draft for Freddy. He may have a few quips or a witty way of speaking, but you won't find any crazy Nintendo Power Glove-type kills. He had to be scary.

That also tied into my big pitch to New Line, which was that *Freddy vs Jason* needed to be high-octane scary. One of my favorite films of all time is *Texas Chain Saw Massacre*. Once the tension begins in that movie, it never stops. My goal was to find a way to hit that kind of energy. I don't know that we could've sustained that level for the whole movie because there's just so much setup in getting Freddy and Jason together. But once we were off to the races, I wanted to get that kind of crazy, kinetic energy going by placing the teenagers inbetween two horrible killers with nowhere to run. I remember a scene where they're trying to get out of a parking structure but they can't. Jason grabs the bumper of the car and the wheels are spinning in place with smoke coming up from them. And in that moment, Freddy then appears in front of the car and things get even worse. The kids are trying to get the hell away but they're trapped. That's the kind of frantic tension I was going for.

DM: Where would you have staged the final fight - in reality or in the dreamscape?

MV: As I recall, the whole point was for Jason to pull Freddy out of the dream and into our world so he could beat him up. That was how the Jason ending from my draft went anyways. If I were going to pick an ending, it would be the one where Jason wins and goes away with some measure of peace having taken out the guy responsible all this havoc in the first place. Lizzie is also around for the final fight and manages to get a few licks in, but it's mostly a battle between Freddy and Jason.

DM: Did you ever think there was room for a *Freddy vs Jason 2*? Or another match-up?

MV: I think that's a difficult task after you've already crossed them over once. Obviously, they're going to continue making separate sequels to both properties, so it's not impossible. I liken *Freddy vs Jason* to *Alien vs Predator* in that they've kind of become their own separate universes. I imagine had this film been enormously successful enough, they would've done a *Freddy vs Jason 2*. But what do you do in the second one after they've already fought? It's much easier to do a sequel with *Alien vs Predator* because they're not physically the same aliens or predators from film to film. That allows you to do new stories in new worlds with new struggles. But you've only got one Jason and one Freddy and they've already punched it out, so how do you up the ante on that? The Jason franchise put him up in space, which certainly upped the ante. But I don't know how you keep staging this fight over and over again. The reboot was probably the best path to take after you put these characters together. I actually thought the new *Friday the 13th* wasn't bad.

DM: You have ties to the *Evil Dead* universe. Would you have considered doing *Freddy vs Jason vs Ash*?

MV: Only if Bruce was into it. I'm friends with Bruce. I've known him off and on for a while. *My Name is Bruce* came out of our conversations together and I wrote that script for him. As I understand it, he was not into the idea of bringing Ash into the mix. That would be the only reason to get involved on that. I was reading a comic book just the other day that had Ash fighting Hitler. I was like '*Okay, now we're really stretching this concept!*' But I'm also the sort of guy that likes to look forward and not back. I've already taken my stab at that kind of crossover, so I've gotten it out of my system, so to speak. But never say never, right? It just strikes me as so gimmicky that unless Bruce was really into it, *Freddy vs Jason vs Ash* wouldn't be worth doing.

DM: These franchises have had legendary battles with the MPAA. Was that ever a concern for you while writing your script?

MV: No, it wasn't. My job was to write the most interesting story with the scariest kills I possibly could. I don't want to sound glib about this, but the MPAA is someone else's problem. With most of these movies, I think they usually did what they wanted and then dealt with the MPAA afterward, not the other way around. In this day and age, all the MPAA can do is say what you can or can't do for your theatrical run. Now you can get the unrated cut on home video or streaming. That almost becomes a sales tool when you add all the hard stuff back in because you can do whatever you want on video.

DM: How about the fan bases? Any concern at how they might have received these changes to Freddy and Jason's backstories?

MV: When you're working with someone else's characters - and I have many times - you need to take great care in how you portray them, even more so when you have a significant fan base who are genuinely interested in what happens to them. You need to pay attention to what's come before… and then you need to put that out of your head and tell the best story you can. I did have a sense of boundary in terms of what these characters would or wouldn't do. They each come with their own incredibly convoluted but mostly cool history, which I didn't want to mess up. But you can't let that paralyze you. You can't let a fear of the fans hold you back.

With our direction at the time, we were saying that Freddy was involved in Jason's backstory at Camp Crystal Lake. I do get how that's a fairly massive addition to the mythos, but you just have to go for it. You just do it and you can't be afraid of the reaction one way or another. That was my attitude going into it. I will admit that I thought it was a cool idea. But sometimes these changes rub people the wrong way. I've worked on many shows that had a very vocal fanbase and I've learned that it's good to acknowledge and understand that, but you can't let it stop you from trying to make the best show you can make.

DM: In the first *Freddy vs Jason* script from '93, Freddy pops back to life and quotes '*Smokin'!*' from *The Mask*, which you were a writer on. Would it have been weird for you to hear Freddy quoting from one of your other works?

MV: Yes, that would've been pretty weird! (laughs) It also would've been pretty wrong for the movie that I wanted to make. That was the antithesis of what I wanted Freddy to be. Not to diss that writer - more power to him - but the idea that Freddy is this variety show comedian who comes out and kills with a wink-and-a-nod was not at all what I wanted. I think if New Line had said to me, '*Do whatever you want, but you've got to open with Freddy coming out and saying smokin',*' I would've said, '*I think you've got the wrong guy.*' That's not the *Freddy vs Jason* I wanted to write. Also, it would've dated the hell out of the movie because references to stuff that colloquial, you watch it now and half the audience wouldn't understand why he was saying it. Or maybe they would? I don't know. *The Mask* was pretty popular. And again, I'm not saying that the guy did anything he shouldn't have done. I'm not trying to level criticisms.

DM: What are your thoughts on striking a balance between the title characters?

MV: Obviously you need to try, but it's not easy. The biggest difference between the two characters, apart from their personalities, is that one speaks and one doesn't. Jason is a silent killer. Freddy is the verbose one, whether he's being funny or not. The fact that Freddy speaks probably means he's going to feel like a bigger presence in the movie because he can interact with the characters. Jason has a much more physical presence than Freddy, which almost dictates that Jason isn't as in-your-face as Freddy. As I saw it, Jason eventually became the protector of the Lizzie character, which is more of a defensive posture. Freddy was the attacker, which makes him a little bigger. I'd say my draft was about forty-percent Jason, sixty-percent Freddy.

DM: When did you realize your script wasn't moving forward?

MV: I don't remember specifically. Having done this for a while, even at that point, I knew it was simply par for the course. It happens. I always wonder what about my draft didn't pop for them? Yet I've also learned not to ask a question if you're not ready for the answer. To actually go in and ask the executives, '*What didn't you like?*' and hear that your script was terrible from start to finish is not fun. I don't need to hear that, so I don't ask! It could've been any number of issues or hold-ups. It also wouldn't help me to get criticisms on the project because I was no longer working on it. I don't think it was personal and I didn't take it personally.

DM: Is it strange still being associated so many years later with a script that didn't get made?

MV: Well, not that I want to tout my ones that got away, but it's not that unusual. In 2004, I wrote a pilot for a *Dark Shadows* revival series, which we actually shot for Warner Brothers. Unfortunately, it never went on the air. So I have my people in *Dark Shadows* that still remember me for that. I also did a script with Ron Howard and Akiva Goldsman for *The Dark Tower* television series that wound up not happening at that time. So I have been involved in other projects with fanbases that have not moved forward.

Here's an example of synchronicity. Yesterday was the 30th anniversary of the *Aliens* movie being released. One of the very first things I ever wrote was a comic book spun off from *Aliens* for Dark Horse comics. They just reissued that, meaning work I did twenty-eight years ago is now being brought back. So the fact that fans are still curious about my take on *Freddy vs Jason* - despite my script not even being made - doesn't really surprise me that much.

DM: My final question I'm posing to all the *Freddy vs Jason* writers; did you see the 2003 film and if so, what did you think?

MV: I saw it and I thought it was perfectly fine. This is the selfish writer in me talking, but I wasn't sure why that script was better than the one I did. They don't seem wildly different. In other words, it was still in the same ballpark. Not sure why that's the one that got them to pull the trigger. That sounds like sour grapes on my part, but it's not. Good for those guys, more power to them. They somehow found the way to align the stars and make it come together. Ultimately, I do think - and I'm cutting myself out of any future *Freddy vs Jason* jobs by saying this - that putting them together probably isn't the greatest thing to try, that the singular movies are way more true to the characters than trying to shoehorn them together. Not that it was poorly done - it was a fine job. I just look back and go '*I understand the commercial impact, but there's a reason there aren't a million of these type movies.*' That's why I thought the *Friday the 13th* reboot was so good. It went back to the franchise's roots and had a fun energy while doing that.

(Opposite page photo credit: Universal Orlando Resort)

FREDDY VS JASON VS YOU!

For some fans in 2016, the terror of *Freddy vs Jason* didn't end at the screen. Their battle crossed over into reality as Universal Studios staged special *Freddy vs Jason* haunted houses on both coasts as part of their annual Halloween Horror Nights event. Although Universal had hosted the titans separately in years past, this would mark the first time they met under one roof. In a surprising departure, the minds at Universal Creative sought to stage their own take on *Freddy vs Jason* separate from the 2003 film. A boiler factory named Craven Industries formed the entranceway to both houses. Although the rooms contained within were different on each coast, they were both were littered with easter eggs for the sharp-eyed fan.

In Orlando, guests started out traversing the scene of a terrible slaughter at Camp Crystal Lake with Jason still roaming around. Severed Freddy heads began to appear and disappear throughout the camp. A moment later, guests found themselves on the front lawn of 1428 Elm Street strolling past jump roping girl corpses. They entered into the iconic house to find Freddy stalking them across a grisly murder scene. The house then transitioned into a familiar boiler room where Freddy and Jason could be seen locked in a bloody struggle.

In Hollywood, guests entered into Freddy's boiler room workshop where the dream slasher was seen tormenting a very young Jason. One horrific room had Snake-Freddy halfway eating his writhing adolescent victim. The setting then changed to Camp Crystal Lake where a crazed Pamela Voorhees was digging up her son's grave. Guests were routed into a nearby cabin where Adult Jason began to attack them. The haunted house ended back at Craven Industries with Freddy and Jason battling each other.

So who ultimately won these two haunted house versions of *Freddy vs Jason*? That depends entirely on when you went. Universal cleverly devised two endings to the haunts, which "scare-actors" alternated throughout the night. Some guests found Jason holding Freddy's severed head as they exited into the park. Others saw it differently with Freddy clutching Jason's head. Even in 2016, the debate over which titan wins continues.

Chapter Nine
The Protosevich Draft

2000

THE SCREENWRITER

The start of 2000 found New Line Cinema barrelling toward a new Jason film they did not wish to make. This was per Sean Cunningham's mandate to Michael De Luca that they either produce something with Jason or lose rights to the character. De Luca's response was a compromise that the studio would greenlight a new Jason movie in early 2000 if *Freddy vs Jason* itself was not greenlit by that time. The recent rejection of the Verheiden draft had marked the final gasp of the Rob Bottin treatment that had fueled the last three years of development. That Bottin had also unceremoniously quit the project meant *Freddy vs Jason* was entering the new millennium without a writer or director. Seriously doubting New Line's ability to turn up a suitable crossover script so quickly, Cunningham began preparations to make *Jason X*. In desperation, De Luca turned to a rising star within the studio - Mark Protosevich - for a quick favor.

Protosevich's first screenwriting credit was 2000's *The Cell* for New Line. The high-concept thriller paired an inventive script with a memorable cast that included Jennifer Lopez, Vince Vaughn, and Vincent D'Onofrio. The strength of Protosevich's work had earned him a favorable reputation at the company even before *The Cell*'s release, particularly with De Luca. The studio boss approached the writer a scant six weeks before Cunningham's deadline. Recognizing the continued failure of existing concepts, he requested Protosevich conceive of an entirely new story for *Freddy vs Jason*. There were no other stipulations beyond this. Protosevich's draft would mark the first *completely original* script for the project in five years.

Following his take on *Freddy vs Jason*, Protosevich would write and/or produce an impressive slate of high-profile projects. In 2006, he would provide the script for Wolfgang Peterson's remake of *The Poseidon Adventure*. In 2007, he would co-write *I Am Legend* starring Will Smith. In 2011, he would provide the story for Marvel Studios' original *Thor*. In 2013, he would write and co-produce Spike Lee's remake of *Oldboy*. Protosevich is currently preparing to make his directorial debut with *Freakshow*, an adaptation of the Jackson Lanzing comic book.

THE PLOT

This *Freddy vs Jason* centers on Rachel Daniels, a young graduate student studying the iconization of monsters and serial killers throughout history. Her research leads her to question the relationship between such legendary figures and the terror they incite. Do monsters create mass fear? Or does mass fear create monsters? Hours after Rachel delivers a presentation on the titans, three people connected to her are slain in the styles of Freddy and Jason. Has renewed fear somehow brought these slashers back to life? Or does their reappearance owe to something else, possibly a secret buried deep in her past?

Protosevich's approach to bringing back the slashers is fascinatingly abstract. Unlike his predecessors, he is less specifically concerned with resurrecting the titans, foregoing details like heart transplants and virgin sacrifices. Instead, his story dips into more supernatural territory by summoning Freddy and Jason from the ether. By treating the titans as spiritual constructs rather than fleshy beings, he changes the rules of the game. In this world, fear is powerful enough to will Freddy and Jason back into existence. Essentially, this is the inverse of a concept introduced in the original *Nightmare*. ("Take away its energy and it disappears.") Protosevich's story reasons that if you give something enough energy, it will then appear.

The screenwriter disseminates this intriguing concept nicely through a doctoral presentation given by the main character early in the story: "Every culture creates monsters. They manifest themselves as vampires, werewolves, goblins, devils, ghosts, and psycho killers. They appear in fairy tales, folk songs, ancient myths, and urban legends. But which came first? The monster or the myth? The killer or the legend? The chicken or the egg? Does fear create the fiend? Or the fiend, fear? [...] Is the goblin who eats babies really any different from Wayne Williams, John Gacy or Freddy Krueger?"

Rachel goes on to note that the titans, who were once real-life serial killers, are officially considered long dead. Yet they live on in infamy, their legends kept alive by our culture's bizarre way of coping with childhood death. The loss of a child, whether by natural causes or murder, is often so devastating for families that monsters are created to blame. Rachel references examples of this from throughout history, citing poems like Johann Wolfgang von Goethe's *The Elf King* and William Butler Yates' *The Stolen Child*. In modern times, many unexplainable deaths and unsolved murders are attributed not to elves or witches, but to Freddy and Jason. She charges that decades of this have made them far more iconic in death than they ever were in life. Clever though this explanation is, it fails to account for what the audience secretly knows to be true. When an Elm Street teen dies suddenly in their sleep or a camper goes missing near Crystal Lake, this truly *is* the work of Freddy and Jason.

First lines of the Protosevich draft:

"Our dreams are a second life. I have never been able to penetrate without a shudder those ivory or horned gates which separate us from the invisible world."

- Gerard de Nerval, Aurelia, pt. 1, ch. 1, 1855

The Elf-King

by Johann Wolfgang von Goethe
Translation by Edwin Zeydel

Who's riding so late where winds blow wild?
It is the father grasping his child;
He holds the boy embraced in his arm,
He clasps him snugly, he keeps him warm.

"My son, why cover your face in such fear?"
"You see the Elf-King, father?
He's near! The King of the Elves with crown and train!"
"My son, the mist is on the plain."

'Sweet lad, o come and join me, do!
Such pretty games I will play with you;
On the shore gay flowers their color unfold,
My mother has many garments of gold.'

"My father, my father, can you not hear
The promise the elf-king breathes in my ear?"
"Be calm, stay calm, my child, lie low:
In withered leaves the night-winds blow."

'Will you, sweet lad, come along with me?
My daughters shall care for you tenderly;
In the night my daughters their revelry keep,
They'll rock you and dance you and sing you to sleep.'

"My father, my father, o can you not trace
The Elf-King's daughters in that gloomy place?"
"My son, my son, I see it clear
How grey the ancient willows appear."

'I love you, your comeliness charms me, my boy!
And if you're not willing, my force I'll employ.'
"Now father, now father, he's seizing my arm.
Elf-king has done me a cruel harm."

The father shudders, his ride is wild,
In his arms he's holding the groaning child,
Reaches the court with toil and dread. -
The child he held in his arms was dead.

THE HUMANS

The main character of this draft is Rachel Daniels, a twenty-year-old studying at The Michael Lucade Graduate School of Psychology (Michael Lucade being a minor reworking of studio boss Michael De Luca). She marks a departure from the last several crossover heroines simply by not being in high school. The script describes Rachel as "keenly intelligent" and hauntingly beautiful." Her boyfriend is fellow student Jim Turner, whom we find to be an untrustworthy ass. Rachel's supportive friends are Amelia and Greta, who would have marked the first openly lesbian couple in either franchise.

The most fascinating new character in Protosevich's script is an Aboriginal Australian known primarily as "The Stranger," real name Dr. Thomas Ezekiel Smith. Formerly an Oxford professor of humanities. We later learn that the Stranger's wife and daughter were killed by Freddy years ago. He has since devoted his life to studying both titans and holds some clues to their mysteries. Although the Stranger is slain early on, he maintains a ghostly presence throughout the rest of the story. He first appears to Rachel - who fears him - following her presentation on Freddy and Jason; "You are forewarned. Be en garde. They'll come looking for you, your monsters."

OPENING SEQUENCE

Protosevich uses his opening sequence to foreshadow one of his script's big ideas - that Freddy (or the evil behind Freddy) has always existed throughout history. This visually thrilling open shows us what *A Nightmare in Bavaria* might have looked like hundreds of years ago. The scene finds an elfin demon chasing Rachel through a dark patch of woods. Upon closer inspection, this demon is revealed to be the black armored, sword-wielding Elf King. Clutching a crying baby in her arms, she heads toward an isolated cottage. Rows of children wearing featureless white masks line the dirt path. The Elf King reaches into his cloak to retrieve a fierce-looking chain-mail glove with bladed fingers. This is all, of course, quite familiar to us.

As she nears the cottage, Rachel becomes disoriented. She accidentally drops the infant, which turns out not to be an infant, but a porcelain doll. Yet when the doll shatters on the ground, the blood and organs of a real child spill out. The Elf King catches up and, standing nose to nose, speaks to her in German; "Vas iss los, mein fraulein?" The demon's face suddenly morphs into Freddy's burned visage. "Everything falling to pieces?" He raises the glove to strike just as she jolts awake.

This sequence, while fun to envision, does seem somehow counter to the original *Nightmare*, which suggested Freddy only haunted Elm Street beginning sometime in the 1980s. Yet later sequels did look to broaden his scope, notably *Freddy's Dead* ("Every town has an Elm Street!") Protosevich's reveal that the dream slasher is not only a global terror, but an age-old one as well, makes for endless new story possibilities. The narrative loophole that would allow for this is the suggestion that Freddy is but the latest disguise of a timeless force. The prospect of seeing Freddy terrorize other cultures in other times could be terrifically fun if not only to see primitive-looking versions of his razor gauntlet.

THE TITANS: JASON VOORHEES

Protosevich's screenplay features what may be the fiercest depiction of Jason *ever*. Although the hockey-masked titan's first appearance comes a little later than his claw-gloved counterpart, it establishes him as an explosive and merciless force. His first kill involves using his machete to sever a drug dealer's appendages "like a golfer teeing off." Jason then slashes open said dealer's mouth in order to pour an entire bag of drugs down his throat, choking him in the process. The next kill is even more savage as the titan turns his attention upon the dealer's coked out girlfriend, who happens to be Rachel's older sister. He cuts open her torso and places her crying infant son *back into her stomach*, as though making a sick social commentary on how drug dealers tend to be unfit parents.

The Stranger later explains that, unlike Freddy, this Jason is the spirit of the once human Jason Voorhees. He is categorically "a supernatural purveyor of vengeance, a wronged human who returns to punish those he deems guilty." Of course, we know this has long been the character's unspoken creed with guilt being defined as anyone partaking in sex, drinking, drugs or trespassing. Interestingly, Protosevich's take on Jason is that he is not only a purveyor of vengeance, but also a protector of innocence. He not only spares the baby in his aforementioned rampage, he later risks his own skin diving after the child when Freddy appears to drop it into molten lava.

This new characterization uniquely sets up how Rachel will eventually side with Jason to beat Freddy. Protosevich is hardly the first screenwriter to align Jason with the heroine, but he may be the one to do it most successfully. He positions Jason as someone the audience can root for without compromising the character's power. Midway through the script, the Stranger appears to Rachel in a dream to prophesize this unlikely partnership, describing Jason as "a pawn without a queen." Later on, the titan interrupts a confrontation between Rachel and Freddy with a tightly gripped machete in one hand, baby in the other. Remembering the Stranger's advice, Rachel calmly instructs, "Jason, give Jake to me. (sincere) Thank you. (equally sincere) Now kill Freddy." He obeys, setting the final battle in motion.

THE TITANS: FREDDY KRUEGER

You might expect a script that explores the monsters of our psyche to include a bleak depiction of Freddy, yet this is not so. Protosevich's presentation of the dream slasher tries to strike a balance between wicked and whimsical. He will often begin a scene cracking wise only to end it on a much darker, more threatening note. The writer's contrast of funnyman Freddy against the story's deadly serious tone makes for a surprisingly good combination. Plus, let's face it… your script *needs* some levity when you have Jason performing a reverse c-section with a machete.

Perhaps the character's campiest moment here involves terrorizing Rachel's psychiatrist in an effort to learn her patient's deepest secrets. An unusual sleep-aid has blocked him from exploring the heroine's subconscious himself. Freddy transforms into a cigar-chomping Sigmund Freud ("What's up, Doc?") and plugs his newest book - *Men are from Mars, Women are from Venus and I'm From Hell* by Dr. Frederick Krueger. He goes on to taunt the psychiatrist by showing her the grisly bodies of former patients who killed themselves. ("Glad I'm not one of your patients. Your track record sucks.")

The Stranger explains to Rachel that Freddy is only a front for the true evil they now face. He describes that force as "an ancient spirit who once took human form, a malevolent thing of pure evil who works his magic in the subconscious." The Stranger further reveals that this demon has assumed many forms throughout history prior to becoming Freddy. Protosevich may be drawing from some of Wes Craven's dialogue in *New Nightmare* and, if so, this makes for a decent callback. Recall the director's lines to Heather Langenkamp in that film: "Whatever you want to call it. It's old, very old, and it's taken different forms in different times. The only thing that stays the same about it is what it lives for. [...] Killing innocence."

THE AUSTRALIAN INFLUENCE

One unique influence on this *Freddy vs Jason* script is that of traditional Australian folklore. While unexpected, these concepts do enhance the titan's mythology in new and satisfying ways. You might come away from this draft thinking Protosevich to be Australian, but he actually hails from Chicago. The most obvious example of this influence at work is seen with the Stranger, who spiritually guides Rachel on her journey to defeat Freddy. He is not unlike Whitaker from the Reiff/Voris draft in that both of their lives were destroyed by Freddy. The difference is that the Stranger possesses a greater, almost existential understanding of the titans and the forces behind them.

The Stranger refers to the dreamscape as the Alchera, which is an Aboriginal term meaning "time out of time" or "the everywhen." This makes for a far more mystical take on the dream realm than seen in earlier *Nightmare* films. Aboriginal folklore tells that death only destroys the body, not the soul. The Alchera then is not only where our subconscious travels while asleep, but also where our souls go upon death. This somewhat equates the dreamscape to the afterlife. Through the Alchera, the Stranger is able to reconnect with his slain family.

Aboriginal folklore also tells that everyone is essentially an incarnation of a totemic being, which can be any object, plant, or animal. In one scene, the Stranger performs an indigenous ceremony around a bonfire in loin-cloth, his chest painted with the totem of a lizard. This ceremony generates a protective force field around him that a taunting Freddy manages to eventually penetrate, killing him immediately after. The Stranger returns later in the story as his totem - a blue lizard - whom Freddy eats (the reincarnated prophet somehow survives this). According to Australian folklore, the lizard can symbolize many things including desert wisdom and protection, which certainly speaks to the Stranger's role in this *Freddy vs Jason*.

In an epilogue scene, we see that the Stranger's teachings have enabled Rachel to visit her fallen loves ones in the Alchera, which resembles an Australian beach. The Stranger and his family also turn up for this reunion.

BLENDING BACKSTORIES

Every screenwriter thus far in the development process has attempted to intertwine the backstories of Freddy and Jason. Protosevich does not disrupt this trend, though his approach is decidedly different than those of his predecessors. He still places Freddy at the scene of young Jason's drowning, but only peripherally. Therefore nothing important actually changes about Jason's history. He still dies of accidental drowning due to neglectful counselors having sex instead of watching him. The twist is that one of those counselors was Freddy… and the other was Rachel's mother.

If this were not twist enough, Protosevich goes on to reveal that young Rachel and her sister were witness to these traumatic events, the infidelity of her mother and the drowning of a peer. Mrs. Daniels is hysterical at discovering Jason's body floating in the lake while Freddy cruelly mocks her panic. He gags the children and places them next to young Jason's corpse, instructing as how they will speak of this day: "You were all swimming, right? *Right?* Me and your Mom were doing a real good job of watching you, too. Then Jason got a... cramp. And he went under. [voice "breaking up"] I tried to save him, I did. But it was too late. (knife at their eyes) *That's what happened!* Got it? Good!"

This long buried piece of Rachel's past gives her the power to become the queen to Jason's pawn and ultimately defeat Freddy. This revelation also explains why her presentation on the titans drew them to her - she has a deep connection to both. The Stranger charges that if Rachel is powerful enough to resurrect these monsters, then she is also powerful enough to destroy them. ("Any weapon, any tool you desire is already at your disposal Use your imagination!")

As intriguing as the implications of this revised backstory are, it fails to line up with the existing continuity. The *Friday* and *Elm Street* timelines tell us that Jason drowned in 1957 and that Freddy was burned alive by the vigilante mob in 1968. This script's Crystal Lake flashback establishes Rachel as being seven-years-old at the time of Jason's drowning. That she is now mentioned as being twenty-years-old means this story unfolds sometime in 1970. This becomes an issue with the inclusion of anachronisms like cell phones, the internet, and the music of Nine-Inch-Nails. Assuming this story plays out in the year Protosevich wrote it, Rachel should be forty-nine-years-old, not twenty.

DREAMS/NIGHTMARES

As previously mentioned, this *Freddy vs Jason* offers up a unique twist on the dreamscape with the Alchera. Near script's end, the Stranger implores Rachel to remember that "the line between your world and his is just an illusion." This transcendent advice paves the way not only for Freddy to attack Rachel in pseudo-reality, but for Rachel to retaliate in the same fashion.

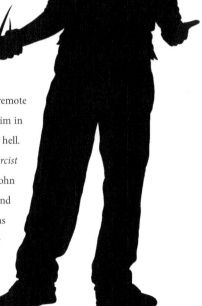

One riveting sequence places Rachel and the baby holed up in a remote cabin. Freddy calls on a terrifying army of demons and serial killers to join him in an assault on the shack. They burst from the ground, as if erupting up from hell. Protosevich details a roster that includes demons Abbadon, Belial, Pazuzu (*Exorcist* fans take note!), Kali, Faerie and Ahriman. On the killer side, Freddy recruits John Wayne Gacy, Ted Bundy, Wayne Williams, Henry Lee Lucas, Jeffrey Dahmer and Charles Manson. Recall that Gacy, Dahmer, and Manson previously appeared as nightmare figures in the Braga/Moore draft and that Bundy was ring announcer in the Abernathy script's Nightmare Arena sequence.

As this monstrous army nears the cabin, they yell out Rachel's name in a ghastly chorus. She turns pale and begins to quake with fear before remembering the Stranger's advice. In a terrific burst of empowerment, she chooses to fight back. ("Fuck that. You know what I have? I have power.") At once, wooden posts burst from the earth, barbed wire connecting them to form a perimeter around the cabin, shredding several demons in the process. Steel shutters slam overtop the windows as an electric fence further lines the cabin exterior. The transition from damsel in distress to fearsome fighter is almost always a fun one in the *Nightmare* series.

Speaking of the dreamscape, this might not feel like a proper *Freddy vs Jason* script if there were not dream drugs somewhere in the story. Protosevich introduces three new such pills. The first is Hytenexoft, which Rachel has been taking for some time to suppress recurrent disturbing dreams. When this suppressant stops working, her doctor prescribes Somnazac, which does exactly the opposite. Rather than suppress dreams, Somnazac encourages them. As her psychiatrist describes, "When you're asleep, you'll know when you go into dream state. And you'll have at your disposal the entire breadth and width of your imagination. An arsenal of thought." Naturally, this eventually empowers Rachel to fight Freddy. The third drug is Mescahedraline Anthropophylax or "Meskie Mex," a powerful hallucinogenic several drug dealing characters take.

THE ENDING

Rachel and Jason eventually tag-team to defeat Freddy in battle, much to the dream slasher's surprise. Upon defeat, hellish vines rip through the floor to drag Freddy down into the underworld. Jason is not entirely victorious as Freddy fatally wounds him in the fight. The script tells that Rachel goes to comfort him in his final moments. Removing the hockey mask, she sees Jason's disfigured face has changed to that of an ordinary man, albeit with a boyish innocence. Protosevich writes, "If he is able to recapture any kind of purity, it happens now. As Rachel holds his hand, he perishes into nothingness."

This has always been one of the riskier moves of any *Freddy vs Jason* script, to so permanently wrap up a killer's storyline. Recall that the Briggs and Braga/Moore drafts also tried for similarly concrete endings. As we have long seen, Jason can overcome any torment imaginable with the exception of emotional closure. This most certainly would not have sat well with Sean Cunningham, who asserted back in Chapter Seven that, "Whoever wins, *you* are able to win if you find a way to keep it going for more movies." For the purposes of *Freddy vs Jason*, this ending makes for a satisfying conclusion. For the purposes of continuing *Friday the 13th*, its constitutes franchise suicide.

THE PSYCHOLOGICAL FREDDY VS JASON

If Protosevich's script has any fault, it may be that his unique vision is simply too high concept. If nothing else, you have to respect the guy for putting such tremendous thought into his story, which does elevate the material to new heights. By all means, this is the most psychological take on *Freddy vs Jason*. Yet at the end of the day, psychological horror is probably not a sub-genre most audiences would think to place this crossover sequel in. It was certainly not the sub-genre of the prior sixteen *Friday* and *Elm Street* films. How might fans have reacted to this, the thinking man's slasher film?

Unfortunately, Protosevich's script flatlined upon submission to New Line. Whatever promise Michael De Luca saw in it, he knew it would not be enough to win over Sean Cunningham and stop the forward momentum of *Jason X*. Perhaps with further development it might have worked, but there was no time left for that. Consequently, the new solo-Jason movie immediately launched into pre-production and began filming two months later.

INTERVIEW: Mark Protosevich
Screenwriter, *Freddy vs Jason '00*

DUSTIN MCNEILL: How did you come on board *Freddy vs Jason*?

MARK PROTOSEVICH: That takes me back about sixteen years. It's an interesting story because it was a bit of a fluke, actually. We had just finished shooting *The Cell* and everything had gone well with that. During production, I had developed a very good relationship with the president of New Line, Mike De Luca. Mike became a friend and we're still friends today. We remain close and always talk about working together again. At that time, which would've been very early 2000, I got a call from him saying, "*Mark, I need you to do me a favor. I'm begging you. Freddy vs Jason is in trouble.*"

I think the scenario was that *Freddy vs Jason* had stalled because they couldn't come up with a draft that everyone agreed on. There was also a deadline approaching that said if *Freddy vs Jason* wasn't in production within six weeks, that Sean Cunningham was free to go do another solo Jason movie, which Mike did not want to have happen. He was hoping to circumvent that by getting *Freddy vs Jason* into production as soon as possible. He said, "*Please, will you write this movie?*"

DM: Were you aware of the project's long history by that point?

MP: No, I wasn't fully aware of its history. I also never read any of the older drafts. I was never even shown them, not that I had time to read through them. Mike was begging for my help with the project. The problem was that I had also just taken another writing assignment, so to do this I had to delay my other project and write *Freddy vs Jason* on the fly as a favor to Mike. I think I wrote my script in four or five weeks because they needed it that quickly.

DM: Were you a fan of either property heading into the script?

MP: I was a really big fan of the *Nightmare on Elm Street* films, especially the first and third films. I also have this peculiar affection for *Wes Craven's New Nightmare*. I've always been a huge Craven fan and admired him tremendously. In terms of horror, he's one of my favorites because he's such a thinker. There's always more going on in a Craven movie than you first realize. I never got to meet him, but I admire his work so much.

So the *Elm Street* movies were very much in my wheelhouse. The *Friday the 13th* movies, not so much. The only one I'd seen at that time was the first one, but I knew Jason had gone on to become an icon. I'm willing to admit that those films were not my cup of horror tea. I appreciated the fact that they were popular and had generated so much interest, but they weren't my thing. That approach to the slasher genre didn't appeal to me on a personal level. Mike was in such a rush to get me to do this he said, '*I'll send you all the movies, all the Friday's and Elm Streets. Immerse yourself as much as you can and do whatever you want!*' He basically gave me carte blanche. I don't think we ever had a face to face meeting about it. He told me to write the kind of movie I would want to see, which is exactly what I did.

DM: That's surprising to hear because your script does not read like a rush job at all.

MP: In all honesty, I hadn't read the script since I wrote it. It's just not something I ever went back to since nothing happened with my draft. I did go back and read it in preparation for this discussion. I was actually impressed by it. I was wondering how I managed to write that in such a short amount of time.

DM: For having come together so quickly, your draft has an internal logic to it that I very much like.

MP: Thank you. That's part of my thing. Every script I write has to make sense to me. The funny thing was that Mike essentially let me do whatever I wanted. I love horror films and I'm obsessed with them, but I also do a lot of reading on horror film criticism and analysis. I incorporated a lot of my reading on critical thinking about horror into the script.

DM: Your script has a certain reputation as being the most psychological take on *Freddy vs Jason*. Do you think that description is appropriate?

MP: I think it's fitting. Looking back, however, I don't know that a psychological *Freddy vs Jason* was the best approach to take in order to reach the widest audience. But again, I was never really a fan of the *Friday the 13th* movies and the *Freddy vs Jason* we later got reminded me a lot of the *Friday the 13th* movies. In many ways, I'm a frustrated psychologist. It's easily a career I could have pursued if I hadn't become a writer. I am completely fascinated by human psychology and also the processes of psychotherapy, both in terms of how we are composed as human beings and also the people who choose to try to understand us from that perspective. It's a really intriguing career choice to me.

I was re-reading my script the other day and there's a scene where they turn onto a street called Robinwood Lane. I laughed out loud at that. Robin Wood was a major film critic in the 1970s and he wrote a famous book on Hitchcock. I took a class in film school where we read one of Robin's books called *The American Nightmare*. If you could ever track this book down, I would highly recommend reading it. He wrote it as a series of essays on films by people like George Romero, Wes Craven, and David Cronenberg. His main thesis was on how horror films were essentially all about a Freudian concept called the return of the repressed. The idea was that all the things we try not to think about ourselves, all our terrible urges, are part of who we are. We repress them, but they're still in us. The desire to hurt and kill people exists in all of us, but most of us succeed in keeping them down. So in horror, it's the monsters that embody everything we repress, the worst things about us. These qualities come back to torment and haunt us in the form of monsters.

DM: Were you concerned about audiences coming in with preconceptions about what *Freddy vs Jason* should be?

MP: I didn't think about that at all. Keep in mind, I had been working as a writer for about five years before I finally had a film made, which was *The Cell*. My approach on *Freddy vs Jason*, as it has always been, was to do it in a way that is unexpected. I wanted to avoid doing something that was just a repeat of what has come before. In that respect, I think I succeeded. When I finished re-reading my script the other day, my first reaction was, '*God I would love have seen this movie!*'

DM: The scene where Jason puts the baby back into the dead mother's stomach. I may need therapy after having read that.

MP: I hadn't really remembered my script all that well, so when I re-read that scene the other day, I just went '*Whoa!*' and put it down for a while. I actually stunned myself reading it again. If I were a moviegoer, I would be like "*Oh my God. That is one of the most troubling images I've ever witnessed onscreen*'. But as a writer I'm like, '*Way to go, Mark! That's really disturbing!*' Had my script been made, I think we'd probably still be talking about that visual today.

DM: Your script set up some pretty amazing visuals. Are you sure you're not a frustated effects guy deep down?

MP: I try to think like a director when I'm writing. When I was in high school, I was convinced I was going to be an illustrator or comic book artist. I was pretty good, but I wasn't great. Having said that, visuals have been important to me for a long time. I try to always create vivid concepts with my writing. People often read one of my scripts and go, '*I can see your movie in my head*,' which I take as a huge compliment.

DM: I know you're more of a Freddy guy, but tell me about your approach to Jason.

MP: For me, the thing about Jason is that - in some ways - I viewed him as a victim. There were aspects of this in *The Cell* also, serial killers who were themselves victims of abuse or injustice. It may not be right to classify Jason as a victim, but there's certainly a victim side to him. What he has done as an agent of evil is not forgivable, but from a certain standpoint, it's kind of understandable. At the very least, it's understandable from his point of view. Whereas Freddy, to me, was just a symbol of pure evil. In my script, I suggested that Freddy was a modern incarnation of an ancient evil, which makes him much, much worse than Jason.

DM: Would you ever consider using some of these concepts in another script? Because they're rich.

MP: To tell you the truth, I was looking at a lot of the aspects of this script the other day and I was going, '*Mark, you can actually take a lot of these ideas and put them into something new,*' which maybe I'll do some day. I'm intrigued by what I came up with because, again, I haven't read this in sixteen years. There are some decent ideas in there.

DM: Did you ever get any feedback on your *Freddy vs Jason* script?

MP: I did get several reactions to it, some good and some bad. There was some announcement in the trades that I was writing a draft of this. I remember an old college classmate of mine commenting that, '*Mark is a hack for writing such trash now,*' and I was like, '*No, that's not my goal at all.*' One, I was doing it as a favor to Mike, but with anything I do, I wanted to do it the best way I can. So my motivation was to go, '*People re going to expect a crappy money grab film about Freddy and Jason. What if I* *gave them something that really shook them up intellectually, physiologically, physically? What if you really gave them something unexpected and fucked with their heads?'* That was my goal.

DM: So you weren't going back and forth with De Luca as you were writing?

MP: Not at all. The time pressure was so intense. I was completely on my own, so I wasn't thinking about anything else. I was purely focused on it from a creative standpoint. Having said that, when I sent the script to Mike, I didn't hear anything back for a long, long time. It was one of the stranger processes that I've been through. The next thing I heard was that there was going to be another Jason movie, so my script must not have been successful in preventing that. Honestly, I don't even know if Mike and I had another conversation about it. I can only guess that the other people involved in the making of *Freddy vs Jason* read my script and went, '*No way!'*

DM: With Freddy, you leave the door open for additional movies. With Jason, you provide closure. Why?

MP: My script does leave the door open with Freddy. I wanted to leave it open. In my take, Freddy is this incarnation of an ancient evil, the kind of evil that never really goes away. And yes, I did try to give Jason some closure. When I read the script the other day, one of my favorite scenes was when they finally remove his mask at the end and he seems at peace.

DM: For me, that scene evoked the old *Wolf-Man* pictures with Lon Chaney Jr. after he changes back into a human.

MP: Doesn't it, though? I grew up on those old Universal classics. Horror films have changed quite a bit since then. That was one of the moments that when I read my script the other day, I wished this movie had existed! I say that from a fan standpoint, not like patting myself on the back. This could've been really something.

DM: You mentioned having seen the 2003 *Freddy vs Jason*. What was your impression of it?

MP: I am going to be completely honest with you here. I did not see it when it came out. I think I had read some of the reviews, which were not great. I really had no great desire to see it. Even when it came out on DVD, for whatever reason, I didn't watch it. I think because I knew I wasn't going to like what I saw. And so in preparation for this interview, I finally watched it. I think I was right in my initial assessment that I wasn't going to like what I saw. When I was growing up, my mother once said regarding people, *'If you don't have something nice to say, don't say anything at all.'* I should probably apply that to this movie.

DM: My take is that they made a fun popcorn movie out of it. Obviously, it won't make anyone's list of greatest films ever.

MP: My thought was that, if you have this opportunity to combine these two great horror icons, why not shoot for something greater? It is what it is. The funny thing is, I remember going through a phase when I was first discovering Hong Kong directors and seeing Ronny Yu's *The Bride with White Hair* and thinking, '*Oh man, he might actually bring something unique to Freddy vs Jason.*' And there were some scenes in the film that have a fantastic, weird, fun, crazy, Hong Kong feel to them. Those were my favorite parts of the movie where it goes into weird territory.

I often equate films with food and that *Freddy vs Jason* isn't the kind of meal I want to eat. I want to be bombarded with flavors that I've never had before or go, '*Oh My God, this chef is amazing!*' Why not do something that provokes a response instead of seeing it and going, '*Yeah, that was just okay?*'

DM: I get that. Why have flank steak when you can have filet mignon?

MP: Exactly. Or beef tartare? Or Thai spiced beef? So many different approaches you could take to this.

DM: Years after you wrote it, your screenplay leaked onto the internet. Did you know that and how do you feel about it?

MP: I had no idea that happened. No idea, whatsoever. When you first e-mailed me, I did a little research and came across it online. Low and behold, it's there in its entirety! I have no problem with it. I'm actually always really pleased when that happens. I know that my original draft of *I Am Legend* is also online for anyone to read. I've had complete strangers who've read it online come up to me and go, '*That was one of the best scripts ever!*'

So to whoever posted my *Freddy vs Jason* script, I don't know who you are or how you did it, but I'm grateful. I actually think if you're a student of film that being exposed to early drafts of projects or alternate versions is great stuff. You can learn a lot.

Chapter Ten
The Bergantino Treatments

2001

THE SCREENWRITER

The next scribe to take on *Freddy vs Jason* would do so from multiple angles. He is a man of many talents and interests, not unlike the project's original screenwriter. As of this writing, David Bergantino's thirty-year career in the entertainment industry has spanned books, video games, movies, television, and even theme park rides. A longtime genre fan, he first boarded the crossover sequel as a script consultant before spearheading a video game effort. When that endeavor fell apart, he pitched his own take on *Freddy vs Jason*.

Bergantino is the author of eleven books with subjects ranging from Shakespeare to Zorro. *Elm Street* fans should recall his clever 1994 novelization of *Wes Craven's New Nightmare*, which was anything but your standard movie tie-in. His adaptation still told the story of Freddy terrorizing the latest *Nightmare* film crew, but with an additional narrative layer. Interspersed throughout the novel are unsettling entries from Bergantino's personal journal that detail his experience translating *New Nightmare* to book form. In adapting the film, he becomes an unwitting participant in its nightmarish story, which is incredibly fitting considering the source material.

The following year saw Bergantino return to the world of *Elm Street* in a big way. He authored four young adult novels in Tor Books' *Freddy Krueger's Tales of Terror* series. These included *Help Wanted, Virtual Terror, Deadly Disguise* and *Twice Burned*. The *Tales of Terror* books were similar to episodes of *Freddy's Nightmares* in that the dream slasher functioned as a Cryptkeeper-like host to new stories rather than as the main antagonist. For *Elm Street*'s most devoted, novels such as these helped ease the nine-year wait between *New Nightmare* and *Freddy vs Jason*.

Most everyone who worked on the crossover sequel gravitated to either Cunningham Productions or New Line Cinema depending on who initially hired them. Bergantino managed to keep one foot in each camp, something virtually no one else can lay claim to. His relationship with New Line allowed him to shop around the rights for a *Freddy vs Jason* video game. He was simultaneously embraced by the development team at Cunningham Productions, who enlisted him as a script consultant. That Bergantino was involved with *Freddy vs Jason* from both ends gives him a unique perspective on the project's turbulent history.

If you are reading this and wondering how you never managed to hear about the great, kick-ass *Freddy vs Jason* video game, fret not. The project was never officially greenlit. This disappointment, coupled with the ongoing rejection of umpteen crossover scripts, led Bergantino to pen his own version of *Freddy vs Jason*. This chapter will look at both his game pitch and sequel treatment.

HELL UNBOUND

The subject of video games adapted from horror films is a strange one. The first slashers to go virtual were *Texas Chainsaw Massacre*'s Leatherface in 1982 and *Halloween*'s Michael Myers in 1983, each on the Atari 2600 system. Both releases courted controversy for their "ultra-violent" gameplay, which amounted to a few pixelated squares of blood. Parent groups were especially outraged that *Texas Chainsaw* encouraged gamers to play as Leatherface with a goal of slaughtering trespassers onto his property. Said outcry led retailers to remove the game from store shelves, all but killing sales. As a result, the release was a massive financial flop. This controversy, coupled with the infamous North American video game crash of 1983, would keep horror icons away from game consoles for six years.

The next slashers to venture into the world of gaming were the titans themselves on the original Nintendo Entertainment System. LJN produced both adaptations with *Friday the 13th* arriving in 1989 and *A Nightmare on Elm Street* the following year. In each release, players took control of human characters to battle spiders, snakes and other assorted creatures, most of which had nothing to do with the film franchises. The titans did eventually show up (as did Mrs. Voorhees' floating head), but their attacks were relatively tame and entirely bloodless. For all their nostalgic charm, these first Freddy and Jason video games set the bar awfully low.

(Interesting to note that LJN's original *Nightmare* game as first announced and previewed in the pages of Nintendo Power #2 would have seen players controlling Freddy as he slashed his way across Elm Street, not unlike *Texas Chainsaw* years before. LJN was most wise to learn from Atari's mistake and modify their approach to avoid any gameplay that simulated mass murder of teenagers.)

Flash forward to early 2000 as the titans are struggling to escape from development hell. Author, screenwriter and game developer David Bergantino looks to produce a *Freddy vs Jason* video game through his own Primal Inc. label. Having already written five Freddy Krueger books for New Line and script consulted for Cunningham Productions, he wins support from both camps to pursue the project. The expectation is that it will release simultaneously with the long delayed movie. Bergantino titles the game *Freddy vs Jason: Hell Unbound*. He intends to finally let gamers control the titans themselves, though not in scenarios that would have awarded points for slaughtering innocent victims with sharp implements.

The project's official pitch read, "At the end of *Jason Goes to Hell,* Freddy Krueger's claw is seen dragging Jason Voorhees's mask down into hell. The game is set shortly thereafter, with Freddy and Jason suffering hellish torments for their crimes on Earth. They are visited by an even more ghastly apparition, Death itself, who has watched them closely. He offers them a challenge: the demon who can fight his way out of Hell and onto Earth, racking up the greatest body count, will inherit Earth forever as their own personal, planet-sized charnel house. The loser will be returned to Hell to suffer its torments for the remainder of eternity. Charred visage turns to scarred hockey mask, blades are raised. Paths are chosen and they are off, slashing their way to a blood-soaked forever!"

Fascinatingly, *Hell Unbound* continues on from *Jason Goes to Hell* with its own alternative storyline independent from any of the proposed *Freddy vs Jason* screenplays. The project was initially envisioned for an arcade rollout with eventual releases on the Dreamcast and Playstation 2 consoles. When Sega abandoned the Dreamcast in early 2001, an X-Box version was considered in its place. The game would have allowed up to four players at a time, except in the case of a PC version which might have allowed up to fifty players to battle online using highly customized characters.

In single-player mode, *Hell Unbound* would have seen gamers raging up through hell as either Freddy or Jason with the game system taking the opposing role. Being hell, these stages would have been populated with monsters, demons, and creatures to slash through. Each level's final boss would have been a unique incarnation of Freddy or Jason from the earlier films, meaning Freddy might have faced off against Hooded Jason or Jason against Snake-Freddy. Whichever titan the player first selected would dictate a unique path throughout the game, allowing for tremendous replay value. This means you could have beaten *Hell Unbound* as Jason and still not seen all of it unless you also did so as Freddy. Two-player mode would have seen gamers race up through the underworld in split-screen. Rather than fight bosses at the end of each level, players would square off against one another before ascending to the next rung of hell.

Bergantino suggested that the titans should transform as they battle through hell, increasing in strength and ability. There would have been unlockable characters (Jason's mother, for example), secret levels, and surprise nightmares. Game environments would have reflected the worlds of the titans themselves, sometimes appearing like Elm Street or Crystal Lake. This meant Freddy-centric levels would have been surreal and nightmarish while Jason-centric levels would have been stark and foreboding. Bergantino also suggested that gameplay dynamics should vary accordingly between worlds. For example, gamers playing as Jason would have had to watch out for Freddy trying to disguise the nightmare world as reality.

So why did we never get to play this amazing *Freddy vs Jason* game? According to Cunningham Productions' Mark Haslett, we can blame it on the film's development woes: "The game was supposed to come out with the movie, but the situation was complicated because the movie kept getting pushed back. You have to understand that we never thought *Freddy vs Jason* was years away from happening. We were always thinking it was more like six months away. No game could come together that fast. I really supported the idea of a game. I thought it was a valuable asset that should have been exploited and wasn't. Plus, there was no one better suited for it than David Bergantino. He was *the* guy to do it."

In the years since *Hell Unbound* fell apart, Bergantino has gone onto great success elsewhere in the gaming industry. He has held vice president positions in both Nickelodeon's Premium Games Group and THQ's Kids & Family Games division. His games have collectively generated more than half-a-billion in revenue and earned him numerous award recognitions. He is currently CEO of Cold Room Entertainment, which specializes in virtual reality horror-genre video games. As for the titans, Freddy and Jason would later feature as guest characters in *Mortal Kombat IX* and *X* respectively. Crystal Lake's most famous son is also set to appear in Gun Media's upcoming *Friday the 13th: The Game*, which has no qualms about letting players slice, dice, bash and mutilate poor campers.

BLOOD KNOWS BLOOD

As previously mentioned, David Bergantino provided feedback to Cunningham Productions on many of the rejected *Freddy vs Jason* screenplays, none of which he particularly liked. His impression was that these scripts consistently missed the mark, failing to reach the concept's full potential. Near the end of this process, Bergantino took it upon himself to formulate his own vision for the crossover movie. You might expect his treatment to be terribly derivative of the many drafts he gave notes on or even the *Hell Unbound* storyline, but this is not the case. Instead, he steers clear of cults, pills and the intertwining of Freddy and Jason's younger days. His treatment, titled *Freddy vs Jason: Blood Knows Blood*, is a refreshingly original take on the material.

Blood Knows Blood finds Freddy trapped in the dream realm as we have long known him to be. He is terribly eager to crossover into the real world and has finally devised a plan to achieve that goal. His three biggest obstacles are the trio of malevolent dream demons we first met in *Freddy's Dead*, the very ones who made him immortal to begin with. In order to break through to reality, Freddy will need to destroy the demons that hold him prisoner and usurp their power. The energy required for such an overthrow can not possibly be obtained by plucking off Elm Street kids one by one, or even by the handful. For this, Freddy is going to need an unprecedentedly high body count.

We soon learn that Freddy plans to become all powerful by manipulating a teen pop sensation into luring thousands of her unsuspecting fans into attending a "dream concert," which takes dream-sharing to a whole new level. Once the dream stadium is filled to the brim, the mass-slashing can begin. A slaughter of this magnitude is sure to supercharge Freddy with the power he needs to overcome the dream demons. From there, he can finally escape into the real world, powers intact. By then, reality won't stand a chance. Forget Elm - this will be a nightmare on every street.

The only person capable of stopping Freddy turns out to be Jacob Johnson, the now teenaged title character from *A Nightmare on Elm Street 5: The Dream Child*. As the dream child, Jacob's special powers enable him to enter and leave the dreamscape at will. He uncovers Freddy's plan for the dream concert and seeks out the brainwashed pop singer, who manages to break free of Freddy's control. Jacob and the popstar then team up to stop their common enemy. They reason that to beat Freddy in his native environment will require a fearless force of comparable power, namely Jason Voorhees. Unleashing the hockey-masked titan in the dreamscape will prove tricky since, technically, he does not dream (and he is also presently dead). Fortunately, Jacob's powers also allow him to pull others into the dream realm with him, which he does with a resurrected Jason. That Jason can now stalk the dreamscape without actually dreaming puts him on more equal footing with Freddy.

Bergantino revives and redeems the ghostly spectre of Mrs. Voorhees in his treatment, who appears to Jason as a friendly spirit. She later helps her son when he seems to be losing to Freddy, who decapitates her for doing so. The story climaxes as the dream concert is about to begin with thousands of people in attendance. Instead of a pop concert, the dreamers are witness to a bloody showdown between Freddy and Jason. The fate of the concertgoers' souls, not to mention reality itself, hang in the balance of whomever wins the fight.

Blood Knows Blood is unique among unused *Freddy vs Jason* pitches for where it stages the final battle. Most screenwriters opted for Jason to beat Freddy in the real world where the latter's dream abilities are not at play, a tradition dating all the way back to the first *Freddy vs Jason* script. Bergantino, on the other hand, envisioned Jason beating Freddy while in the dreamscape, Freddy's homefield advantage be damned. That the final clash plays out inside a packed stadium evokes the same "fight of the century" spirit that earlier drafts had with the Nightmare Arena. Having thousands of onlookers would also have surely allowed for some gore-tastic collateral damage as the titans brawled. You can almost hear special effects makers gleefully cracking their knuckles at the very prospect of such a throwdown.

The treatment's title refers to a line of dialogue from said final battle. Just before killing Freddy, Jason grumbles out three words ("Blood knows blood!"), which was in reference to how his story addressed the titans' bloodlines.

INTERVIEW: David Bergantino
Game Developer, *Freddy vs Jason: Hell Unbound*
Screenwriter, *Freddy vs Jason: Blood Knows Blood*

DUSTIN MCNEILL: How did you get involved in all of this *Freddy vs Jason* business?

DAVID BERGANTINO: It started when I was trying to get a book published on the *Friday the 13th* series years ago. Back then, I was what you might consider a professional fan boy. I had written some four-hundred pages of this really weird satirical film criticism book that walked through each of the *Friday* movies. I even had a publishing deal for it and an agent, but the project fell apart because of some complicated licensing issues involving the series.

Later on, I heard that New Line had taken over rights to the franchise. I reached out to their head of marketing, a guy named David Imhoff, and I managed to get through to him. I pitched him my *Friday the 13th* book over the phone and the line went silent for a couple of seconds… and he goes, '*Wow, that's better than our book!*' And he put me in touch with their book packager and she became my agent. We shopped that book around but nobody wanted to buy it. New Line liked my idea, though, so they came back to me and said, '*We're actually doing an adaptation for this new meta Elm Street sequel, New Nightmare. Would you be interested in writing that book?*'

DM: And of course, you were!

DB: Yeah, I definitely was. I wound up doing the official novelization of that film. They were just looking for a straight transcription of the movie as usual, but I pitched them on something even more meta where it's the novelization but it's also about the writing of the novel and my finding out that Freddy is actually real. New Line heard that and went, '*Yeah, do that!*' And *New Nightmare* remains the least edited book I've ever written. They only changed one paragraph and that's because I mentioned another studio's property.

When I moved back to Los Angeles, I ended up talking to Mark Haslett and kind of imposed myself on his crew, which is how I became friends with all those guys. That's when Sean Cunningham asked if I wouldn't mind providing feedback on some of the *Freddy vs Jason* scripts that had been coming in. I was happy to do that. Keep in mind, I was still friends with New Line's licensing guy, Imhoff, so I was sort of connected to these characters from both sides of the equation, the Cunningham side and the New Line side.

DM: Any idea how many scripts you wound up reading?

DB: I think I read and gave notes on over thirty different versions of the story. That number includes full scripts, revised drafts, and treatments. All of that I was doing on Sean's end. On the other side of things, I had stayed in touch with Imhoff at New Line and learned they weren't doing all that much licensing-wise with the characters. So I convinced him to allow me to pitch around a *Freddy vs Jason* video game that could go hand-in-hand with the movie. That project I was developing separately from Sean.

DM: What were your impressions of the drafts that were coming in?

DB: My biggest impression was that they were all being approached politically rather than creatively, which is why I ultimately decided to write my own treatment. I don't think anyone, even to this day with the movie that came out, solved the issue of how Freddy and Jason can fight each other given what their origins are. Freddy is pure dream and Jason is pure physical violence. How do you get them together when they literally exist in opposite worlds?

DM: Your treatment was very mindful of the existing continuity whereas most proposed scripts were not. Why go that route?

DB: I was really into this concept of bringing the universes together in a meaningful way. If you look at the *Freddy vs Jason* that came out, it makes almost no reference to anything that came before it, not really. My movie would have done that. I kind've saw it as the *Star Wars* of *Freddy vs Jason*'s. I thought the kid from *Dream Child* might be an interesting concept to revisit, that he could serve as a bridge between the real world and dream world. We never found out what happened to him after that sequel, so I brought him back.

DM: Did you have anyone in mind when you were writing in the pop star character?

DB: I don't really know. I guess today it would be Taylor Swift or someone like Taylor Swift, someone who all the girls wanted to be and all the guys wanted to sleep with. In retrospect, that sounds really silly. But the whole idea was that Freddy wanted to get everyone dreaming about this giant pop star in order to get everyone's souls in one place. Normally he just cherry picks his victims, but this dream concert thing gives him an opportunity to kill everyone at once. That would generate the huge surge of dream power needed to overpower the dream lords and then all of reality.

DM: Your treatment was one of several pitches that had Jason finally speak. Tell me about that.

DB: That was a big thing they were pushing for at the time. They wanted him to finally say something onscreen, which was going to be their big surprise to the audience. He didn't jabber the whole movie. It was sort-of like a punchline as one of the very last things he did after killing Freddy. He would then deliver one line.

DM: Oh, right. I think one of the previous drafts had him gurgling '*Freddy's dead!*' after killing him.

DB: Yes, I remember that. Mine had him saying "*Blood knows blood*," right before he decapitates Freddy.

DM: I laugh a little at the idea of Jason speaking, but that's not to say you can't do it. You just have to pull off a really solid execution of it or else it's gonna be bad.

DB: Absolutely, but to me that was secondary to reasonably having Freddy and Jason in the same room together. I overthought it then and I'm probably overthinking it now. Conceptually, they are such different entities. I just thought the writers needed to try harder. What they wound up doing was simply skipping over that part. They all reasoned that Freddy obviously had the advantage in the dream world since Jason is not a creative dreamer. So in every script they would bring Freddy into the real world where he would get the crap beaten out of him because Jason is so strong. No one wanted to try that any other way.

DM: That's where I give you major points for having Jason defeat Freddy in the dream world because I think your audience would've been expecting the exact opposite.

DB: This is actually what I believe is the crowning achievement of my concept! In most scripts and what's already been well established is that if you pull Freddy into the real world, he is very vulnerable. In a way, they've sort of muddied those waters because he still sometimes exhibits magical powers in the real world. Also, you never really kill Freddy either, which is why he keeps coming back for sequels. In his case, the reason is a rule I stole from *Dungeons and Dragons* on what happens if you kill a god in our real world. You don't actually kill them so much as banish them to their original plane of existence to recharge. That way, you don't really cause universal chaos by destroying a god. And so it goes with Freddy. Killing him in the real world doesn't ultimately achieve anything. He needs to be destroyed in *his* plane of existence, which of course is near impossible because he is practically a god in the dream world.

What I proposed, I think, solves the issue of how you get Freddy and Jason together and have a battle with stakes. In my construct, Freddy can't really affect Jason because he has no imagination or fear, which is really what Freddy preys upon. And unless Jason, who is grounded in physical reality, can get to Freddy, he can't stomp him. And if Freddy is pulled into our world, Jason stomping him only banishes Freddy, not really destroying him.

And so the reversal of the Dream Child pulling Jason into the dream world accomplishes something that's not really been done before: someone physically entering the dream world *not* via a dream. Every other time, someone had to fall asleep to confront Freddy. This is why Freddy always wins, because he has more access to people's fears than the people who dream. Because Jason has no fear or imagination, other than images of his mother being killed, Freddy's usual unbeatable advantage in the dream world is mostly negated. Thus, Jason physically entering the dream world via the Dream Child's powers makes Freddy vulnerable in a way he never has been before. And that's why ultimately not only does Jason *truly* destroy Freddy, he gets a little help from Mom, in a way turning Freddy's own power against him. His image of his mother is his strength, not his weakness or fear. And so she appears, grabs hold of Freddy and Jason mutters "blood knows blood" and beheads Freddy.

DM: I also appreciated the fact that you didn't recycle existing concepts as so many of the other drafts did. I like the murderous cult, but you can only do that idea so many ways before it feels played out.

DB: Yeah, I thought the Freddy cult felt a little forced. I just don't remember them ever doing anything with it that united the mythologies effectively. The only story that I remember liking was Rob Bottin's and his was just a treatment when I saw it. He seemed to do it the most justice.

DM: What an interesting choice for director, right?

DB: Absolutely. He was a shoe-in from his past experience in the genre, plus you'd get him overseeing great special effects at a discount.

DM: Why did you never expand your treatment into a full script?

DB: The feedback I got was that it was way too expensive. Look at what they spend on a typical *Friday the 13th* - not much at all. What I was doing in my treatment was fairly epic and would've cost a lot. You could probably do it now much cheaper, maybe cut in a stadium full of CGI people instead of hiring thousands of extras.

DM: Did Jason rack up any kills in your treatment?

DB: Jason did get some kills in. He has to be directed by the heroes to fight Freddy. It's one of those things where they resurrect him, but they do it wrong and he kills a bunch of people right away. They eventually have to lure him like a bull into the dream world. It's not like he comes back and suddenly he's on their side. He's not easily controlled. He's still Jason, after all.

DM: Tell me about the game you envisioned for *Freddy vs Jason*.

DB: Well, it was not a recent thing. We're talking around the time of X-Box and Playstation 2. It was supposed to be a platform brawler where you would go around punching and slashing things. You could have done it single player, but it was ultimately meant to be a two player versus kind of game where one person is Freddy and the other is Jason. As those characters, you would fight towards each other, battle it out, split up, and repeat that a few times. It was a straightforward approach, I thought. Based on the strength of the licenses, I got pretty close to GT Interactive and THQ, but there came a point at which it was really clear that they weren't going to be able to release the game day-and-day with the movie. That resulted in the game falling through. The reason they couldn't release it simultaneously with the movie was because the movie never had an actual release date, not while we were trying to plan the game anyway.

DM: That's terrible because the game sounds fantastic. You absolutely *had* to tie this in with the movie release?

DB: Yeah, that was a huge stipulation, although I always advocated against it. It can make it very hard to do something of quality when you have an external factor guiding your design rather than your design guiding itself. I do understand it from a marketing perspective, though, why you would want the movie and the game to hit at the same time. You could get away with it today because there are so many more platforms. But at the time, these games needed to be in-step with the movie release.

DM: So Freddy and Jason were playable characters. Was there an option to play as a human character?

DB: I never created a human character to play as. My game was more like you were battling through hell. That plot came about from one of the big challenges I was facing back then, which was that nobody wanted to have a game where you went around killing teenagers. That crossed a *big* line, so it all had to be fantasy-based. Imagine Freddy and Jason trapped in the lower levels of hell. Those all became fantasy environments in which you could slash through demons and monsters instead of teenagers.

DM: You can see how the NES games dealt with that. Suddenly we had bats, devils and zombies in Crystal Lake.

DB: Oh, it was even more of an issue back then. They definitely didn't want you playing as Freddy or Jason. There's no way they would have wanted you to be the monster doing the killing. So they created human characters just for the game and then made up a lot of creatures for you to fight through. That makes it difficult for a game developer when you have to dance around your subject matter. The next evolution happened around the time of my game where you could now play as Freddy and Jason, but only if none of your targets were human.

DM: Did you ever stop and ask yourself why Freddy and Jason? Why not Freddy and Pinhead? Or Jason and Leatherface?

DB: Not really. People just love crossovers. They really do. After *Hell Unbound*, there was an attempt by THQ to bring together everybody. Freddy, Jason, Pinhead, you name it. I was consulting on that for a bit. It was clear to me that whoever wrote the treatment for that game probably only watched the movies for the first time the weekend before they wrote it. I say that because the treatment kept talking specifically about Jason's axe and I go, '*Jason has used a lot of weapons, but if you're going to talk about his iconic weapon, it's a machete.*' And obviously, that game never happened. The rights were so complicated to negotiate. You had a bunch of weird stipulations like '*Well, we're going to let you use Jason in the game, but Pinhead can't be the one to kill him. That's our rule.*'

DM: Speaking of bringing in other characters, what did you think of the *Freddy vs Jason vs Ash* comics?

DB: I didn't read them. I know about them but didn't read them. Ash makes perfect sense to insert into the middle of all this. Leatherface would've also been interesting because he's not supernatural in the least bit. The other reason you would've wanted to add in Leatherface is because New Line already owned that license.

DM: So the big question; In *Blood Knows Blood*, who has to win the title fight and why?

DB: My impression was always that Jason should win because Freddy is ultimately more dangerous and more purposeful. In my treatment, I figured out a way for Freddy to wipe out thousands of people at one time. Jason would never do that. Jason is like a machete whereas Freddy is more like a bomb.

DM: I want you to know that you're really bumming me out. You wrote an original *Friday the 13th* book I can't read, developed a *Freddy vs Jason* video game I can't play and pitched a *Freddy vs Jason* movie that I can't watch. My last question would be about the existing movies. As a fan, which ones do you like best?

DB: Obviously the first of each. On *Friday 13th*, I also liked *Jason Lives* because it has the best line from any of these movies. It's a great comedy, but it's also kind of scary because it's the only sequel that really threatens young children. Two kids are hiding after Jason's been rampaging and one turns to the other and asks, '*So what were you gonna be when you grew up?*' I also find *New Blood* interesting because it's almost like creative bankruptcy where they're not sure what to do next. It's like someone said, '*How about we do Jason vs Carrie?*' and they just went with it because that's exactly what *New Blood* was. *Part Five* is another one that I like.

As for the *Nightmare* series, number one, of course. *Freddy's Revenge* is probably everyone's least favorite. I think *Dream Warriors* should have been the best of the series because it almost became like Freddy versus the X-Men. They just happened to kill off the better characters before there was a really great fight scene with everyone together. They probably couldn't have afforded that many big effects in one scene, come to think of it. To me, *Dream Master* is the movie that *Dream Warriors* should have been. *Dream Child* was a good idea, I thought. I didn't like *Freddy's Dead* much and, of course, *New Nightmare* has a special place in my heart.

Official Titan Statistics

Below are each slasher's official stats as given by New Line Cinema in '03.
These figures were printed on t-shirts, trading cards and mentioned
in press releases, so you know they *must* be right.

Freddy Krueger

Hometown: Elm Street

Height: 5' 10"

Weight: 175 lbs

Victim Death Toll: 1,039

Times Resurrected: 7

Weapon of Choice: Finger Knives

Jason Voorhees

Hometown: Camp Crystal Lake

Height: 6' 6"

Weight: 275 lbs

Victim Death Toll: 1,254

Times Resurrected: 10

Weapon of Choice: Machete

(Okay, so these figures are riddled with outrageous errors. For starters, streets and camps are not the
same thing as towns. Freddy hails from Springwood and Jason from Crystal Lake. And don't think
too hard about the "Times Resurrected," as it appears someone just counted the prior movies for
each franchise. The body counts are also curious. Freddy barely crested thirty victims across the first
seven Nightmare's, which is a smidgen off from 1,039. With more films, Jason's count is far higher yet
even liberal estimates put it below two-hundred, which is nowhere near 1,254.

So much for official stats!)

Chapter Eleven
The Shannon/Swift Draft

The 2003 film crew's logo.

2001

THINGS GO BAD

The year 2000 was not a great twelve months for *Freddy vs Jason*. Mark Protosevich's script had failed to circumvent *Jason X* from happening as Michael De Luca hoped it would. The studio chief had wished to remain focused on the crossover sequel, not another solo-Jason production. Yet he did not dislike the new direction of *Jason X* and greenlit the project just as he had agreed to do. At best, it would be another profitable slasher movie. At worst, it would continue the financial decline of *Jason Goes to Hell* and *New Nightmare*, further impeding efforts to make *Freddy vs Jason*. Filming would begin in March '00 just outside Ontario, Canada.

News of *Jason X*'s greenlight would be overshadowed by a bombshell announcement. Internet giant America Online would be buying Time Warner for $162 billion in the biggest corporate merger of all time. The House that Freddy Built now had new owners to answer to. Had AOL Time-Warner reviewed New Line's performance in 2001, they would have seen box office toppers like *Rush Hour 2* and *Lord of the Rings: Fellowship of the Ring*. Unfortunately, their new corporate overlord was instead evaluating their 2000 slate, which was abysmal. The studio released sixteen movies in 2000, none of which hit the $100 million mark. Their biggest hit had been the Protosevich-scripted *The Cell*. Beyond that, New Line had suffered a handful of box office underperformers and outright flops.

Consider the case of *Little Nicky* starring Adam Sandler, which grossed $40 million domestically against an $85 million budget. There was also *Dungeons & Dragons*, which grossed $15 million domestically against a $45 million budget. Worst of all was *Town & Country* starring Warren Beatty and Diane Keaton, which managed a shocking $6.7 million against a $90 million budget. This last project reportedly suffered from runaway production costs and extensive reshoots, not to mention beginning filming without a completed script. All three films also earned scathing reviews, further staining De Luca's reputation at the company.

Near the end of 2000, De Luca made two important decisions regarding *Freddy vs Jason*, formative moves that would lead to the film we now know today. The first was taking a story pitch from Damian Shannon and Mark Swift, whom executive Bryan Hickel had recommended to him. Shannon and Swift had impressed the studio boss with their work on an abandoned comic-to-film adaptation of *Danger Girl*. He liked their crossover pitch and requested they submit a treatment, despite the fact that neither writer had any film credits to their name. De Luca's other important move this year was allowing intern and horror aficionado Jeff Katz to join *Freddy vs Jason's* development team.

FROM BAD TO WORSE

If 2000 was a bad year for *Freddy vs Jason*, then 2001 was even worse. The year began with the firing of Michael De Luca on January 18 by New Line chairman and once mentor Robert Shaye. Some reports cited the studio's recent box office losses as cause while others blamed De Luca's tabloid-making bad boy behavior. Several reports suggested that Shaye and De Luca's professional relationship had grown tense from so many years of conflict and disagreement. Whatever the reason, *Freddy vs Jason* had now lost one of its biggest supporters. The studio chief who had developed the crossover with Sean Cunningham for seven long years was gone. His time running the company had yielded such hits as *Austin Powers, Rush Hour, Blade,* and *The*

Wedding Singer, among many, many others. More bad news followed several days later with AOL Time-Warner announcing the slashing of more than 2,400 jobs. One hundred of these cuts would come from New Line's 600-person workforce. This, along with De Luca's firing, resulted in a complete turnover of executive talent including all development personnel who had worked on *Freddy vs Jason*.

The new studio chief was music executive Toby Emmerich, who had written and produced *Frequency* for New Line the previous year. This appointment was justifiably cause for concern. De Luca was an enormous fan of genre fare, having written/produced *Freddy's Dead* and numerous episodes of *Freddy's Nightmares*. Emmerich, on the other hand, was admittedly no fan of horror. This put the crossover sequel on shakier ground than ever before considering *Freddy vs Jason* presently had no script, only a treatment ordered by the outgoing development team.

Also concerning was that this new regime was inheriting *Jason X* for release, a sequel you might expect to do poorly in the hands of those not vested in the property. Although it premiered internationally at Germany's München Fantasy Filmfest in July, the sequel was considered low priority by the incoming team and shelved for an astonishing eighteen months. During this time, the finished movie leaked out onto the internet where it was downloaded countless times through file-sharing software, which in turn generated negative reviews en masse before *Jason X* saw an official release. As if the leak and poor word-of-mouth were not bad enough, New Line pitifully dumped the sequel into theaters on April 26, 2002 with a half-hearted release. The new Jason movie opened on 1,878 theater screens, roughly the same as *New Nightmare* had seven years before. Compare that to the company's rollout of *Final Destination* in 2000 on 2,587 theater screens. The new sequel did not perform strongly, earning $16 million worldwide against an $11 million budget. We can debate the merits of *Jason X* all day long, but less debatable is the fact that it was the clear victim of a studio in transition.

A NEW HOPE

There now seemed to be a real possibility that *Freddy vs Jason* might actually die in development hell, particularly in the time following *Jason X*'s box office failure. Sadly, there were no more horror fans left within New Line's ranks, which might also have resulted in the crossover sequel being fast-tracked into production by people who simply did not care. Among the project's few remaining champions were Damian Shannon and Mark Swift, who, technically, had not even been hired on as writers yet. Armed with a forty-page treatment and a slew of reference documents (character histories, beat sheets, franchise guides), they continued to advocate for their vision. They even commissioned a series of concept paintings by artist Dave Damron to show New Line's executive brass.

To fill Bryan Hickel's executive vacancy on *Freddy vs Jason*, Toby Emmerich hired Stokely Chaffin, who had produced the first two installments of the *I Know What You Did Last Summer* franchise. Chaffin considered herself a genuine fan of the titans and sought to make the crossover with like-minded individuals. In searching out talent, she was vocal about valuing passion for the material over years of experience. She sensed such passion in Shannon/Swift's presentation. Also seeing great promise in their treatment, she ordered them to expand their pitch into a full screenplay.

Before starting work on the script, Shannon and Swift took full account of their situation. So many talented writers had already tried and failed at the task they now faced, their work rejected for various reasons. These latest scribes were not looking to write just another version of *Freddy vs Jason*, but the *final* version of *Freddy vs Jason*. To do that, they would need to understand where the project had stumbled in the past and use that understanding to guide their writing. By specifically avoiding the pitfalls of previous drafts, they might finally devise a script that could launch the project out of development hell.

EIGHT SIMPLE RULES FOR WRITING FVSJ

After careful thought and reflection, Shannon and Swift created eight rules to govern the direction of their script. These were designed both to help distinguish their draft from previous iterations and to result in the best movie possible. They formed a creative bible for the project that would ensure it did not betray either of the parent franchises. These eight rules were first summarized in *Fangoria #226* and will be further paraphrased here.

(1) The new story must be set in the fictional universes of the *Friday* and *Nightmare* film franchises. This took aim at drafts by Braga/Moore, Goyer/Robinson, and Aibel/Berger, which appeared to take influence from *New Nightmare* by contextualizing some or all of the preceding movies as being fictional.

(2) The new story will remain faithful to existing mythologies, which should not be changed to suit the present conflict. This referenced practically every previous draft of *Freddy vs Jason*. There would be no more intertwining of backstories, meaning Jason never lived on Elm Street nor did Freddy ever visit Camp Crystal Lake. If Freddy was going to kill Jason, he would have to do it now in the present, not secretly in the past. This also meant that Jason would remain silent.

(3) The new story's tone will be "scary and fun, not campy and absurd." This rule appears to reference several older drafts, most notably the Abernathy script. Shannon and Swift decreed that *Freddy vs Jason*'s humor should come from the teenage characters, not the titans themselves, which placed a limit on how campy Freddy could become.

(4) Continuity must be maintained, meaning *Freddy vs Jason* should begin where the previous sequels, namely *Freddy's Dead* and *Jason Goes to Hell*, left off from. The titans will begin the story trapped in hell, not inexplicably back in action leaving audiences to wonder what has transpired between sequels.

(5) All non-slasher characters should be new. Characters should be either in the *Nightmare* tradition (strong-willed and independent) or in the *Friday* tradition (young, dumb, and fun).

(6) The new plot must come from Freddy and Jason and not be "a dream within a dream." This rule ensured that the new story would be titan-driven and actually have something at stake in the central conflict.

(7) The kills will be evenly split in the distinct styles of Freddy and Jason. The Freddy kills should be suspenseful and character-based while the Jason kills should be brutal and shocking.

(8) The new story should strive for tonal balance in all meanings of the word, feeling at times like a *Friday* sequel and at other times like a *Nightmare* sequel. Importantly, the final battle should unfold in both reality and the dream world.

THE PLOT

This *Freddy vs Jason* finds the world a much different place than we last saw. With Freddy now gone, the residents of Springwood have erased him from all documented history. They don't speak his name. They don't even dream anymore thanks to a suppressant drug called Hypnocil. Since fear equals power, these efforts have prevented the dream slasher from escaping hell and resuming his wicked ways. Down but not out, Freddy hatches a comeback scheme. He resurrects Jason Voorhees from the bowels of hell and, disguised as Mrs. Voorhees, tricks him into terrorizing Springwood. With Elm Street fearful again, Freddy can finally return to his former glory. This plan goes awry when he loses control of his hockey-masked puppet, setting the stage for an explosive confrontation with the youth of Elm Street trapped in the crossfire.

The genius of the Shannon/Swift draft calls to mind a truism from singer-songwriter Woody Guthrie. "Any fool can make something complicated. It takes a genius to make it simple." Such wisdom so perfectly summarizes this take on the crossover sequel. Shannon and Swift's vision for *Freddy vs Jason* is appreciably straightforward and uncomplicated, simple but not simplistic. It somehow manages to avoid overthinking itself, which was a terminal problem plaguing so many of the preceding drafts.

Per their own Rule #6, the screenwriters do a fantastic job of centering their story around Freddy and Jason. The plot is so titan-centric that I was able to summarize it above without even mentioning the teenage protagonists until the last sentence. Freddy's opening monologue both catches the audience up to speed and sets in motion the wheels of the new story. It also educates the uninitiated who may not have seen all of the previous seventeen movies (or any of them, for that matter). This makes the Shannon/Swift version of *Freddy vs Jason* incredibly accessible for new audience members.

One of this draft's many strengths involves how it portrays Crystal Lake and Springwood following the events of the previous movies. The screenwriters charge that years of butchering will have tanked the real estate market in Crystal Lake, paving the way for a new luxury resort to be built on top of the former camp. (This echoes a similar plot from the Braga/Moore draft.) Yet this detail barely survived into the 2003 film. While not directly mentioned, background signage at the construction site where Freddy and Jason battle references the former camp as the future home of a Crystal Lake resort project.

FREDDY vs. JASON

The town of Springwood, on the other hand, has enacted an aggressive plan to keep Freddy from returning, which makes sense considering how they've endured six movies' worth of terror. They have purged him from their history and do not dare speak his name. Anyone who does is immediately quarantined to Westin Hills Psychiatric Hospital. The town elders continue on with their lives, quietly fearful of his return. Freddy is an especially sore subject within the Springwood Police Department, who refuse to even acknowledge the possibility of his involvement when a teen is found murdered inside 1428 Elm. ("No outsiders. We can handle this. We've stopped him before. We don't say his name aloud anymore. You're not from around here. I don't expect you to understand.")

THE HUMANS

This draft's teenage heroine is Lori Campbell, who lives with her physician-father in the house at 1428 Elm Street. The Campbell's have had a rough go of it in recent years. Both Lori's mother and boyfriend, Will Rollins, abandoned her under mysterious circumstances four years ago. Neither have been in touch with her since. When Will sees a news report detailing Jason's carnage on Elm Street, he returns to Springwood to check on Lori's safety. (In the 2003 film, Lori's mother is said to have died in a car accident.) Lori's two best friends are tomboy party-girl Gibb and the tougher, smarter Kia.

One of the more interesting new characters in the Shannon/Swift draft is Lori's father, the suspicious Dr. Campbell. The screenwriters are strategic in their slow unraveling of the Campbell family mystery. Partway through the script, we learn that Dr. Campbell had Lori's boyfriend institutionalized at Westin Hills after claiming he saw the doctor murder Lori's mother. This disturbing accusation, coupled with Dr. Campbell's strange behavior, is so alarming that even Lori begins to distrust her father. The later revealed truth is that Freddy actually killed Lori's mother. Dr. Campbell only covered up her death to keep the town from fearing and thus empowering the dream slasher. Part of that coverup included institutionalizing Will at the hospital to keep him from spreading fear among the town's youth. Shannon and Swift spend much of their draft setting up Dr. Campbell as an unsettling secondary villain only to reveal him near story's end as a loving father trying desperately to save his daughter from Freddy.

THE OPENING SEQUENCE

In a detail omitted from the 2003 film, the Shannon/Swift draft opens with a passage from John Milton's *Paradise Lost*. "So frowned the mighty combatants that hell grew darker at their frown; so matched they stood; for never but once more was wither like to meet so great a foe. See, with that heat these dogs of hell advance to waster and havock younder world..."

The foreboding Milton passage then gives way to a Freddy monologue delivered overtop clips from previous *Nightmare* entries. Now trapped in hell, he reveals that Springwood has managed to forget about him, a fate worse than death. He does have a plan to force his way back into their minds, however. The montage then transitions to a new scene of Jason stalking and killing a skinny-dipping camp counselor, which we quickly recognize as the dream of a dormant titan. Freddy appears to Jason in this dream disguised as Mrs. Voorhees, instructing her son to "wake up" in order to carry out a bloody mission on Elm Street. We next see Jason's rotted-out corpse as it appears in reality. Suddenly, his black heart begins to beat once more. Muscles and tissue re-form around his massive frame. The hulking slasher gets to his feet and begins his journey toward Springwood.

It is remarkable how much narrative ground the screenwriters manage to cover in this draft's first eight pages. In a bold move, Shannon and Swift allow Freddy to directly address the audience. Sure, the character has regularly broken the fourth wall throughout the *Nightmare* series (and in every episode of *Freddy's Nightmares*), but never before with such a sizable exposition. Freddy quickly reminds us who he is, why he is not currently haunting the kids of Elm Street, and what he plans to do about it. That Shannon and Swift's opening includes a pre-burned Freddy flashback and the quasi-return of Mrs. Voorhees (after an eight-film absence, no less) makes for terrific fan-service. In a fun moment absent from the 2003 film, Freddy hides in the fog of Crystal Lake during Jason's dream and mockingly whispers to him; "CH-CH-CH-HA-HA-HA."

This opening sequence also lays the groundwork for why the titans will clash later on. In the script (but not the film), Freddy specifically commands that Jason only kill *one* person on Elm Street in order to generate the fear necessary to bring Freddy back. However, the hockey-masked titan is unable to stop killing, slaughtering a handful of teenagers instead. This infuriates Freddy, who feels his home territory is now being encroached upon. As Freddy learns, unleashing Jason was the easy part. Controlling him is something else altogether.

THE TITANS: JASON VOORHEES

You could make an easy case that Jason's characterization here is among the most faithful of any *Freddy vs Jason* pitch. Critics of the 2003 film might debate that, but the claim certainly holds up at the script level. More or less, this is Jason as we have always known him. He does not speak, period. He also does not hallucinate Freddy's face onto his victims. Nor does team up with any of the teenage protagonists. Shannon and Swit's depiction shows mercy to no one, even pausing to kill two of the heroes in the final act. That Freddy is able to manipulate Jason by impersonating Mrs. Voorhees is a nice nod to *Friday the 13th: Part 2* wherein that film's final girl does much the same.

The screenwriters allow Jason several memorable attack sequences in this draft, the most memorable of which may be the nighttime party attack scene. Partway through the script, the titan tracks the Elm Street kids to a cornfield rave and begins indiscriminately slashing. Three kills in, a partygoer douses him with everclear and sets him on fire. The script notes that Jason "seems unfazed, even as he cooks." Indifferent to the pain, he chases after the arsonist. This then becomes one of the film's most iconic images - a fiery Jason attacking a cornfield of panicked youth.

JASON IS NOT AFRAID OF WATER

One of the biggest controversies of the Shannon/Swift draft involves the misconception that their Jason is categorically afraid of water. This is simply not true, not in the 2003 film and not in any version of the screenplay. Yet countless moviegoers have walked away from *Freddy vs Jason* with this impression. There is even a Facebook group called

"Jason Voorhees Is NOT Afraid of Water," with a membership 600-strong. So how has this happened? The answer is partly that Shannon and Swift got a little too high concept for a *Freddy vs Jason* movie, but moreso that Ronny Yu's direction of a key scene, while visually interesting, failed the material.

The key scene unfolds midway through the script. The titans are battling each other in Jason's mind with Freddy unable to inflict any real damage upon his opponent. ("Why won't you die? Oh, you're not afraid. *Yet*.") Jason throws the dream slasher against a wall of pipes, which burst and release water. This downpour separates the two titans. Jason suddenly halts his attack, refusing to cross the water. Freddy is momentarily perplexed before he realizes what is happening ("So there is something you're afraid of. Ah, to be young and drowning again.") Jason then devolves into his thirteen-year-old self, who lays helplessly quivering on the floor. Do not conclude from this that the titan is afraid of water - he is obviously not. Instead, let's read between the lines.

For clarity of point, let us first establish that dreams take place in the subconscious mind while the conscious mind is sleeping. So the above scene depicts Freddy tormenting Jason in his own subconscious. Let us also establish that the subconscious mind is a catalogue of all our experiences. There is no way to erase bad experiences from the subconscious mind, though we can create new positive experiences to outweigh the bad ones. The old information still remains there, just buried. So it would be reasonable to suggest that if Jason had any fear, it might be of drowning, which water can certainly be symbolic of. Yes, we know from previous *Friday* sequels that in reality Jason has no conscious fear of water and can traverse it just fine. But the scene above does not depict Jason's conscious mind nor the real world. We are inside Jason's subconscious, which deals in symbols and metaphors. This is, after all, why we try to interpret our dreams. The downpour of water is a symbol that triggers the memory of childhood trauma, the last fear Jason ever felt as a boy. This is why he immediately regresses to a childhood state. Noticing this strong response, Freddy places a single razor-claw upon his temple and begins to probe in. ("Let's dig a little deeper.") Descending further into Jason's inner-psyche brings us to the memory of his drowning.

Having said all that mumbo-jumbo, what does it mean for the movie? It means that Freddy is going especially deep into Jason's mind and exploiting buried trauma. We already know that Freddy has enormous access to a dreamer's secrets and fears, which is precisely what is happening here. Jason is not specifically afraid of the downpour that separates him from Freddy - that would be a direct fear of water. Instead, he is afraid of what the downpour symbolizes in his subconscious mind. Imagine the helplessness you would feel while drowning, desperately unable to overcome the water flooding yours lungs. This is precisely what Freddy reminds Jason of with the waterstream. Adult Jason quakes with fear, drops his machete, and becomes a child again.

To summarize this sequence as *'Jason is suddenly afraid of water'* is an erroneous oversimplification and does a disservice to the writers. If we have to simplify it at all, a more appropriate phrasing would be *'Jason has a deeply rooted childhood fear of drowning,'* which is what Freddy exploits.

THE TITANS: FREDDY KRUEGER

Like with Jason, Shannon and Swift adhere faithfully to Rule #2 in their depiction of Freddy. Their opening sequence immediately reveals him to be a schemer, which lines up with existing *Nightmare* mythology. This particular draft stands apart from other *Freddy vs Jason* scripts, however, for limiting rather than expanding the scope of his plan. In earlier drafts, the dream slasher sought apocalyptic world domination. Here, he simply wants to get back to haunting the dreams of Elm Street's youth ("I've been away from my children for far too long.") and is that not classic Freddy?

To enact this plan, Freddy resurrects Jason and guides him to Springwood in order to incite fresh fear. The dream slasher reasons that any new blood spilled on Elm Street will be automatically attributed to him, thus generating the power required for a comeback. The trouble arises from Freddy's instructions for Jason to kill only one person, which is hardly Jason's style. The hockey-masked titan instead dispatches a slew of people, even killing one passed out teenager seconds before Freddy can lay claim to her in the dream realm. This then becomes the central conflict of Shannon and Swift's *Freddy vs Jason*. The titans are battling over the youth of Elm Street, winner kills all.

All things considered, this depiction of Freddy ranks among the more comically restrained of any throughout the development process. This is less about what the character does, but rather how he does it. Take the scene where Freddy morphs into a hookah-smoking caterpillar during the stoner's nightmare, which sounds kind of ridiculous when you say it out loud. Shannon and Swift play this scene surprisingly straight with zero puns whereas previous drafts would have doled out endless weed jokes. This Freddy also avoids pop culture references, so no Rocky, Freud, or Popeye impressons here. He does, however, mockingly impersonate one character's suicided brother in a nightmare sequence. Submerged in a bloody bathtub with slit wrists, Freddy taunts his victim mercilessly before plucking veins from his feet, slashing his face, and setting him on fire. Such brutality works well to offset what few puns the writers still allow him.

If *Nightmare* fans had any bone to pick with the Shannon/Swift draft, it may be that Freddy has the lowest body count of any sequel or *Freddy vs Jason* script ever. Going by the 2003 film, Freddy only gets to kill one person versus Jason's twenty-plus body count. This draft's sole nightmare victim is Carlos, who was re-named to Mark in the final film. But then again, isn't that kind of the whole point of the story, that Jason has pissed off Freddy by stealing his kills? That's what they're fighting about!

BLENDING BACKSTORIES

In terms of blending backstories, Shannon and Swift do not, per their self-imposed Rule #2. The only backstory revelation in the script involves what truly happened to Lori's mother and boyfriend four years ago. Still, the screenwriters manage a clever cheat that allows Freddy to meddle in his opponent's backstory without actually changing anything. Upon discovering Jason's subconscious fear of drowning, Freddy modifies Jason's nightmare to resemble Camp Crystal Lake circa the 1950s. On this sunny day, the campgrounds look pristine. We see children playing unsupervised by the dock while the counselors flirt with one another off in the distance. The children taunt young Jason, throwing a sack overtop his head in another nod to *Friday the 13th: Part 2*. The bullying campers then push Jason into the lake and leave him to drown.

An also dreaming Lori witnesses this and turns to the indifferent counselors for help, one of whom turns out to be Freddy. She runs back to the dock in an attempt to save young Jason herself. Just before reaching him, Freddy bursts from the water and pulls him under. As child Jason drowns in the dreamscape, adult Jason begins to vomit water in the real world. He barely manages to escape Freddy's attack by waking in reality, thus exiting the nightmare. How can Lori possibly enter into Jason's dream in order to see this unfold? The script does not provide a concrete explanation, though the answer may owe to the fact that both she and Jason have been dosed with the same high-powered tranquilizer.

HALLOWED GROUND

With regard to classic locations, the Shannon/Swift draft engages in a bit of welcome fan service. Their story begins and ends at Crystal Lake with a long visit to Springwood in between. More specifically, the writers take us back to the dilapidated cabins of Camp Crystal Lake and the iconic house that sits at 1428 Elm Street. This draft also travels back to Westin Hills Psychiatric Hospital from *A Nightmare on Elm Street 3: Dream Warriors* where they are still prescribing hypnocil for dream suppression. Westin Hills is also revealed to be where Lori's father has imprisoned her boyfriend for the past several years.

Another nitpick many have with the 2003 *Freddy vs Jason* is that it seems to magically relocate Crystal Lake and Springwood within miles of each other. In fleeing Westin Hills with a tranquilized Jason, the teenagers figure the best place for him to wake up would be an abandoned Camp Crystal Lake. At best, Lori will be able to pull Freddy out of her dream to fight a waiting Jason on the latter's home turf rather than the more populous Springwood. At worst, Jason will awake from his coma and hopefully wish to remain at his old stomping grounds. In the film, the passage of time from one location to the next is unclear, leaving many to assume Crystal Lake and Springwood are now neighboring towns. Hardcore fans will already know that Springwood is in Ohio and Crystal Lake somewhere in New Jersey, which puts an easy nine hours of drive time between the two locations. The original script managed to sidestep this problem completely with a simple line of explanatory dialogue by Will on the way to Crystal Lake. ("We've been driving all night. It can't be much further.") Had that line been included in the 2003 film, this would have been a non-issue.

The original script also featured a slightly longer opening sequence than the 2003 film did, which would have shown us more of Crystal Lake. Upon resurrection, we would have seen Jason burst from the asphalt ground outside the old Voorhees homestead from *Jason Goes to Hell*. He would have then walked into a nearby bait-and-tackle shop, stolen a machete, and headed off in the direction of Springwood, leaving behind a stunned store owner and customer. In the 2003 film, Jason simply rises up already holding his machete.

DREAMS/NIGHTMARES

If there is one thing the Shannon/Swift *Freddy vs Jason* provides in wonderful abundance, it's nightmare sequences. There are so many nightmares here that you could make the case that this draft feels more like an *Elm Street* sequel guest-starring Jason than an equally balanced crossover. Per Rule #7, these nightmares are very much character-based. The virginal Lori's nightmare involves sex. The physically insecure Kia's nightmare involves plastic surgery. Carlos' (later Mark) nightmare involves his dead brother. Jason's nightmares involve fear of drowning and his mother's disapproval.

One nightmare in particular returns us to classic Freddy territory. As Gibb stumbles drunkenly away from the cornfield rave, she passes out. In her dream, she continues stumbling and follows her recently slain boyfriend into an abandoned barn. Once inside, Gibb finds that she is not in a barn at all, but the labyrinth-like boiler room of Freddy Krueger. The dream slasher scrapes his claws against the steamy pipes, morphs his face out from the wall (channeling the original *Elm Street),* and, of course, fires off a few quips. ("There is nothing to fear, but fear himself!")

THE ENDINGS

Near the end of the second act, the heroes uncover Freddy's plot to spread new fear on Elm Street using Jason, whom he has now lost control of. Upon learning this, they devise a plan to use the hockey-masked titan for their own purpose - to kill Freddy. After tranquilizing Jason at Westin Hills, they load the unconscious killer into their van and head for Camp Crystal Lake. Once there, they intend to wake him up just as an also tranquilized Lori pulls Freddy from the dreamscape. If everything goes according to plan, this will set the stage for the title battle in the real world.

Unfortunately, all does not go according to plan. An angry Jason wakes from his slumber too soon, resulting in chaos at Crystal Lake. The titan turns his fury upon the teenagers, who struggle to stall him until Lori can wake from her Freddy nightmare. Once that happens, both the original script and 2003 film depict a savage battle between the two slashers. Their brawl spills out of the camp, across a construction site, and finally onto a dock overlooking Crystal Lake. Both titans sustain terrible wounds. Freddy slices off Jason's fingers. Jason rips off Freddy's right arm. As the carnage unfolds, Will begs Lori to escape with him to safety. In a fine moment of badassery, she refuses: "He killed my mother, Will. It was Freddy. My Dad covered it up to protect me. He didn't do it. Freddy ruined both our pasts. But we can still do something about the future and I am not leaving until I see him die!"

The original draft reveals an interesting dialogue absent from the eventual film. As Jason gains the upperhand on the dock, Freddy begins to beg for mercy: "Wait, we should be a team! I've got the brains, you've got the brawn. Let's kill shitloads of people! Arrgh! Wait! Wait! You win, okay? It's over! Now please, let's stop this! We can still get them!"

As the titans tear each other to pieces, Will and Lori douse the dock with gasoline and light it, causing a massive explosion. The heroes briefly believe they've emerged victorious until a one-armed Freddy rises up holding Jason's machete. Before he can strike, Jason appears behind him and impales his rival using his own razor-gloved arm. Seemingly fatally wounded, both fall back into the dark waters of Crystal Lake. Here is where things start to get a little crazy. Between script and screen, at least four different endings were considered for the Shannon/Swift version of *Freddy vs Jason.*

In the initial draft, a glowing red portal opens beneath the dock, sucking Freddy, Jason, and the entire lake down into hell. Dr. Campbell and the police arrive soon after. He apologizes to Will for committing him to Westin, explaining how he was only trying to protect against Freddy's return. As Lori and Will debate who won the battle, the doctor goes to retrieve Freddy's razor-glove from the empty lakebed. Suddenly, a familiar arm bursts from the ground to grab Dr. Campbell, pulling him down into the earth as Lori watches on in horror. The next moment unfolds in slow motion inside a fiery hellscape. We see Freddy slipping his razor-glove back on. As the image speeds up to real-time, we see Jason wielding a massive battle axe, all of this to the sound of a cheering crowd. The final line reads: "Freddy and Jason move at each other, battling in a deep pit, surrounded by the eyes of a thousand dark demons and a million tortured souls. CUT TO BLACK"

Shannon and Swift later envisioned an alternate take on this epic conclusion. Instead of cutting to black, Freddy and Jason's hell match would have continued on before being interrupted by none-other-than *Hellraiser*'s own Pinhead. Reportedly, the cenobite was to deliver a single line to end the film: "Gentleman, what seems to be the problem?" The issue that prevented this cameo from happening was financial in nature as it would have cost New Line a small fortune to license out the character from rival distributor Dimension Films, who were still regularly pumping out direct-to-view sequels.

The Shannon/Swift draft's third ending was not actually written by Shannon or Swift, though it was filmed and initiially incorporated into the 2003 film. This epilogue returned to 1428 Elm Street some two months after Freddy and Jason had seemingly destroyed each other. The candle-lit scene found Lori and Will in passionate embrace, which soon turns into overaggressive sex. When Lori pushes her partner away for being too rough, he looks back at her with a maniacal grin. Suddenly, razor-claws spring from Will's fingers! Lori screams as he slashes at her, hard cut to credits and cue Freddy's distinctive laugh. It's unclear even fourteen-years-later who originally conceived of this ending or what it meant for the characters. What is known is that test audiences unanimously found this to be a confusing and unsatisfying finish. Was Lori dreaming? Did Freddy possess Will? If so, why wait two months to attack? Did Freddy manage to get back into the dreamscape? Did Lori die? Too many questions, not enough answers.

Like the third ending, the fourth and final conclusion to the 2003 *Freddy vs Jason* was one that did not originate with Shannon and Swift.. In fact, it was suggested by Robert Shaye months after filming had wrapped when the Will-becomes-Freddy conclusion was deemed unsatisfactory. Shaye's ending unfolds in slow motion on the fog-drenched shore of Crystal Lake. In it, Jason slowly rises up from the water holding his machete in one hand and palming Freddy's severed head in the other. As the titan walks off-camera, Freddy's head turns to the audience and winks. Cut to black and cue Freddy's laugh. The advantage to this particular finish was that it allowed the audience to draw their own conclusion as to who, if anyone, won the fight. Can one truly claim a Voorhees victory if Freddy lived on?

THE GREENLIGHT

In March 2002, New Line finally committed to moving forward with the Shannon/Swift draft. Although Sean Cunningham saw promise in this version of the project, he strongly felt there were several story issues that needed addressing. Yet he feared voicing such concerns now might threaten the film's newfound momentum. Rather than plunge the script back into development hell, he agreed to sign-off on it and submitted extensive notes on how it might be improved upon, which were not utilized. Unfortunately, Cunningham ultimately had no involvement in the development of the Shannon/Swift draft, not that he was bitter about that. In fact, he gave the production his full blessing and helped extensively in promoting it.

"I've read most of the previous scripts for *Freddy vs Jason*," Todd Farmer told *ArrowInTheHead.com*. "From the beginning I've said this script was the best. It was the best at bringing them together, the best at delivering both a Jason movie and a Freddy movie. It was fun and it was smart. It was true to both Freddy and Jason. Look, I'm bitter. I've got more reason to hate *Freddy vs Jason* than most…but I can't. [Shannon and Swift] did it. Damn them."

Upon joint script approval, the studio immediately began their search for directorial and producorial talent. They also circulated the new draft among the major players such as Robert Englund and Kane Hodder. While Stokely Chaffin liked Shannon and Swift's work, she felt their script contained too much material for a ninety-minute slasher film. To this end, she enlisted David Goyer, who was then under contract to New Line, to do an uncredited polish on the script. Goyer streamlined much of the Shannon/Swift draft, merging or removing scenes in order to bring down the runtime. These cuts required the creation of new expository dialogue to help bridge the narrative. Goyer combined characters, reduced the kill count, and removed a nightmare sequence inspired by 1958's *The Fly*. This polish was much less about changing the story and more about condensing it. One unfortunate deletion was a reference to Tommy Jarvis trying to stop the construction of a luxury resort overtop the ruins of Camp Crystal Lake. Although Goyer's polish did help in bringing down the runtime, the first cut still clocked in at nearly two-hours long, requiring another fifteen minutes of deletions in order to reach the eventual ninety-eight minute runtime.

INTERVIEW: Bryan Hickel
Creative Executive, *New Line Cinema*

DUSTIN MCNEILL: When and how did you come on at New Line?

BRYAN HICKEL: I came on in '96 as a temp and went to work for the head of distribution soon after. Then I moved over into development working for Richard Brener and Donna Langley. I was fortunate to rise through the ranks pretty quickly at New Line and I remained there until the De Luca regime was over.

DM: What marked your first involvement with *Freddy vs Jason?*

BH: This is all a little hazy because it's so long ago. As I remember it, I got promoted and they started giving me my own projects. Up until then I had been a junior executive on other people's projects. I don't even know at that point how many executives had worked on *Freddy vs Jason*. It was quite a few. Mike De Luca handed the project to me and said, '*Here, see what you can do with this.*' The film was a big priority for the company. We had already spent a lot of money on development simply because of how many drafts we had gone through.

DM: How familiar were you with the franchises heading into the project?

BH: Not at all! The irony is that I didn't come to Hollywood as a horror fan. Of all the genres, it was probably my weakest. I was more into comedies and Academy-caliber dramas. But I knew that working for New Line meant you had to be cool with horror. So over the course of one long weekend, I marathoned both franchises. I watched all the Freddy's and all the Jason's. I also read through all of the previous *Freddy vs Jason* drafts. That was all neccesary so that I could start talking to writers about the project on Monday morning. I had to familiarize myself with the genre and those franchises very quickly.

DM: That must have been a lot to take in all at once for a non-horror fan.

BH: It might actually have helped a little that I was an outsider to the genre. Some of the people that had worked on *Freddy vs Jason* previously were huge fans, which might've made it harder in a way. I say that because I was just trying to overlay basic story structure and ideas onto this milieu that you would pull from any genre. I wasn't necessarily as caught up in the mythologies as the people that grew up on these properties might have been. I honestly have no straightforward explanation as to why the project wasn't cracked by the time I got there. I'm just speculating, but maybe my mind was a little bit more open as an outsider simply because I was not a fan of the genre? Hard to say.

DM: What were some of the issues that were preventing *Freddy vs Jason* from moving forward?

BH: That's a great question. My immediate observation was that we had drafts from some darn good writers who had done good work for us on other projects. What I came to believe was that the Freddy mythology was just so much more complex and sophisticated than the Jason mythology that it was difficult to merge the two together. There's a lot of interesting psychological elements to the *Nightmare* films about entering into someone's dreams whereas the *Friday* movies seemed like pure slasher films. I think people were having trouble reconciling the disparity of sophistication in the two series.

DM: How much direction did you give out to prospective writers?

BH: At first, I just called everyone I knew who was a decent writer to see if they were interested. Then I had those who were interested come in and give me a pitch. I can't remember how many pitches I heard - quite a few. I do remember bringing in Damian Shannon and Mark Swift to give us a story pitch. Right away, De Luca told me he thought theirs was the best approach. As soon as they left the room, he turned to me and said, '*Let's go with these guys.*' There was a discussion at the time about hiring someone else to develop a parallel draft to keep the energy going, but I don't think we ever implemented that plan. Looking back, that sounds so crazy to even consider doing, but it wasn't that crazy in the context of *Freddy vs Jason*.

DM: Was *Jason X* considered a setback in terms of *Freddy vs Jason*'s development?

BH: To me, it wasn't as much a setback as it was a placeholder. You've got these two hugely popular franchises just sitting there. If you can't crack the combination of the two, you've got to do something else. I don't blame anyone for going off and making *Jason X*. It's kind of economically stupid to have them be dormant for too many years. I would attribute it more to that than anything else.

DM: In your opinion, who should've won - Freddy or Jason?

BH: Well that was part of the problem. How should it end? No one seemed to be in agreement on that. I thought Freddy was much more sophisticated than Jason, so I always figured he would end up winning that battle, but you also could've had them fight to a draw. That would allow you to continue on to more sequels with those characters. I don't know if that neccesarily meant doing another *Freddy vs Jason* movie because it's hard to maintain a fight like that across multiple movies.

DM: After De Luca, was there a concern *Freddy vs Jason* might be dead in the water?

BH: Anything could've been dead in the water at that point. We were also going through a merger with AOL that was turning out disastrous for New Line. I don't think anybody really knew what was going to happen once Mike was gone. They wiped out most of the executives. Actually, they wound up letting too many people go too quickly and had to rehire some back. Personally, I moved on to Warner Brothers for a production deal over there. At that point, *Freddy vs Jason* wasn't my project anymore, so it wasn't my problem. I moved onto a new agenda and didn't hear anything else on it until it came out.

DM: Did you go see it?

BH: No, I didn't. I had no interest. I just literally had no interest. Well, I guess that's not entirely true. I did have some interest, I was just busy working at Warners on movies that were more to my taste, historical epics and things like that. I was glad that *Freddy vs Jason* finally worked out. I also kept in touch with Shannon and Swift because I thought they had done such an excellent job and professional job in delivering the *Freddy vs Jason* script. I tried to get them going for *Clash of the Titans* over at Warner Brothers, but ultimately the studio decided to go with another team.

DM: How frustrating was it to get kicked off *Freddy vs Jason* just as you felt you'd found the right pitch?

BH: It was painful. The whole thing was painful. I loved working at New Line in those days as it was a very special place. Mike had created a very unique atmosphere. Keep in mind, I was leaving a whole slate of movies, not just *Freddy vs Jason*. That was the one that I would have been senior executive on first, but I had other passion projects as well. You have to realize that *Freddy vs Jason* was a big opportunity for me. This was the first movie they handed me that, if I got it right, would allow me to start overseeing other much bigger productions. I couldn't have possibly imagined we'd all be laid off before it got made. But it happens. We just moved on as best we could.

DM: I really hate it for De Luca considering how many years he spent developing *Freddy vs Jason*.

BH: Oh yeah, but you have to remember that De Luca lost so much more than just *Freddy vs Jason*. He lost this whole world that he had created. There's nothing like it anywhere else in Hollywood. Yes, he was aware of the bottom line and of the fact that we had to make money, but he was also occasionally willing to make something simply becasue it was interesting and it was going to be good. I remember when we were making Paul Thomas Anderson's *Magnolia* where Mike almost conceded in the room that it wasn't going to make money, but that were were going to do it anyway because it was going to be a great film. And it was. I've never met anyone else since then that had that perspective at all. It has always been about the bottom line everywhere else. Mike lost an entire slate and had to start over at Dreamworks. I'm sure *Freddy vs Jason* was incredibly frustrating for him to lose, but again it was among much bigger frustrations he was surely feeling at the time.

DM: You're so right. I often think of De Luca's slate in terms of just *Freddy vs Jason*, but it was much bigger than that, wasn't it?

BH: Oh yeah, it was. Consider the *Lord of the Rings* films. The larger credit for those films go to other people, but Mike was certainly involved in first deciding to make them. Ironically, as I remember, we were in a bad slump at the company just before we got laid off. But everything that was coming into production at the time we left wound up working very well. So New Line went on a hot streak after we all got fired that lasted several years and one of those hot movies was *Freddy vs Jason*. But that's all just part of being a studio executive. Your job can be so involved with a certain slate of movies and then suddenly you have to move onto someone else's slate to pick up where they left off. It's ultimately why I left the industry. I ended up getting slates that I wasn't passionate about. If you're not passionate about what you're working on, this then becomes a rough industry to be in. I might as well be making cars or something.

DM: How unusual was it that it took ten years to get *Freddy vs Jason* made?

BH: It's funny because I've been out of the industry more than ten years at this point. I went back to business school and I'm getting a PhD right now. I'm currently doing investment management. I'm completely removed from movies except for watching them when they come out. Yet I'm still seeing stuff coming out now that I worked on ten years ago, fifteen years ago. I just saw HBO made *Westworld* into a series, which is something I was working on at least ten years ago at Warner Brothers where Schwarzenegger was attached at the time. It keeps happening. That movie *Clash of the Titans* went through multiple iterations of writers and what came out had nothing to do with what I developed for it. If there's good underlying material, people will keep pushing for it. And if it doesn't fit the film world at the time, people will try to push it onto television now.

INTERVIEW: Jeff Katz
Development Executive, *New Line Cinema*
Screenwriter, *Freddy vs Jason vs Ash*

DUSTIN McNEILL: As I understand it, you grew up a horror fan in Detroit knowing the families of Sam Raimi and Robert Shaye. At just twenty-years-old, you dropped out of college to drive across country to begin an unpaid internship at New Line Cinema in hopes of working on *Freddy vs Jason*, which you actually did! You went from unpaid intern to development executive practically overnight. That journey is like something from a movie. You know that, right?

JEFF KATZ: Yeah, it is. I will do a book at some point because I've had a very weird career. I was very fortunate and a lot of it was good timing. Had *Freddy vs Jason* not been in development hell for so many years, I wouldn't have gotten to work on it. I actually have Wes Craven's *Scream* to thank for delaying the movie until I was able to get out there. I would keep track of *Freddy vs Jason* in high school by getting the latest draft of it every year at the Motor City Comic-Con. You could tell that *Scream* had a big impact on it because the drafts started getting very self-referential after that movie came out. That's so the nature of Hollywood, to chase something that works. It's just the business. And so that dragged the project in a different direction for several years, which was the wrong direction. *Scream* was actually integral to delaying it enough for me to get out there when I did.

DM: So you get to New Line as an intern. It should've been easy then to navigate toward *Freddy vs Jason*, right?

JK: You would think that, but not really! When I arrived, they stuck me in the production office, which was not development. I was in a totally separate building. I did six months there free. I basically lived on ramen noodles and I loved every goddamn second of it. It was phenomenal. Everyone on the production side knew my deal pretty early on, that I wanted to work on *Freddy vs Jason*, and they were generally pretty supportive. Near the end of my internship, I was able to move over to Fine Line a few days each week just to be in the right building to get into position to work on *Freddy vs Jason*. And ultimately, I made my move at the New Line Christmas party at the old Century Club, which is no longer in existence. Those parties were pure Hollywood legend and there's nothing else since quite like them. So I bumped into De Luca, who sort of knew who I was. I cornered him and said, '*Listen, I know this project like the back of my hand. I would kill just to be able to give you a fan's point-of-view on it.*' And De Luca, bless him, agreed to let me work on it and connected me to Bryan Hickle. And that was the start of my involvement.

DM: If you're talking Christmas 2000, that would've been right before De Luca was fired and AOL took over, right?

JK: Yeah, it was a huge shakeup. A whole new regime came in. Sometimes those situations can create opportunities for people to suddenly move up and I was able to do that. Once Toby Emmerich took over, they brought in Stokely Chaffin and Renee Witt. I got to Stokely very early on and offered to consult on *Freddy vs Jason* as a fan. To her credit and to Toby's credit, they were very open to letting me do it. And my role grew from there. I got to live the fan's dream. It's still surreal to me that I even got to do it. It was very important that we get *Freddy vs Jason* at least halfway right. It wasn't going to be perfect. I had worked on enough movies by then to know that. We just had to get the spirit of it right because when you're working with an existing property, fans of that property are really good at sniffing out whether or not you're being authentic. If you're being cynical, they'll know.

DM: What was your first impression as to why the project was so long delayed? They started back in '93!

JK: There were a lot of factors affecting it. *Jason X* had an effect on it. *Scream* had an effect on it. The corporate shakeup had a huge effect on it. Lots of things were affecting it, which is kind of crazy because these movies are not that hard to make. How long has it been since the last *Friday the 13th*? Eight years since the remake, right? Why has it been that long? How hard is it to make these movies? Not that hard, but it becomes incredibly hard when people overthink it or get caught up in budgets and politics. The nature of the Hollywood beast gets in the way. You could make a new Freddy movie with Robert Englund for ten million easily and it would make a very nice return on investment. Don't you think there would be some interest if today Robert Englund announced he was coming back to play Freddy again?

DM: Of course. That would be huge.

JK: Right! It shouldn't be that hard to get a new *Elm Street* out, but it's incredibly hard to people that don't understand the material. It's the same way with *Star Wars* or the Marvel movies or any of those properties, no different at all. I worked at Fox for a while and I can tell you that's why the *X-Men* movies are so hit-and-miss. I worked on them. At the top, they just don't get it. They go '*Oh no, this is so geeky,*' but they've gotta make those movies because they make huge money every time. That's how horror gets muddled in a lot of ways, by people who don't understand or appreciate it.

But again, it's due to all of those factors that I was able to rise up and work on *Freddy vs Jason*. Midway through production on the movie, I was brought into a conference room and told in front of the entire development staff that I was being promoted to executive. I had no idea that was coming. It made my career and it's something that really only could've happened at New Line. It was something very unique to the environment that Robert Shaye fostered. At some point, I'm sure someone will do an oral history of New Line Cinema and that will be one of the great reads of all time. The New Line story itself is just incredible.

DM: What kind of effect do you think *Jason X* had on *Freddy vs Jason*?

JK: Well, it had an effect in the sense that *Jason X* didn't really work. Don't get me wrong, I enjoy *Jason X*. I think there's a lot of fun stuff in there and it's clearly written from a very knowing perspective. Todd Farmer is a friend of mine and obviously a huge fan. But because it didn't work, it first made people stop and ask if we really wanted to make *Freddy vs Jason,* which, of course, we did. We did if for no other reason than to get our investment back that we had spent on umpteen drafts of the damn thing. But also, it drove people to reconsider the whole approach to Jason going forward. I've heard a lot of different rationales for why Kane Hodder wasn't brought back. I can tell you that, internally, *Jason X* was looked on as something that just did not work and from that came a huge desire to simply do something different with the character. We first started looking at the mask. Before *Jason X*, the hockey mask was almost gone, right? It was pretty much caked into Jason's mutated flesh. We wanted to go back to the *Friday*'s we liked most, which were *Final Chapter* and *Jason Lives,* and see that Jason again. Especially part six, which was the first zombie-Jason. That way we could get the guy a fresh hockey mask that we could now fuck up. That was what started the train to taking Jason in a different direction, which eventually resulted in the actor switch. I do feel badly for Kane because I know he was wanting to do this particular film for years and years.

DM: I think most fans would agree with you on *Final Chapter* and *Jason Lives*. Those are greatly loved movies.

JK: Damn right they are. Those are the two I remember watching and connecting to the most as a kid. Part of that was because of Corey Feldman and Crispin Glover in *Final Chapter*, but also because the Tommy Jarvis stuff really resonates with people. They built three movies on that one character. Those are also the Jason's we all remembered and liked best. Lean, lanky, and tall. Plus, if you're gonna have him fight Freddy, you want him to start with a somewhat clean mask so that Freddy can fuck it up, right? That's what we were aiming for. The rotted-out zombie Jason had run its course for us. We wanted to go back.

We did that with Freddy as well. As a fan, I really felt that the Freddy makeup took a huge downturn in quality when they moved away from the Kevin Yagher look to go back to how David Miller did it. The character also wasn't as great in those later movies. That's no knock on Miller, who's an incredibly talented guy, but I thought the Freddy of the first three sequels was the scariest looking Freddy. In *Dream Child* and *Freddy's Dead*, he just looked like a burnt-up, dirty old man. I think, because of that, I never connected to those films the same way. And so my big push was to get Freddy looking and acting scary again like in *Dream Warriors*, which was my favorite beyond the original. I'm sure that's not an unusual statement.

DM: Not unusual at all. I find it interesting that you were able to follow *Freddy vs Jason's* progress before you even got to New Line by way of the bootleg scripts you were finding at conventions.

JK: There was a place in Boston called Mick's Poster Cellar. I have no idea if it's still in business. I assume it's shut down at this point. Every year at the Motor City Comic-Con, they would go and have boxes of the latest in-development scripts that they somehow gotten. They'd be $15 or $20 each. They also had fantastic one-sheets, one of which I took with me to LA and hung in my kitchen for several years. It was this gorgeous Italian *Army of Darkness* poster. Great stuff like that.

DM: What did you think was or wasn't working in the scripts you were reading?

JK: I remember reading the Briggs draft when I was a kid in high school. There were several things in that I liked. Actually, I wound up stealing that script's ending for one of the *Freddy vs Jason vs Ash* comics I later did. I'm friends with Peter and I told him I was doing that. There was one that had a Freddy-mobile, which was ridiculous, and another that had some cultists called Fred-heads that didn't work for me. A lot of the scripts either didn't get Freddy right or didn't get Jason right or didn't get either of them right. Or they had too much extra stuff piled on top.

I seldom rewatch my own stuff because doing so drives me crazy, but when I rewatch *Freddy vs Jason*, I can honestly say that I think we got Freddy right and I think we got Jason right. I know the water thing is kind of a reach, I'll admit that, and we're also missing a traditional Freddy nightmare kill, but we nailed the characters. I think what was missing in a lot of the earlier drafts that Shannon and Swift seized upon was that this is one of the greatest fights of all time, therefore you don't need to sell it like it's Wrestlemania with a bunch of extra shit. Just give people the fight and the truest versions of these characters, okay? Don't sell people an orange and try to make it look like an apple. And God, don't try to make it like it's *Scream*. There was one script where a character sees Jason's white hockey mask and calls him Michael Myers. Don't do shit like that. You don't need that. You just need to get back to basics. *Jason Goes to Hell* is not one of my favorite movies, but that last scene of Freddy grabbing Jason's hockey mask gives you a phenomenal place to jump off from. I remember when I was in high school hearing about that scene at school because I didn't see it opening weekend. I was like, '*Oh my God*.' Jump off from that moment and keep it simple, stupid. That's why the movie we eventually made worked and clicked. It's *Freddy vs Jason*. It's not rocket science.

DM: So the cultists didn't thrill you?

JK: Can you imagine going to see *Freddy vs Jason* and getting a movie about Dominic Necros? Are you fucking kidding me? It's like seeing *Batman vs Superman*, which I did not particularly enjoy, but seeing that and suddenly Lois Lane is now the main character. Not even Lois Lane - it's like getting Chump Zworski, the new Jimmy Olsen replacement. You can't get pretentious with these movies because they've never been that. Even Wes Craven, who I was lucky enough to meet and was an artist of the highest order, was never pretentious about his films or himself. Generally speaking, it's when you get executives and filmmakers involved with pretensions about making these movies that you run into trouble. *'I need to put my stamp on it to make sure that it is different and elevated!'* That's when you get into trouble.

DM: What did you think about the constant attempts to intertwine Freddy and Jason's origins?

JK: Had we done it, it would've been fairly predictive of where a lot of movies are going now with the interconnected cinematic universes. Ultimately, you get that intertwining in its own weird way in Jason's dream sequence, which is good. You scratch the itch without really committing to the backstory. It would've been ahead of its time. I remember in the Briggs draft that Jason was actually an Elm Street kid, right? I get why all the writers wanted to do it, but I don't know if it would've been received all that well at the time.

DM: How about the handful of scripts where Jason spoke a line at the end of the film?

JK: Oh God, I had forgotten about those. Is there really any way to do that well? I think with *Freddy vs Jason*, you've got to remember it's the irresistible force vs the immovable object. Remember who these characters are. You have Freddy, who's a chatty, almost song-and-dance man fighting against Jason, the silent wrecking machine. That's why it works. It all goes back to keep it simple, stupid. Distill the best things that have worked in the past and you'll be good. Jason speaking is not one of those things. That's just not Jason.

That's like my biggest complaint on *Batman vs Superman*. I'm a big Superman guy. I actually got to write several issues of Superman for DC Comics and I honestly don't recognize Superman in these new movies they're giving us. He just doesn't look like any version of the character I've ever seen and I've known this character for thirty-something years of my life. I've written this character and I don't see him up on the screen anywhere. In a world where you fully control the property, how do you not understand your own character? It speaks to the nature of Hollywood and executives and the system. You can't teach fandom. You can't teach that innate connection to a character or the material. That's why you get these conversations like, 'Wouldn't it be cool if Jason spoke?' And anyone who knows the character would go, 'There's a 99% chance that's going to be ridiculous.' It's not that you can't ever do anything new with the characters. Just don't overdo it. Michael Myers cried in one of the later *Halloween*'s and I thought that scene was very effective. It worked for me. Now if he had jumped out and gone '*Hello, sister!*', that's not going to work for me.

DM: How did you think the final film did with regard to balancing the characters?

JK: Balance is utterly essential. It's the whole point of doing a crossover like this. You're kind of doing two greatest hits packages in one. Or two great rock acts playing on the same stage. You've gotta remember that New Line was the House that Freddy Built and Jason was the step-brother, if you will, because he was a late arrival into New Line's portfolio. And he's not even there anymore! He's now gone back to Paramount, which is something I'll never understand. How did someone let that happen? But the only way this story works is if it's even handed and I would argue our movie almost leans Jason.

DM: Did the film's success kill the prospects of future solo-sequels? Because both franchises were rebooted afterward.

JK: We tried for two years to make *Freddy vs Jason vs Ash* happen. That was very serious and very real. We had long negotaitions with Sam Raimi's camp on it. That was even before the movie came out. The idea was that if you're going to end Freddy and Jason, you may as well have them ended by the one guy horror fans would accept ending them. We tried to do that for years! I wrote a treatment for *Freddy vs Jason vs Ash,* which was eventually turned into the comic. Everybody was onboard with the concept. Robert Shaye and Michael Lynne were both wanting to do it. They just couldn't make a deal with Raimi despite their best efforts. It got very agressive towards the end in terms of the dealmaking.

When that fell apart, there was talk of trying to do a Freddy prequel with Robert. Think something like *Henry: Portrait of a Serial Killer.* That's when talk of remaking *Nightmare on Elm Street* started bubbling up. I'll be honest, I'm not a fan of remakes. I just don't see the point. I worked on the *Friday* one for a minute, but left when I was approached by Fox. I just never understood it. You could make a very low budget Freddy movie with Robert and it would do quite well. At this point, you just need to do *Freddy vs Freddy.* I've even told this to the guys at New Line. You need Jackie Earle Haley's Freddy fighting Robert Englund's Freddy and end with Robert giving Jackie's Freddy nigtmares in his head, sort of losing but winning. Then you can take the Jackie character in a different direction. That movie gives people what they want, a passing of the torch. I think you should have a new Freddy and Jason movie every other year. If I owned them, we'd alternate them every other Halloween. That would be good business.

DM: What did you think of the film's alternate ending with Jason Ritter's character becoming Freddy?

JK: That ending just did not work for anyone. I think it was one of those things where it was meant to be like the old Freddy tags, but it wound up undercutting the fight itself. We knew we had to cut it from the very first time we saw it. We struggeld for a long time to figure out what the right ending would be. Both the ending and the opening took a long time to figure out, but I think we eventually got them both right.

DM: *Freddy vs Jason* has a marvelous opening, though. It was pitch-perfect!

JK: Thank you for saying that. I ended up writing the opening with a line from Toby Emmerich, which was 'He may get the blood, but I'll get the glory.' That opening was a very collaborative effort for a lot of people. Those were the two things that lingered well into post. I had the job of picking clips from the *Elm Street*'s for the opening, which I loved doing because I picked all my favorite shit from the movies. We almost didn't get Rodney Eastman from *Dream Warriors* because he got really religious after he did it and was hesitant to sign off on the footage. As a fan, it was so much fun getting all of those actors to sign off on the clips. We were suddenly running around asking each other things like, '*What the hell ever happened to Yaphet Kotto and how do we find him?*' It was funny to me that we did our recap opening with the Nightmare films, because recap openings were really something that the Friday movies had long perfected. Not so much in the later ones, but the ones right in the heart of the series. They'd open with a bunch of kids sitting around a campfire telling the story of Jason Voorhees while you watch kills from earlier movies. I always loved that stuff and to be able to do that for Freddy is something I'm very proud of.

INTERVIEW: Damian Shannon & Mark Swift
Screenwriters, *Freddy vs Jason (The 2003 Film), Friday the 13th (2009)*

[The following interview was originally conducted for Bloody-Disgusting.com by film journalist Trace Thurman and appears here with permission. You can find Trace on Twitter @TraceDThurman.]

TRACE THURMAN: What was your original pitch to Michael De Luca?

DAMIAN SHANNON/MARK SWIFT: Original pitch to Mike was very close to what ended up on screen. We had a very strong take from the beginning on what the movie should be and what the movie should *not* be. So he got the full pitch: characters, story, action set pieces, everything. We got the opportunity to pitch because De Luca loved what we did with a project called *Danger Girl* at the studio, and asked if we were Freddy and Jason fans. We jumped at the chance. De Luca had explored so many different ideas at that point that he was really lost as to where to start. We came from a place where we didn't want to change their backstories at all. We didn't want to throw out the other movies. We wanted everything to count. We pitched what we as fans would want to see. De Luca loved it and hired us soon after.

TT: Did you know anything about De Luca planning to release two endings, one with Freddy winning and one with Jason winning?

DS/MS: Mike may have thought about that before we came onboard, but we never discussed having multiple endings like that. Personally, I think it was a terrible idea. It would have sent the message that we didn't care about the ending and were just looking for an extra cash grab.

TT: Were you nervous when De Luca was fired that the film might be dropped again?

DS/MS: Of course! It was a disaster! You have to understand, this is around the same time that *Jason X* came out and bombed at the box office. De Luca had been the champion of that movie, and he was the champion of *Freddy vs Jason* and now he was gone. We had to re-convince New Line that even developing *Freddy vs Jason* was a good idea, and believe me, it took some convincing. We had to re-pitch a whole new set of execs, write summary documents about how and why Freddy and Jason were in the same movie and what they were fighting about. We had to do a beat sheet. We gave them a list of rules about things Freddy and Jason should and shouldn't do. On and on. All this before we even wrote the script. De Luca was a huge fan of the franchises, but after he left, we were sort of the only fans left.

At one point, the studio hired a consultant to test the concept with the public, to see if there was any interest in the movie. I think they sent teams to malls with a questionnaire. They found that there was indeed some interest, but recommended that it be rated PG-13. When we heard this, we wrote an impassioned e-mail to the head of marketing at the studio, begging him to not only to back the movie, but to keep an R rating. It was a long uphill battle to get *Freddy vs Jason* made, over a few years. When it finally came out, and with very little advertising, *Freddy vs Jason* had the biggest horror opening of all time. But we're just proud to have gotten it made. We felt like there were so many fans out there who had been dreaming about this matchup for so many years, us included! that we did everything we could to get it done for them. The fact that it was such a success was icing on the cake.

TT: What were your thoughts on Kane Hodder being recast with Ken Kirzinger?

DS/MS: We were as shocked as anyone when Kane wasn't brought back. After all, Kane played Jason more times than anyone else, and kept the torch of the franchise alive between movies. At the same time, we also think Ken did a great job in the role, and we like the fact that there have been many interpretations of Jason Voorhees throughout the years. Personally, our favorite is Derek Mears, but we're pretty biased. It's a fun thing for fans to debate. But obviously, we feel bad for the fans who fell into the 'no one but Kane' camp. Our goal was to deliver for the fans, but you can't make everyone happy.

TT: There have been conflicting reports on his recasting. Do you know why Kane wasn't brought back?

DS/MS: You would have to ask the director and the studio. Writers usually don't have a lot of influence over casting decisions. But we can dispel some rumors. No, Kane wasn't recast because he didn't have sympathetic eyes. That was a strange rumor that got started because someone wrote that description on a casting sheet. No, Kane wasn't recast because he was too precious with the character. Kane is a pro and he would have been great in the role. If I had to take an educated guess, I would say they probably felt that Ken matched up better visually with Robert as Ken is a bit taller and maybe they saved some money.

TT: Reportedly, your original script would have resulted in a movie nearly two-and-a-half-hours long before David Goyer was brought in to cut it down. What were some of the subplots and scenes that were removed?

DS/MS: No, it wouldn't have been two and a half hours. Our script never strayed far from 120 pages, which is about a two-hour film. However, most studios like their horror films to be around ninety minutes, but we always felt this was an epic matchup that required a little more time. They disagreed. Subplots and characters were cut and combined at the request of the studio. We did at least three drafts with Ronny before the studio brought in David. He did an excellent job of trimming every ounce of fat from the movie, but he also had to cover up what was cut. So in the end, you had characters explaining the plot to each other, rather than talking like real people, which is a real pet peeve of ours. It made for a shorter movie, but one filled with some hilariously bad dialogue and glaring holes.

TT: Call me crazy, but I would have loved a two-and-a-half-hour *Freddy vs Jason* movie.

DS/MS: Of course! We would watch a five-hour movie of Freddy and Jason going at it, but we're deranged fans.

TT: What one part of your original script were you most disappointed to have seen cut?

DS/MS: Lots of little smart, funny, and interesting character moments, mostly. Nothing too big in terms of sequences lost. Although, there was one larger scene that we had to cut. During the end fight, we had a pretty cool scene in a construction trailer. The gag was, one of the kids was trapped inside with Freddy. But then Jason was on the outside, stabbing his machete through the thin metal walls, trying to kill everything inside. So then Jason gets in, and our kid is trapped in an enclosed space between Freddy and Jason, who are going at it. The trailer is on wheels, and during the fight, it becomes unmoored, and starts rolling and bouncing down a hill as they continued to fight. It was pretty crazy and would have been spectacular on screen.

TT: What made you want to frame Jason as a somewhat redeemable anti-hero in the film?

DS/MS: How dare you. Jason was never presented as redeemable or as an anti-hero. The way we portrayed Freddy and Jason in the film was always closely rooted in their respective backstories and mythologies. Freddy was a child killer. That makes him, at his origin, a victimizer. Jason drowned when the camp counselors weren't watching him. That makes him, at his origin, a victim. Therefore, those identities needed to be carried over into the story, and be at the core of their dynamic. However, that doesn't mean that Jason is good or redeemable or even an anti-hero. Jason is a remorseless killing machine. But the fact that he has more layers than that only makes him a more interesting character in our eyes.

TT: One criticism from many fans is that the film feels a lot more like a *Friday the 13th* film than a *Nightmare on Elm Street* film. In fact, Freddy only kills one person in the entire movie. Was there a reason you went in that direction?

DS/MS: It's funny, we usually hear from people '*It's more of a Nightmare film than a Friday the 13th film*'. And our answer is that, yes, Freddy is the one pulling the strings of the plot. He's the one in control, manipulating events, and dominates the story. Jason is more of a tool in that sense. However, Jason cannot be controlled. As you rightly point out, Jason gets most of the kills. Again, this is rooted in their respective franchises. The *Nightmare* series has never been about body count like the *Friday* series. Therefore it was only natural that Jason would have most of the kills, but Freddy would be driving the story. Perhaps not so coincidentally, Bob Shaye, the head of New Line, was always more of a Freddy guy. We were the ones trying to make sure Jason didn't get short shrift. From the very beginning, we strove for balance. For instance, we felt it was very important that Freddy and Jason fight in both the real world and the dream world, and you have to fight for this balance and these decisions through every step of the development process. It's a miracle it came out as balanced as it is.

TT: What was up with Jason's fear of water in the movie?

DS/MS: We've answered this question a thousand times over the years, but we're glad you brought it up, once again. Of course, Jason isn't afraid of water. The intention was — if Jason has any fear at all — it would be rooted in his drowning. This is what Freddy exposes — Jason's memory of his childhood at Crystal Lake. However, the way it was shot, it could be interpreted that Jason is afraid of water. After all, he doesn't cross the water stream, right? But remember, this is taking place in Jason's psyche. In his dream. Ronny was being symbolic. It's interesting, the casual fan is usually the one who brings up this 'fear of water' thing. Generally in the same breath with 'Jason doesn't run!!!' and then we have to point them to *Friday the 13th Part 2*. But the more serious hardcore fans usually get that it's a fear of drowning issue and not fear of water.

TT: This isn't that important, but how did they drive from Springwood to Crystal Lake in what seemed like an hour?

DS/MS: In the original script, they are driving all night. There was even a scene where they are stopped by the cops, and need to keep Jason in the back, hidden. This really bugged us the first time we screened the movie. Jason also got to Springwood pretty quickly in the beginning, too. But hey, what are you gonna do? They wanted the movie to fly by and boy does it fly!

TT: Both of you have commented on Kia's use of the word faggot, but it seems like no one is willing to take credit for it. Do either of you know who came up with that line? And if people were against it, why wasn't it edited out? I know the word was more commonly used in 2003, but I'm just curious. Horror has a rather large gay audience so it seems curious to even leave that line in the film.

DS/MS: It was offensive then, and it's offensive now. All we can tell you is… we didn't write it, and we were really shocked when we heard it in the movie. We complained about it after the first screening, but it was never changed. It's a real stain on the movie, in our opinion.

TT: You have mentioned the many different endings that were considered for the film, one of which included Pinhead. Was that Pinhead idea taken seriously? And can you talk more about the ending that took place in hell?

DS/MS: Pinhead was only in the end of our very first draft. New Line liked it, but didn't like the idea of having to get the rights. They also ultimately had reservations about bringing in a third character. That didn't bother us. We noted that in the end of *Abbott & Costello Meet Frankenstein*, they bring in the Invisible Man in the end. So we got rid of Pinhead, and most of the remaining drafts had Freddy and Jason ending up fighting in hell. How they got to hell was something that changed probably a dozen times. In one version, the lake drained, leaving only Freddy's severed glove at the bottom of the dry lake. Will goes to pick it up, and he gets yanked down in a nod to the original *Nightmare on Elm Street* ending.

Another was that Ronny had an idea about a giant hand rising up out of the lake and pulling Freddy and Jason down. We tried all kinds of things, but in the end we lost the idea of hell altogether. The studio said something that stuck with us, and that's 'hell never looks good onscreen.' They're probably right about that. Hell is more powerful in our imagination. When you try to actually shoot it, nine times out of ten it looks cheesy. So we have no regrets about not ending up in hell.

TT: The film's other alternate ending involves Jason Ritter's character essentially becoming Freddy. Tell me about that.

DS/MS: We didn't write that ending, and we were so happy when test audiences hated it, because we hated it more. To this day, we have no idea what the intention of that scene was. Will is now a killer? Freddy is inside him? It made absolutely no sense to us, and we never stopped complaining about it. Thank you test audiences!

TT: Who came up with the ending that was eventually used in the film, with Jason holding Freddy's severed head?

DS/MS: Robert Shaye, head of the studio. New Line pitched it to us, we thought it was perfect and typed it up. That scene was a reshoot. New Line definitely wanted to get this thing right. They really should be commended for pulling the trigger on the movie. It was expensive for a horror movie, even at the time, and a crazy idea to begin with. I don't think *Freddy vs Jason* would get made today. Today, studios want to make horror movies that cost next to nothing, and are all shot in a couple of rooms. *Freddy vs Jason* was a big epic horror action movie with a ton of different scenes and locations. We give New Line and Ronny Yu a lot of praise, thanks, and credit for making our script a reality.

TT: I get that you can't really kill either character, but the stalemate of the ending feels like a copout. Was there ever a winner?

DS/MS: Will have to disagree with you here. We don't think the ending plays like a stalemate or a cop out. The intention was always for the ending to be a Rorschach test for fans: Freddy fans would think Freddy won, and Jason fans would think Jason won. Having talked to hundreds of fans since the movie came out, I'd say we were mostly successful in that goal. We loved the idea of fans leaving the theater debating who won, and clearly, that still goes on to this day. But if you ask us? We would say that Jason won the fight, but the war continues. We think it's the perfect ending, but obviously, others may disagree. Again, you can't make everyone happy.

TT: We have all heard about *Freddy vs. Jason vs. Ash* as penned by Jeff Katz. Supposedly the success of *The Grudge* killed the sequel. Do you know anything about that? How far did you get into planning before having to scrap the project?

DS/MS: A direct sequel to *Freddy vs Jason* was never seriously considered by New Line, much less one involving Ash. The plan was always to make standalone movies with Freddy and Jason if *Freddy vs Jason* was successful, and lo and behold, that's exactly what they did. We even wrote one of them. Not sure how *The Grudge* fits into that — but no, it didn't alter any plans. *Freddy vs Jason vs Ash* was an idea that Katz had by himself. We're glad that he got to explore it in comic form! However, as much as we absolutely love Ash and the *Evil Dead* franchise, that's not the way we'd go with a direct sequel.

TT: If a sequel were greenlit tomorrow, what would it entail? What is the *Freddy Vs. Jason 2* story you're dying to tell?

DS/MS: We do have lots of ideas for a sequel to *Freddy vs Jason*— and yes, we've discussed it generally with New Line — but they just don't have any need for it right now. However, you never know what the future holds, so we'd rather not share the ideas here. Hopefully we'll have a chance to make it someday. Getting the chance to write for these two iconic characters was a real honor and a privilege, and we'd love the chance to write another chapter in their story. But this time, we'd *really* push for that two hour running time.

Chapter Twelve
Lights, Camera, Slash!

2002-2003

FINDING THE RIGHT DIRECTOR

Upon approval of the Shannon/Swift draft, New Line began shopping *Freddy vs Jason* around to a handful of prospective directors, all of whom declined. The studio offered it once more to Wes Craven, who had no interest. They also tried again for Guillermo Del Toro, though he chose instead to direct *Blade II*. They even sought Rob Zombie, who was already committed to making *House of 1,000 Corpses*. New Line flew in Hong Kong filmmaker Ronny Yu to pitch him on *Freddy vs Jason*, though he declined, citing script issues and an unfamiliarity with the two franchises. Yu, an internationally celebrated auteur, was then best known stateside for having re-invigorated the *Child's Play* franchise with 1998's *Bride of Chucky*.

Following this string of rejections, Stokely Chaffin established what she called an open door policy on *Freddy vs Jason*. Per this, she agreed to personally meet with any filmmaker interested in helming the crossover, an approach she would later come to regret. The studio exec would eventually meet with more than seventy candidates, none of whom impressed her enough to win the job. Spanish filmmaker Jaume Balaguero of the *[REC]* franchise was among the hopefuls campaigning for the director's chair during this time.

After this long and fruitless search, New Line would reapproach Yu and beg him to reconsider his decision. Robert Shaye insisted that the filmmaker's unfamiliarity with the previous movies was a non-issue, that it actually gave him a fresh perspective on the material. Furthermore, he personally guaranteed the director enormous creative freedom over the project including final say over the ending. Given these terms, Yu accepted New Line's offer to direct *Freddy vs Jason* in early May '02. He would immediately begin working with the screenwriters to further develop and refine their screenplay across several more drafts.

A HOLLYWOOD NORTH PRODUCTION

In 1997, the Canadian government unveiled an aggressive tax credit program in hopes of attracting international film and television productions. Producers could become eligible to claim these lucrative credits provided their projects were cast and crewed with Canadian citizens. For movie studios, relocating production from Los Angeles to Canada often meant millions of dollars in savings on any given venture. By 2002, New Line Cinema had fully embraced the program, shooting films like *Blade II, Final Destination, Willard,* and *Elf* in whole or part within the country. Jason Voorhees was certainly no stranger to Canada having filmed *Jason Takes Manhattan* and *Jason X* there years before. Even Michael Myers went Canadian on *Halloween Resurrection*. Hoping to stretch their *Freddy vs Jason* dollar as far as possible, New Line moved the production north.

Early studio estimates found the Shannon/Swift draft to be overly long and overly expensive. The script's projected runtime, which Stokely Chaffin had hoped would be a lean ninety-minutes, was more than two hours long. The budget required to realize this vision was said to be in excess of $50 million, more than twice what New Line had initially wanted to spend on *Freddy vs Jason*. That figure failed to include the $4 million in development costs the project had already accrued across the past nine years. To his credit, Toby Emmerich reportedly pushed Robert Shaye to increase the budget closer to $30 million and to not include the runaway development costs in that figure. (To put that number into perspective, *Freddy vs Jason* cost more to produce than the first nine *Friday* movies combined!) Ronny Yu would work with the screenwriters to pare down their script, reducing both the runtime and budget in the process.

Several script drafts later, Yu was paired with executive producer Douglas Curtis to begin production planning. Curtis, a veteran of New Line productions like *All About the Benjamins, Next Friday,* and *Friday After That,* scrutinized every detail of the screenplay to ensure it could be achieved on the film's budget. *Freddy vs Jason* seemed to have all the trappings of a challenging production, including but not limited to a large cast, elaborate character makeups, children, wire stunts, fire, water, green screen, practical effects, digital effects, outdoor filming, and underwater filming. The script's tall order of visual effects would require the help of no less than seven effects companies, often working arm-in-arm.

CASTING THE CROSSOVER

For the most part, *Freddy vs Jason* was cast using experienced yet relatively unknown performers. After an extensive search, twenty-three-year-old actress Monica Keena, a veteran of such shows as *Undeclared* and *Dawson's Creek,* was cast into the lead role of Lori Campbell. Actor Brad Renfro, who first came to prominence in Joel Schumacher's *The Client,* was initially cast as Lori's boyfriend, Will Rollins. Unfortunately, the performer's much publicized struggle with substance abuse would ultimately cost him the role, forcing the production to recast him a scant week before filming began. The part eventually went to *Swimfan* star Jason Ritter, whose father - John Ritter of *Three's Company* fame, had previously appeared in Ronny Yu's *Bride of Chucky.* The only celebrity cast into the crossover sequel, apart from horror icon Robert Englund, was Destiny's Child singer Kelly Rowland as Lori's strong-willed friend, Kia. *Freddy vs Jason* would mark the singer's feature film acting debut.

Much of the supporting cast was comprised of Canadian talent including Brendan Fletcher as Mark, Tom Butler as Dr. Campbell, David Kopp as Blake, Jesse Hutch as Trey, and Zack Ward as Bobby. Actor Lochlyn Munro, who portrayed Deputy Stubbs in the film, previously appeared in a 1992 episode of Wes Craven's *Nightmares Cafe* alongside Robert Englund. Fellow Canadian Kyle Labine, who portrayed stoner Freeburg, also had a small part in 2002's *Halloween Resurrection.* Future scream queen Katharine Isabelle was cast in the role of Lori's wild-partying friend, Gibb. Even in 2002, Isabelle was already gaining a reputation within the horror genre with roles in films like 2002's *Carrie, Ginger Snaps,* and *Disturbing Behavior.*

Original *Friday the 13th* actress Betsy Palmer was sought to reprise her role as Mrs. Voorhees, though she would ultimately decline to return citing issues over salary and the size of her role. The part was eventually recast with Paula Shaw, who had appeared in Christopher Nolan's *Insomnia* the previous year along with Isabelle. Palmer would not be the only Voorhees recast on *Freddy vs Jason.*

A screen-matched hero machete used by Ken Kirzinger and a Canadian Effects Technician during production.

(Photo courtesy Charles Mineo)

A NEW JASON

One of the film's biggest controversies involved who would ultimately play the part of Jason Voorhees. Many had simply assumed that series veteran Kane Hodder was a shoe-in for the part, which would mark his fifth time behind the hockey mask. To the fans, this sequel was as much about Freddy and Jason as it was Robert Englund and Kane Hodder. Although numerous actors and stuntmen had portrayed the slasher in years past, Hodder was the only to have done so more than once and therefore held the record at four films. The story goes that New Line gave Hodder a copy of the Shannon/Swift draft just prior to meeting with him in-person to discuss the project.

"The excitement I had over getting to make this film was comparable to winning the lottery," Hodder wrote in his autobiography, "All I could think about, day in and day out for several months after I heard it was going to be made, was what was the script going to be like? The waiting didn't last long as New Line called me down to pick up the script. [...] With this script I was like a kid on Christmas morning waiting to rip open his presents. This was the one, the one we all have been waiting for. This time, instead of pulling over and reading it in the parking lot, I forced myself to wait until I got home to read it, so I could savor every word and page to its fullest. [...] The script was good. There were some things I didn't like, but overall, I was impressed how well the writers had woven the two worlds together."

Hodder then had an initial face-to-face meeting with an unnamed studio executive, who made a lowball offer for him to reprise the role. The stuntman-turned-actor asked whether this included residuals or not, which the executive was unsure of. Hodder left the meeting expecting to continue the conversation in the near future. Many weeks passed without further word from the studio. Then came an open casting call for the role of Jason Voorhees. Stunned, the performer lobbied for his old job back to no avail. He was eventually recast with Canadian stuntman Ken Kirzinger, who had previously donned the hockey mask for two scenes on *Jason Takes Manhattan*. (Kirzinger also played the diner cook that Hodder's Jason throws into a mirror in that sequel.) Rumors circulated that Hodder had been recast for someone taller (not true, his replacement bested him by a scant inch), someone with more sympathetic eyes (also untrue) or that Hodder was demanded too much money (even more untrue).

Hodder publicly maintains to this day that he has never been given a reason for his recasting on *Freddy vs Jason*. No one from the production has officially taken responsibility for the move. Casting director Matthew Barry has blamed Ronny Yu, who then blames studio brass, who in turn generically place the blame back onto the production team. Hodder's suspicion that New Line's decision was economically-motivated is backed by the fact that the Canadian Kirzinger would have counted toward the company's tax credit. Although Hodder has discussed his displeasure over the recasting at length, he has remained mostly silent on Kirzinger's performance as a professional courtesy.

"Ken Kirzinger made a great Jason," *Jason X* screenwriter Todd Farmer wrote on ArrowintheHead.com: "He was big. He was unstoppable. I got nothin' but love for the man, but, I'm sorry. Why wasn't it Kane Hodder? Yes, Ken pulled it off, but tell me what in his performance was so amazing that Kane couldn't have done it? From the beginning I wanted to see *Freddy vs. Jason*, but I also wanted to see Robert vs. Kane. From a fanboy point of view that would have been utter perfection. Thanks New Line. Thanks for taking that away from me with your stupid executive politics. Bozos."

Kirzinger's performance would earn him a special place in horror history and lead to more work within the genre. In 2007, he would play the mutant-cannibal patriarch of *Wrong Turn 2: Dead End*. Two years later, he would spoof his most famous role by playing the hockey-masked Mason (get it?) in the horror-comedy *Stan Helsing*. Some projects would even reunite him with his *Freddy vs Jason* costars. In 2014, Kirzinger would portray deranged trucker Rusty Nail in *Joy Ride 3: Road Kill* where he would again face off against actor Jesse Hutch (*FvsJ*'s Trey), whom he beheaded as Jason years before. In 2015, Kirzinger was cast as a disfigured killer in *The Blackburn Asylum* where he would again kill actor Lochlyn Munro (Deputy Stubbs in *FvsJ*).

FILMING

In retrospect, 2002 was a busy year for *Freddy vs Jason*. The Shannon/Swift draft was approved in March. Ronny Yu came on as director in May. Pre-production began in June with filming slated to begin in September. The production was scheduled to film for fifty-three days across eleven weeks in Vancouver, Canada. Coordinating the many facets of this ambitious project would prove a herculean task. For starters, the film was heavy on stunt work, requiring dedicated stunt doubles for eleven cast members. The project was even heavier on visual effects with some shots requiring makeup, practical, and digital effects work. Cast and crew would work around the clock with up to three units shooting simultaneously.

Freddy vs Jason's cameras first rolled on the morning of Monday, September 9, 2002 with Kia's school infirmary nightmare sequence. Although Freddy slashes Kia's face in this scene, the titan would be composited in later on as Robert Englund had not yet arrived on location (nor had Ken Kirzinger). The company would spend this first week working from locations depicting Springwood High, the Sheriff's Department, and some Westin Hills Asylum interiors. The production did film on Friday, September 13, but sadly not on scenes involving Jason or Crystal Lake. The crew would instead capture Elm Street exteriors on the *Friday* franchise's namesake holiday.

The first titan to arrive on location was Kirzinger's Jason on the night of Friday, September 20. This material depicted the slasher's early arrival on Elm Street as well as Gibb unknowingly flicking a cigarette onto his mask. Englund's Freddy would appear on set several days later on September 20 for 1950's-era Camp Crystal Lake exteriors. ("It's not my fault this bitch is dead on her feet.") Five days later, Englund plunged into the chilly waters of British Columbia's Buntzen Lake in order to film scenes of Freddy dream-drowning young Jason. The actor wouldn't don his full Freddy regalia (makeup, hat, sweater, and glove) until the evening of Friday, October 4 for the scene where Freddy fails to kill Blake on Elm Street. ("Not strong enough yet.")

The week of September 27 saw filming move into an actual cornfield for the rave attack sequence where a flaming Jason slashes through several partygoers. Despite being an experienced stuntman, the producers would not allow Kirzinger to perform the fiery attack himself due to the enormous risk involved. Had the performer been badly injured, *Freddy vs Jason* would've struggled to find a replacement midway through filming who looked and moved exactly the same way. The hockey-mask instead went to stuntman Glen Ennis, who would later stunt-double the CGI bear that attacked Leonardo DiCaprio in *The Revenant*. Of some concern was that Ennis had no experience with fire-stunts, though he performed the rave-attack scene numerous times without injury or incident.

The shoot was in large part frontloaded with dialogue scenes involving the teenage protagonists. This was purposefully done to allow the various effects teams time to prep for the more challenging nightmare and fight sequences later on. One of these larger sequences was the climactic dock fight and explosion, filming on which began in week five. This sequence alone involved makeup effects, stunt fighting, heavy blood spray, dismemberment, decapitation, and fire. After wrapping the main actors, a second unit stayed behind to capture the propane tank explosion that sends Freddy and Jason (doubles, naturally) into Crystal Lake on Tuesday, October 22. That day's production notes simply read, '*Kaboom!*'

On Tuesday, October 15, *Freddy vs Jason* moved into the abandoned Riverview Psychiatric Hospital in Coquitlam, which would become Westin Hills in the film. Riverview's facilities have frequently hosted film and television productions including *Smallville, The X-Files,* and *The Butterfly Effect*. Horror fans might also recognize the property as Grace Andersen Sanitarium from the opening scenes of *Halloween Resurrection*. The *Freddy vs Jason* team did not have full run of the property as New Line was also utilizing the space for interiors on Jon Favreau's *Elf*. Unfortunately, Will Ferrell's Buddy the Elf never actually crossed paths with the titans as *Elf* had only just begun set construction in October. Still, it's strange to imagine Westin Hills and Gimbel's Toy Store both being under the same roof.

The following week would see the production travel to yet another abandoned hospital, the Woodlands Asylum in New Westminster, for scenes depicting Freddy's nightmare boiler room as seen throughout the film. One of the scenes captured this week would see Paula Shaw stepping into the role of Mrs. Voorhees. ("I should've known you wouldn't be able to stop killing!") This particular work week ended on Thursday, October 31 - yes, Halloween - with Englund's Freddy tormenting actor Spencer Stump's young Jason in the nightmare realm, a scene that saw Shaw's character reduced to a staked head. From there, the cast and crew would go on to film scenes depicting Jason's attack on Westin Hills and Freeburg's stoner nightmare.

Weeks nine and ten had all units back in full battle mode for Freddy and Jason's fiery confrontation inside the dilapidated cabin near film's end. This complex sequence required filmmakers to rapidly cut between six cast members and six near-identical stunt doubles, the transitions of which appear seamless in the film. Week ten would end with the main unit filming Trey's early death scene at 1428 Elm Street. Second unit would end the week inside a water tank at the University of British Columbia's Ocean Research Center, which was previously utilized on *Jason Takes Manhattan*. Here the company would stage scenes such as Freddy nightmare-drowning young Jason.

The final days of *Freddy vs Jason*'s production saw all three units capturing various shots to complete earlier sequences. The second and splinter units were charged with grabbing numerous inserts, background plates, and green screen shots during this time. One of the production's final scenes involved Kia attempting to give mouth-to-mouth resuscitation to a drowning Jason in the van. Beyond that, one of the final shots of principal photography involved Jason coming

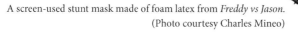

A screen-used stunt mask made of foam latex from *Freddy vs Jason*.
(Photo courtesy Charles Mineo)

back to life in Freddy's prologue; his black heart beginning to beat once more and his one good eye opening. *Freddy vs Jason* officially wrapped principal filming on Tuesday, November 26.

Four months later, the filmmakers had reached a watchable cut of the film, which was test-screened around Los Angeles in mid-April. Despite having unfinished effects and a temporary soundtrack culled from earlier sequels, this early *Freddy vs Jason* scored wonderfully with test audiences - all except for the ending. An overwhelming majority of respondents disliked Will becoming Freddy in the film's final moments with many confused as to the ending's implications. The filmmakers were in agreement. Robert Shaye and Ronny Yu then collaborated to create the ending we now know of Jason emerging from Crystal Lake holding Freddy's severed head. This last-minute reshoot was filmed in Southern California not with Kirzinger behind the mask, but with stuntman Douglas Tait, who became the third person to portray the slasher on the sequel.

RELEASE AND RECEPTION

The cast and filmmakers of *Freddy vs Jason* went all out to promote the sequel leading up to its August 15, 2003 release. On Thursday, July 10, Robert Englund, Ken Kirzinger, and Ronny Yu signed autographs and took fan questions at San Diego Comic-Con. Five days later, New Line staged a mock pre-fight press conference at Bally's Las Vegas Hotel, complete with famed announcer Michael Buffer as host. ("Let's get ready to rumble!") On stage left, Kirzinger's Jason sat silently beside Sean Cunningham. On stage right, Englund's trash-talking Freddy sat alongside Yu. Behind them all stood a small army of security guards in case things got out of hand, which, of course, they did. ("Momma's boy here, he's big, he's dumb, he's slow, he's stupid and he ain't got no style!") The titans fielded questions from reporters with Cunningham responding on Jason's behalf with "No comment." The tongue-in-cheek event ended with both titans having to be restrained after lunging at one another.

Freddy vs Jason had its world premiere on Saturday, August 9 at a unique outdoor event in Driftwood, Texas organized by the Alamo Drafthouse and *AintitCool.com*. The all-day event, which was called Camp HackNSlash, featured camp-inspired activities for one-thousand lucky horror fans. Attendees could learn how to custom-build Freddy gloves, decorate Jason masks, make smores, go swimming, play dodgeball, and attend (or participate in) a wet t-shirt contest. After dusk, *Freddy vs Jason* was projected onto a giant inflatable screen by the lake. Following the movie, Englund, Yu, Kirzinger, and Cunningham participated in a late night discussion panel.

Robert Englund's Freddy boxing robe from the Las Vegas event.
(Photo by Joe Delfino courtesy The Nightmare Museum)

The film had its proper red carpet premiere at Hollywood's Arclight Theatre on the evening of Wednesday, August 13. The major players and their families were all present. Jason Ritter attended with his celebrity father while Monica Keena brought her grandmother. The premiere also featured a slew of tinseltown luminaries including Jessica Biel, Kaley Cuoco, Jennifer Tilly, Lance Bass, Chris Evans, and the band Slipknot. Englund would travel east the following week in order to personally donate a screen-used *Freddy vs Jason* razor glove to New York City's Planet Hollywood.

After ten long years in the making, *Freddy vs Jason* finally opened onto more than 3,000 screens on Friday, August 15, 2003. The reviews were, as expected, brutal in their assessment of its merits. Many critics appeared to dismiss the sequel based on its title alone. Other reviewers seemed reluctant to praise any part of the production, begrudgingly delivering even backhanded compliments. *The Chicago Tribune* said that *Freddy vs Jason* "succeeds as a guilty pleasure." *The Miami-Herald*'s positive review called it "a surprisingly ambitious entry into a genre that felt bankrupt," revealing an inherent prejudice towards horror. But then again, *Freddy vs Jason* was never aiming to please mainstream critics.

The crossover sequel debuted in first place at the domestic box office with a stunning $36 million dollar weekend marking the biggest horror opening of all time. Even more shocking was that *Freddy vs Jason* remained in first place the following weekend as well. The titans would eventually be knocked from their top spot by *Jeepers Creepers 2*, but would remain in the top ten for another two weekends. All in all, *Freddy vs Jason*'s theatrical run grossed more than $115 million dollars worldwide, by far a high mark for both franchises.

INTERVIEW: Douglas Curtis
Executive Producer, *Freddy vs Jason (The 2003 Film)*

DUSTIN MCNEILL: How did you become attached to *Freddy vs Jason*?

DOUGLAS CURTIS: I had made a series of films for New Line, all of which just happened to star Ice Cube. I did two of the *Friday* movies and *All About the Benjamins*. One day, I got a call from one of the executives and she said, '*I know this is a little outside your realm, but what would you think about doing Freddy vs Jason?*' I didn't know anything about it. She sent me the script and I thought it was terrific. I said, '*Let's do it!*' So Ronny Yu came over and we spent weeks going through the script line by line so that I could figure out what his vision for it was. Once we did that, I was able to figure out how much this was going to cost in terms of the budget. We got to know each other very well and had a great working relationship.

DM: How aware were you of the two franchises before you joined the production?

DC: I was certainly aware of them, but I hadn't seen any of them. You can't work for New Line and not know about *Elm Street*. But I didn't dive into them to catch up. Ronny and I both decided that we didn't want to get too attached to the older movies. We were wanting to make an original film, not something influenced by someone else's work. We didn't so much as even look at a single frame from the other sequels until about two weeks before filming began.

DM: Really? Why start watching any of them then?

DC: We started getting a lot of flack about casting Ken Kirzinger as Jason instead of Kane Hodder. We wanted to be confident in that choice. So we sat down to watch three of his Jason movies, which did nothing to change Ronny's mind. He said, '*We're still going to use Ken Kirzinger for this movie.*' And I think he was right. Ken was great in the role. I remember the first time I saw him in full wardrobe. We were doing a night shoot on Elm Street. He came up behind me, tapped my shoulder and scared me to death! Standing six-foot-seven in that costume, he was so, so frightening. And his attitude as that character was just great too.

DM: That's a bold move to have an executive producer and a director that hadn't seen the earlier films, like either it's a great idea or a really terrible one. Obviously, it worked out pretty well here.

DC: I think Robert Shaye was literally insisting on it. He didn't want a movie that looked like any of the other ones. It was his intention to now do something new and original with these characters.

DM: Did you have any sense of the immense fan anticipation as you were making it? Were you guys feeling any pressure?

DC: The only pressure we felt on *Freddy vs Jason* was getting it made in the amount of time we had to do it for the amount of money we had to work with. I think we had around fifty-five days to shoot and it was a very ambitious picture. We did ten weeks of prep and ten weeks of shooting, so we hit the ground running fast. We were working twelve, thirteen hour days even in pre-production just to get everything ready for the cameras. We didn't feel any pressure from the fans or audience anticipation, at least not until the first screening. That was unbelievable. We didn't get too wrapped up in the older movies and the fanbase, so we just had no idea. Our first test screening was in a theater that sat a thousand people and we were turning people away at the door. The moment the first scene came on the screen, we knew it was going to be a hit. They were so overjoyed at what they saw. Even though we went back and made a number of changes, we could have opened with that cut and still been successful. That was Ronny's cut that we first screened and, as always, the studio wanted some changes to it. They were good changes, nothing too substantial.

DM: How was New Line while you guys were making the film? Were they hovering or were you on your own?

DC: They're a great company to make films with. If they trust you, which they did me, they don't bother you at all. They only get involved if you call them and say you have a problem, which I never did. I did call once to say that I didn't think we could finish the cornfield scene in the amount of time we had budgeted. Our production executive was Dana Belcastro, who is now Senior VP over at Alcon. She said, '*Okay, that's fine. You can cover it, right?*' That was another way of asking if I could find the money somewhere else in the budget. They weren't going to give us anymore. I said, '*Yeah, I hope I can,*' and she said, '*Well, you better!*' (laughs) But we had no pressure, none whatsoever. They loved the movie.

DM: Which scene or scenes were most challenging from a production standpoint?

DC: One big challenge we had was the fight in the boiler room. In the script we were working from, all it said was '*clash of the titans.*' That was it. There was not a single descriptive sentence for what happened between Freddy and Jason in the boiler room beyond that. So we had to interpret what that meant including the fight choreography. Fortunately, we found the perfect location for the boiler room that allowed us to do everything we wanted to do. That conversation between me, Ronny, and the production designer didn't even begin until week ten of preproduction, so it was quite a challenge to make happen. I think our hardest scene to shoot was the rave scene in the cornfield simply because it had so much going on. By the way, that was all our corn in that scene. We planted it ourselves. A farmer advised us on how early we'd need to plant it so that it would be tall enough by filming. So we did the math and planted it exactly on the day we needed to and it was camera-ready by the time we came back to it. But that scene was tough. We had a week of first unit, followed by a week of second unit. Every day was a different challenge. We had fire. We had extras. We had stunts. We had Jason walking through the cornfield on fire, which the stuntman could only do for thirty seconds at a time. That whole sequence had to be filmed in tiny pieces and put together. Ronny was also a perfectionist , so everything had to be exactly how he saw it in his mind. We had a very good working relationship, so I was usually the one sitting next to him during filming. If he really didn't like something, he would not be the nicest guy to be around. So I was the negotiator on many nights.

DM: It's difficult even imaging how many aspects of production there must've been to balance on a project like this.

DC: You can't even imagine. It was, by far, the hardest film I've ever done. One of the things that helped us a lot was that we had perfectly matched stunt doubles for Freddy and Jason because they sometimes needed to be in two places at once. It also helped that Robert Englund was so committed to his role. There were times, believe it or not, where Robert was filming twenty-four hours a day. He would finish with the first unit and we would all go home to sleep, but not him. He'd then go over to work with second unit for twelve hours until we came back. I consider him the hero of that movie. He just never said no and he never complained. He gave that role his all and the results are up on the screen. On a personal level, he's just one of those exceptional people you so rarely meet in this business. I just can't say enough about him. He's also the one piece of *Freddy vs Jason* that you can't go without. You can't possibly replace him. No one in their right mind would try to do that film if he wasn't on board.

INTERVIEW: Ken Kirzinger
Stunt Double, *Friday the 13th Part VIII: Jason Takes Manhattan*
"Jason Voorhees," *Freddy vs Jason (The 2003 Film)*

DUSTIN MCNEILL: Stuntman, actor - what came first?

KEN KIRZINGER: First came stunt work. Then, because I'm a big guy, I started getting bit parts as Goon #1 or playing a background cop or having a line right before I get blown up or shot or crash the car. The acting stuff was sort of a natural blend of the two. When I retired from stunt work, that's when I decided to focus more on my acting.

DM: How did you become involved with *Jason Takes Manhattan*?

KK: I got a phone call from Randy Cheveldave, who was the production manager. He left a phone message saying '*Hey, do you* *want to be the stunt coordinator and play Jason?'* and I said, '*Sure!*' And the next call I got said that the guy who played Jason last time was going to be playing him again, but that they still wanted me for the stunt coordinator. I obviously still wanted that job.

DM: You took on Jason in that film. I'm sure you're asked this all the time, but how would that encounter have gone in real life?
KK: (laughs) It depends on which version of Jason we're talking about. There's supernatural Jason and then there's real-world Jason. In the latest version of *Friday the 13th,* I think Jason is much more human, right? Because they explain how he can get from one place to another using tunnels, whereas in other sequels he just appears, which seems more supernatural. I mean, if Jason can just appear anywhere he wants to, you don't stand much of a chance. But if he's flesh and blood in front of you, that's different. If I was up against real world Jason, I would like to think that I could hold out a little bit longer.

DM: When did you first become aware of *Freddy vs Jason*?
KK: I remember seeing *Part Nine* where Jason got dragged to hell and Freddy's glove comes up to grab his mask. Like everyone else, I went, '*Oh, they're about to put them in a movie together,*' but I didn't think much more of it. Then when they finally came to Vancouver to make it, I thought, '*Wow, it's been a long ten years since we saw that scene.*' It didn't originally occur to me why it would've taken so long to get that project going. You figure it might've had something to do with getting the right script. Certainly it couldn't have been because the studio didn't think it was economically viable.

DM: You were cast as one of the most-beloved characters in the horror. Did you have any idea what you were getting into?
KK: I had no idea what I was getting into. I did *Jason Takes Manhattan,* but I wasn't a huge part of that film. It was just another job to me. I had no concept of the audiences, the conventions, or the fanbase that are out there. At first, I was only interviewing for the stunt coordinating job on *Freddy vs Jason*. It was the producer who said to me, '*You know, we're looking for someone with your build and stature. Would you be interested in meeting with Ronny Yu and possibly playing Jason?*' Of course I was interested. I did the audition, met with Ronny, and they gave me the job. I was very grateful to have been a part of it.

DM: What's the audition process for Jason like?
KK: It wasn't complicated. They set up a video camera and gave me a cheap hockey mask. Then someone read aloud the opening scene of the girl swimming in the lake. The camera was focused really tight on my eye. They would have me react as they were reading the scene. Then I had to walk around the room a few times in different ways. That was the extent of it.

DM: Did you have any concept of the controversy surrounding your replacing Kane Hodder as Jason?
KK: I had no idea of that controversy, not at the time. I don't think it was something that was being talked about a lot on set. I didn't really hear that much about it until after we finished shooting the movie. I started doing some promotional stuff and people began asking about it. I think there's been what, seven or eight guys that have played Jason by now? Maybe more? The producers liked to hire local people to save money, so I assumed that played a part in their decision. I really didn't make too much of it.

DM: Did you feel the need to re-watch any of the older films prior to starting production?

KK: I had seen all the movies in the years gone by, but I did not rewatch any of them prior to taking up the role. I had actually worn the Jason suit in *Takes Manhattan*, so I felt that I had a pretty good grasp from that heading into *Freddy vs Jason*. Most of my approach to the role came from Ronny Yu and his direction. He wanted me to move very, very, very slowly until I did something like chopping someone or folding the bed up. He thought that would accentuate the character. I liked that idea, so I went with it. I also liked that we made Jason just a tiny bit more sympathetic in this film. We got to see a side of him that you don't see much in the other movies.

DM: Some of the unused *Freddy vs Jason* scripts had Jason speaking a line or two. Would you have been up for that?

KK: I don't think so. I'm glad that wasn't in our script. You can definitely go out of bounds with a character like this. Having Jason speak is taking him too far away from the character that audiences and fans have come to know and love. That's what I thought our screenwriters did really well. They'd obviously taken a really long time to think about it and get it right. The script had this great balance between keeping him this elemental force you shouldn't mess with, but also making him sympathetic. And he's still Jason. At the same time, it was my job as an actor to do justice to both the script and Ronny's vision for the picture. They would've had to have asked me to do something really un-Jason for me to go against it.

DM: Did being the main actor behind the hockey mask limit your stunt work on the film?

KK: It definitely did, but you have to accept that when you become an actor. They don't want you to do very many stunts because of insurance. Plus, these days you often have a second unit handling stunts and you can't be working with both units at the same time. On *Freddy vs Jason*, I had specifically asked early on in production to be allowed to do the burn in the cornfield because I knew it was going to be amazing. I also knew that it would get nominated for a World Stunt Award. It was more than one burn, actually. I think they did something like eight burns in order to complete that sequence. But they wouldn't even consider letting me do it. The producer kept saying, '*Look, Ken. You've got to realize we hired you as an actor.*'

I did get to do one of my stunts on the very last night of filming. They were doing two scenes with Jason at the same time and they had both myself and my stunt double, Glenn Ennis, made up in full as Jason. I was supposed to rise up out of the ground and he was supposed to go flying out of the back of the van as it rolls. They came up to me and said, '*Ken, would you mind doing the ratchet out of the back of the van?*' And my first thought was, '*Oh yeah, I'm expendable now that it's the last night of filming!*' But I didn't mind doing it. I went flying out of the van and Glenn ended up doing my scene coming up from the ground.

DM: As a stuntman, did not being able to do your own stunts bother you?

KK: It didn't bother me that much. I know it bothered Kane pretty bad when I doubled him on *Jason Takes Manhattan*. He actually asked me not to tell people that I doubled him as Jason. So for years and years, I didn't tell anyone. But people eventually found out. Now it's almost thirty-years-later and I don't think it's a big deal anymore because people just know it's how these films work. You can't be in two places at once and the insurance company has some say in what you can and can't do. It's just business.

DM: What's your preferred ending to *Freddy vs Jason*?

KK: I think I'd most like to see the one we didn't do, which was the alternative ending of Jason and Freddy fighting each other in hell. But I really do like how we ended it in the film and how we left it open for another movie, which was pretty cool. I'm talking about where we see Jason coming out of the lake holding Freddy's head. A lot of people like that ending because it doesn't give you a clear winner, not really. Personally, I like that ending for another reason. Ever notice how that misty lake is kind of dream-like? And how Freddy winks at the audience? I've wondered about that. Is that ending meant to be literal? Or has Freddy somehow put Jason back into a dream state and Jason doesn't know it yet? Does Jason only *think* he's beaten Freddy? You don't really know. I like that a lot. It's quite satisfying.

DM: I've never considered that possibility. That's terrific. So you feel like the film didn't have a clear winner?

KK: It's fun to debate, but who's to say, really? I have an ongoing joke with Robert about it. I always tell everyone at the conventions that I won by a head! You could argue that Jason won the battle simply because there was more of him left at the end of the film than there was of Freddy. So whenever we're signing autographs, I often like to write stuff like '*Robert's a loser!*' and have fun with it. He'll often write something funny back.

DM: Expectation for the long-awaited title fight was pretty big. How did you think the film did in meeting that?

KK: I thought it did fantastic! I think we gave it the attention the audience wanted. You're right about the expectation being big. I thought Ronny did a good job of meeting that expectation in very creative ways. Having part of the fight go down on a construction site was great because it gave them so many toys to play with. That it also unfolded a little at Camp Crystal Lake was good also because that tied into Jason's backstory. That's a special place for him, obviously. It was fun to help bring that to life and it was even more fun to watch it all go down once it was cut together. Ripping Freddy's arm off and Jason getting stabbed with his own machete, I mean - I just thought the writers did a really great job of figuring out that fight.

DM: Tell me about the hilarious Las Vegas weigh-in event you guys did. Was that scripted out beforehand?

KK: That was pretty much all ad-libbed on-stage as we were doing it. We also had a lot of interviews to do after the weigh-in, like fifty or sixty interviews with different people. They'd have Robert and I sitting together answering questions, but the catch was that we were doing all this in-character. And everyone knows Jason doesn't speak, so I wasn't able to respond verbally to anything anyone asked me. I could only react with my body language. And, of course, Freddy is a loudmouth, so he's making tons of jokes about Jason and I had to sit there and take it. It was tough! But also pure fun and great marketing.

DM: Were you able to keep a straight face during that?

KK: No, I was definitely not. I remember many moments where I was cracking up underneath the mask, but still trying to do my best to remain in character. It helped some to remember how I did it in the movie. When you're doing a role like this, you really need to be in character. The hockey mask hides a lot, but it doesn't mean you're not still acting. I remember one night where Ronny caught me out of character and started yelling from behind the camera. '*Ken, you're not in character!*' Despite the mask, the makeup, and the wardrobe, he could still tell. You could only see one eye through the mask, which is like one

Backstage RIP passes from the Las Vegas event. (Photo by Joe Delfino courtesy The Nightmare Museum)

percent of my entire body, but he could still tell. With only one eye showing, I had to find other ways to convey the character by how he walks and moves and even breathes. It's like the old saying goes, '*If you believe it, they'll believe it.*'

The big challenge was getting his body movement right and maintaining his posture. What you see on camera feels so much slower in person. It's more mental endurance than physical endurance. You have to keep how you're moving in the back of your mind. Jason's body movement is his language and it's how the audience relates to him. The nuances of his movement are really no different than how you deliver a line. What's his motivation? Is he angry? Is he cocky? Is he frustrated? Doing all that on set was a lot easier than doing it in the interviews because Robert was constantly doing things to make you break character.

DM: So the movie comes out and it's a box office smash, two weekends at number one. Was there sequel talk?

KK: They wanted to do another one as soon as the first came out. I remember them saying that. Of course, Robert and I were both onboard right away. They talked about wanting to do *Freddy vs Jason vs Ash*, but were never able to pull it together. And I'm still asked all the time if we're going to do another one. At this point, I don't think so. It's been too long, but it would be cool.

DM: How your experience been on the horror convention circuit these past years?

KK: I'll be honest with you. In the beginning, it was a shock to see people so into these films, but it's really grown on me and I love going to those shows. I'm very appreciative to the people who show up and still want to meet me more than a decade after the film came out. I hope it's nothing I ever take for granted. It completely boggles my mind that this character is still so popular. I couldn't even begin to guess how many masks and machetes and posters and t-shirts I've signed over the years.

A 2003 Japanese promotional flyer. (Photo courtesy Charles Mineo)

INTERVIEW: Robert Englund
"Freddy Krueger," *Nightmares 1-7, Freddy vs Jason (The 2003 Film)*

DUSTIN MCNEILL: *Freddy vs Jason* - when do you think this idea began?

ROBERT ENGLUND: The idea behind it is very old. I like to demonstrate it by giving an example of young fan boys in the 1930's and 1940's who would go see a *Frankenstein* or *Wolf-man* picture. Afterwards, they would sit around on their stoop outside their brownstone in New York or lay out in sleeping bags in their suburban backyard somewhere in America, wondering who would win in a throwdown between Frankenstein and the Wolfman. That kind of fan energy eventually made its way to Hollywood and they began making those movies. There were lots of movies made way back in old Hollywood or what we call Golden Age Hollywood where they did match ups between monsters and superheroes. You also had comic books doing things like Superman vs Batman. So the idea is very old.

DM: How early were fans talking to you about this match-up?

RE: Almost immediately following the original *Nightmare on Elm Street*. On the street, fans would ask me who would win, Michael Myers or Freddy Krueger? Or who would win with Freddy versus Jason? At the time, I had a hit television series called *V*, and curiously enough on Thanksgiving of 1984 I was in a parade for NBC. They sent me up there to do publicity for *V* and to ride on a float in the Thanksgiving Day parade in Sacramento, the capitol of California. I remember it like it was yesterday. It was cold and I was kind of dressed like my character with a bow tie and a sweater vest, which is not how I normally dress. As the parade ended, a biker pulled up to me. He was muscular guy on a Harley with long flowing prematurely gray hair. I thought he was a Hell's Angel. The guy took off his shirt and he had a full torso, Japanese-style, Yakuza tattoo of Freddy and Jason grappling wrapped around the muscles of his torso. It was on his back, chest, shoulders, and upper arms. That was the first time that I had ever seen anything like that. It was also the first Freddy tattoo I had ever seen. He just happened to be in a wrestling pose, wrapped around this guys muscles and body, with Jason Voorhees from *Friday the 13th*. That is when I knew that this was a serious fan fantasy. That was when the seed was planted for me in the back of my mind. It was a Hell's Angel in a parade parking lot with a *Freddy vs Jason* tattoo in 1984.

DM: Were you kept aware of the project's development throughout the 90s?

RE: Nobody was calling me, but I sometimes heard things through my agent, sometimes from fans, sometimes even from drive time morning DJs who were very fan oriented. There was a guy, Jeff Katz, who was one of my conduits into the truth about *Freddy vs Jason*. He was a nice guy, very friendly and open with me. I remember running into Jeff one year at either an Oscars party or a New Line party. He revealed to me that it was really starting to shape up, that it was really, really, really going to happen. They had a script they liked and they were trying to get Ronny Yu to direct.

Here's the irony. In the '90s, I was doing a lot of judging at film festivals in Belgium, the US, and in Italy. I had done a wonderful festival at this beautiful resort in France. It was a very eclectic jury I was on with people like the great John Landis, the very glamorous Asia Argento, and the Elvis of France himself, Johnny Holiday. We were watching movies from nine in the morning until four in the afternoon with a big huge break for lunch and a couple bottles of wine. I remember one cold morning sitting in this beautiful little theatre with my giant cup of good French coffee with John Landis. We were there to watch *Bride of Chucky* and we loved it! John and I really got it. We liked it so much we gave Ronny Yu a special award a that festival. So I was a fan of his before he ever came on board *Freddy vs Jason*. When he was announced as our director, I was really, really happy. I just knew he was going to bring this eccentric comedic, violent vision to the project.

DM: With the script, how protective were you of Freddy? Could there have been something you might have objected to with the character? Or were you more willing to leave that up to the writer and director?

RE: Normally, I am very protective because we've made a few mistakes with him before. We violated the Wes Craven bible on a couple of the sequels, most notably on *Part Two*. We took Freddy out of the dream in a weird way on that one. We also jumped the shark a bit on *Freddy's Dead*, although we did that intentionally. That movie has some great imaginative sequences that I love, but we pushed the envelope a little too much. I kind of learned my lesson on *Part Two* because there were a couple of scenes I hated in that one like Freddy, who has all these amazing powers, rolling around on the floor with a teenage girl. To me, that violated his power.

In retrospect, the only problem I had on *Freddy vs Jason* might have had something to do with my age and my confidence. I had always seen Freddy as a wiry junkyard dog who probably wouldn't fight fair. He'd fight dirty. Ronny brought over his amazing stunt coordinator from Hong Kong and together they envisioned Freddy doing martial arts or kung fu anytime he got into a fight. Now I understand the fun of that, seeing Freddy ricocheting off the walls and doing those crazy kicks, but that just wasn't him. He wasn't going to karate chop Jason. He was going to kick him in the balls! I had to defend that to both of them and I argued my point on it. Doing martial arts would have violated the essence of the character. Freddy was not going to play fair. He was going to cheat. I know we did go down that road in one of the sequels where an invisible Freddy kung fu fights a kid, but that was different because the kid imagined himself as a martial arts master. That came from the teenage character. It was rooted in something.

DM: Speaking of the Wes Craven bible, several of the unused drafts attempted to revise the backstories, often with Freddy having molested and killed Jason as a boy. Would it have been a mistake to finally reveal Freddy as a child molester?

RE: Here's the problem with it. There's a certain cold, dark poetry to the phrase child killer. It's such a dark concept that is so impossible to understand, but it does have a certain punk resonance to it. You can imagine a band called The Child Killers playing at a dive bar in Seattle or New York. There's also a symbolism to the phrase. What are you doing when you kill children? You're killing the future. Why does Freddy kill the future? Because there's no place for him in it. To also make Freddy a pedophile is like gilding the lily. It's just too much icing on the cake. Does he fuck them and kill them or kill them and fuck them? That opens a door that is so depraved and so hard to really comprehend.

For me, the mythology of *Nightmare on Elm Street* is just so perfect. Freddy Krueger, this child killer, was burned by a bunch of vigilante parents. Only he never made it to hell and now operates out of some subconscious purgatory where he infects the offspring of the parents that killed him. That makes for a nice, clean revenge motif. You muddle that when you make him a pedophile, which isn't to say there's not a sexual element to him. When he's facing off against a seventeen-year-old girl, there is a level of *Beauty and the Beast* sexuality there. But I think that's a lot more understandable than suggesting Freddy has the hots for one of those little jump rope girls and wants to do naughty things to her. It's too much evil. I think wise voices at New Line always knew that and were smart to keep it out of *Freddy vs Jason*.

DM: You're absolutely right with all of that, but these screenwriters that tried to add that detail in didn't pull it from thin air. There are subtle implications all throughout Freddy's characterization, aren't there? You can certainly read into it.

RE: Absolutely. Whether you're reading a book, watching a movie, or going to see a play, something special happens. Between the page and the mind's eye, between the dark of the theatre and the lip of the stage, or between you and your flat screen in your man cave, something happens. The distance between all those spaces gets filled in by the reader, the guy in the audience, and the viewer. That's called free projection and it's different for everyone.

One of the great losses that we had when music videos came along was the opportunity to listen to a song and fill in the meaning with our own imaginations. We created mental images that depicted what songs looked like and meant. Now with MTV, we are told what to see in our mind's eye. We are shown it. Music videos fill in those details for us. In the *Nightmare* films, Freddy is evil personified and you can take him on a lot of levels, be it symbolically or viscerally. That evil can mean a lot of different things. I don't think we ever need to qualify it beyond child killer. That seems like enough. We can let people free project between the screen and their eyes sitting in the dark. They can decide for themselves what all Freddy has done based on their own human experiences. But child killer? Boom. That's enough on our part.

DM: Lewis Abernathy, who was the first screenwriter on *Freddy vs Jason* in '93 likened his more comedic direction to *Abbott and Costello Meet Frankenstein*. New Line rejected this approach. What are your thoughts on the tone of *Freddy vs Jason*?

RE: I can see how they might be a little gun shy with that script in '93 coming off *Freddy's Dead*, which was definitely horror-comedy. There would have probably been some backlash after

Screen-used wardrobe from the scene where Jason slashes Freddy's arms off.
(Photo courtesy Charles Mineo)

we pushed it too far in that one. Some parts of it were almost like a Warner Brothers cartoon. Plus we had the 3-D stuff and all the celebrity guest stars. But I remember saying before that how we should have done an *Abbott and Costello Meet Frankenstein*-type movie with Freddy and The Fat Boys. I got to work with them on a music video years before. We hung out together some and I even went to the first BET awards show with them. They were so talented and so funny. They also represented a new wave of hip hop culture that was emerging at the time. I just thought it would be great! Let Freddy play it straight and let The Fat Boys do all the comedy around him. At least, it seemed like a good idea at the time. Then *Freddy's Dead* happened and I now see there's a limit. So with *Freddy vs Jason*, you had to limit how much comedy you put into it.

DM: Sean Cunningham has mentioned how Freddy and Jason can't both be pure evil in the match-up, that the audience needs someone to get behind and root for. He strongly felt that had to be Jason. Do you agree with that?

RE: I know what he means. Jason's evil is ex post facto. He was a child who was tormented and bullied and he's been reacting to that experience ever since. That's very key to Jason's core identity. Given that, I think you can sympathize with his revenge on a certain level. Freddy, on the other hand, was simply bad to begin with. His revenge is very different because there's no sympathy to it. There's also no joy to Jason's revenge or at least he doesn't exhibit it. Whereas Freddy is very content in his purgatory and revenge. Freddy likes his work.

DM: I have to ask the obvious question. If you were put in charge of it, who would ultimately win?

RE: I kind of like the gimmick of our ending. But also, you know that if Jason ever falls asleep after that ending, Freddy's going to get him. Freddy can regenerate, much like a lizard that's lost its tail. We've seen him do it before. He dwells in the world of the subconscious, so you know he's just waiting for his next opportunity to get back at Jason. It's difficult for me to really consider any other ending to the film now. I've lived with *Freddy vs Jason* for so long that I can't really see it any other way. If you had asked me this question before I made the movie, I might've wanted to defend Freddy a little more and argue that he should more clearly win.

DM: Would you have been game for a rematch?

RE: I think so. I know before Michael Bay came onboard with Platinum Dunes, there was talk of wanting to make *Freddy vs Jason vs Ash*. I heard secondhand rumors that Sam Raimi had sat down with some executives at New Line to discuss doing it back around the peak of his *Spider-man* success. And the story was that Ash had to win for them to consider doing it, which I thought was great. I had this vision of a poster with a shirtless Bruce Campbell showing off his three-hundred spray-painted abs. He'd have Jason in a headlock under one arm and Freddy in a headlock under the other arm and then the words, '*Freddy vs Jason vs Ash - keeping the world safe from sequels!*' I'm just speculating here, but I think New Line ultimately put the kibosh on anymore versus movies because - of the three properties we're talking about - *Nightmare on Elm Street* is vastly the most successful and maybe they felt they had to protect that a bit. I do think by not doing a rematch they left an awful lot of money on the table after *Freddy vs Jason*. There probably should've been a rematch a couple of years later, maybe around 2006 or 2007. If I were a producer, I would've pushed for it.

DM: As of now, this film stands as your final Freddy performance. Do you feel it's a good cap to your legacy as that character?

RE: Yes, I do think it's a nice capstone to my time playing Freddy. It was a huge hit here and also internationally. I think it has a nice deconstructed, graphic novel quality to it. I love the cast. I think the cast is very strong. You can pop it on the flat screen digitally remastered and it looks great. It still holds up more than a decade later. Had *Freddy vs Jason* not been the monster hit that it was, I might have wanted to come back one more time. But as it stands, I'm glad to have gone out with a home run.

A screen-used hero glove used in the final battle of *Freddy vs Jason*.
(Photo courtesy Charles Mineo)

Chapter Thirteen
The Katz Treatment

2004

THE SCREENWRITER

The Hollywood rise of Jeff Katz is the stuff fanboy dreams are made of. The Detroit-native dropped out of college at twenty-years-old and moved to Los Angeles with hopes of landing at New Line. He may have begun work on *Freddy vs Jason* as an unpaid intern, but he finished the film as the youngest executive in studio history. He immediately became New Line's foremost horror expert. Four years later, he had been promoted to Vice President of Production overseeing films like *Snakes on a Plane* and *Shoot 'Em Up*. He would then transition to 20th Century Fox in the same role to supervise *X-Men Origins: Wolverine*.

Prior to *Freddy vs Jason*'s release, Katz began to sense the potential for a follow-up crossover that brought *Evil Dead*'s Ash Williams into the mix. To this end, he wrote a seventeen-page treatment for the project, which was well received internally. From there, Katz began reaching out to the major players behind each franchise. The next year-and-a-half was spent developing the project to no avail. The treatment eventually leaked in full onto *Bloody-Disgusting.com* in October '04.

PLOT

Set in the weeks before Christmas, *Freddy vs Jason vs Ash* finds the dream slasher trapped in Jason's mind following the events of the last film, an arrangement neither particularly like. Freddy reasons that he can escape this unseemly prison if his host retrieves the Necronomicon Ex Mortis (aka the Book of the Dead) from the basement of the old Voorhees mansion. He talks Jason into running this errand by promising to use the book's power to revive his dead mother and give him intelligence. Unfortunately for the titans, Ash Williams has recently arrived in Crystal Lake for the grand opening of a new S-Mart store. In actuality, he also seeks the Necronomicon and has tracked the book to the Voorhees family home. The titans manage to reach the book first, which results in Freddy being released from his cerebral prison. He promptly betrays Jason and reveals his true plan to unleash his nightmare powers upon reality by way of the Necronomicon. The task of saving the world from an ultra-powerful Freddy and an extra-furious Jason now falls to Ash.

By his own admission, Katz' approach to *Freddy vs Jason vs Ash* is not unlike a three-way greatest hits package. The writer's attention seems evenly split between telling a new story and reminding us why we came to love these characters in the first place, bringing back classic locations and iconic weapons in the process. Whether by accident or design, his treatment adheres to Shannon and Swift's eight golden rules for writing *Freddy vs Jason* (excepting number five). This helps enormously in making this second crossover feel like an organic continuation from its predecessor. Had this sequel been made, it might have formed a bizarre

trilogy of sorts. *Jason Goes to Hell* first introduced the Necronomicon into the *Friday* series and ended with Freddy's glove claiming Jason's mask. That final scene led directly into *Freddy vs Jason*, which itself leads into this treatment where the Necronomicon comes back into play. Little could writer-director Adam Marcus have known back in 1992 that he very nearly set up two crossover films simply by including horror easter eggs into his sequel.

OPENING SCENE

Freddy vs Jason vs Ash's pre-credit sequence takes a page from *Friday the 13th Part VI: Jason Lives* by having the last film's surviving couple return to Crystal Lake. Why would Lori and Will want to return to where their friends were horrifically slaughtered? To make sure Freddy and Jason are truly dead, of course. They arrive to find the town heavily snowed over. Construction on the lakefront housing project - partly destroyed in the last film - has been temporarily suspended for the harsh winter. The old Voorhees house, last glimpsed in *Jason Goes to Hell*, is slated to be demolished shortly into the new year. With the camp and house gone, the town might finally begin a new chapter in its history.

The sequel survivors aren't far into their search of the area before Jason appears and slaughters Will. Lori gives chase through the halfway finished neighborhood with her attacker following close behind. The titan seems distracted in his pursuit, which allows her to dodge several of his machete blows. We soon learn that distraction is Freddy, who appears to be watching Jason throughout the chase. He does eventually catch her, killing the last remaining survivor of *Freddy vs Jason*. The scene ends with Jason stalking off into the darkness, dragging Lori and Will's bodies behind him. Cue credits. Katz' treatment notes, "Both Jason Ritter and Monica Keena have said they'd love to come back and get killed."

THE HUMANS

The treatment introduces two new groups of slasher fodder youths for Freddy and Jason to tear through. The first, more likable bunch all work alongside Ash at Crystal Lake's new S-Mart. Most prominent from this crew is Caroline, your standard wholesome final girl. Next up is jovial Indian guy Raoul, whom Katz likens to Kal Penn. For tough black guy Jarvis, Katz invokes Kincaid from *A Nightmare on Elm Street 3: Dream Warriors*. Rounding out the group is average white guy Dave, whom Katz writes "would typically survive, but has to die because, damn it, Ash *always* gets the girl."

The second group are a bunch of rich, spoiled out-of-towners, who seem well deserving of Jason's machete. They drop into S-Mart early in the story and run across Ash, who sells them camping supplies. He's dismayed to learn they've planned an overnight trip to the old Voorhees house for a quick thrill before it's torn down. The longest surviving member of this second crew is Bree, a flirtatious bombshell who seduces Ash into selling her camping gear on his company discount. She barely manages to escape the slaughter that occurs shortly after her group's arrival at Jason's family home.

THE TITANS: ASH WILLIAMS

Ash's characterization here is consistent with his depiction in the *Evil Dead* trilogy, which is to say he remains an unlikely hero for this or any story. Although still very much a self-serving trash talker, Ash appears a more proficient fighter than last seen in *Army of Darkness*. This works as it stands to reason his combat skills would have sharpened after so many years of killing deadites. Katz is quick to incorporate Ash's signature weapons into this new clash. By now, the character's boomstick and chainsaw have become iconic armaments on the level of Freddy's glove and Jason's machete. In true Ash fashion, he loses both in an early scuffle with Jason, barely escaping with his chainsaw-stub intact. Ever resourceful, the anti-hero uses everything within his reach to fend off the attacking titan including pots, pans, and gardening tools. Losing these trademark items early on allows Ash to create a new, upgraded arsenal just before the final battle. He scours S-Mart for a new sawed-off boomstick and comes across "the mother of all chainsaws," which Katz writes is "industrial quality and very badass."

(Random trivia: This treatment notes that AC/DC's *Highway to Hell* should be blasting in Ash's '73 Oldsmobile as we first meet him. The band's *Back in Black* would later feature into the first season of *Ash vs the Evil Dead*.)

THE TITANS: JASON VOORHEES

This treatment aligns with Ken Kirzinger's theory on *Freddy vs Jason*'s ending - that Jason emerging from Crystal Lake with Freddy's head was actually a dream inside the titan's own mind. As revealed in this new story, Freddy is now trapped inside Jason's subconscious, barely surviving on what little fear the titan has left (most of that related to mommy-issues). As we are quick to see, this Jason is haunted by persistent visions of his nemesis, visions he is powerless against. The titan rages against them to no avail, his machete gliding through the dream slasher's ghostly form.

This treatment's characterization of Jason affords the titan more depth than we're used to seeing, though in a way that aligns with existing mythology. That Freddy is trapped inside Jason's mind means he has access to the slasher's deepest, darkest secrets. Freddy exploits these in order to bribe his rival into retrieving the Necronomicon from his old family home. The incantations contained within will allow Freddy to escape his host's subconscious among other, much worse things. In return, he offers to revive Jason's dead mother and bestow the titan with some intelligence. Freddy's promise to make Jason smarter reveals a huge insecurity on the latter titan's part. How does Jason know he is of lesser-intelligence? Likely from memories of childhood bullying, possibly even from his abusive father.

In a way, this adds another tragic dimension to the character. Jason's deepest desires in this life are to have back the one person who actually loved him and to be smart, a quality he feels separates him from everyone else. (He may honestly be too dumb at this point to realize his appearance is also a distinguishing factor.) Freddy gives his host an initial glimmer of heightened intelligence before commanding him to stop Ash from reaching the Necronomicon. This makes for several interesting moments such as when Ash sets a trap for Jason using his S-Mart coworkers as live bait. The brainier titan is quick to notice this setup and pauses to assess the situation. He shakes his head "no," before pulling out an additional machete and heading in another direction to avoid the trap. Katz writes several jaw-dropping moments for Jason into his treatment. The first occurs as the titan tromps through snowy woods to his old family home. Along the way, he slashes through a group of overly-cheery Christmas carolers as Freddy comments from within his mind ("Ah, holiday spirit all around...") The second big moment occurs as the titan storms into S-Mart to retrieve the Necronomicon from Ash. This is Jason as we've seldom seen him - out in public in broad daylight hacking through waves of customers and employees. Another moment sees Ash lop off Jason's hand at the wrist mid-battle. In a gag that originated in the Reiff/Voris draft, the titan stabs a machete handle down into his bloody stump and continues fighting. Near story's end, Ash points his boomstick point blank at Jason's mask and blasts it off to reveal a hideous maw underneath.

THE TITANS: FREDDY KRUEGER

Being that the story takes place in Crystal Lake, the young protagonists are familiar enough with the legend of Jason Voorhees to know that he isn't much of a planner (or a reader), so Jason carrying around the Necronomicon seems out of character. Though the heroes suspect that someone else may be behind this development, it isn't until halfway through the story that Ash learns of Freddy's involvement.

Katz' Freddy differs from the Shannon/Swift Freddy in that his ambitions are now much greater. In the first crossover, the dream slasher wanted only to return to Elm Street. Here he wishes to enter reality with dream powers intact so that may destroy our world one town at a time, though he'll first need to escape the prison of Jason's mind. He rightly figures that the Necronomicon can help him achieve both goals. Of his current predicament, Katz writes, "In essence, he's imprisoned inside the mind of his greatest enemy and holding on to the last shred of fear that allows him to exist. Freddy is seemingly doomed to roam the demented mind of Jason Voorhees for eternity, a fate worse than hell. He's desperate to escape and it's his desperation that drives our story."

Part of this treatment's fun is seeing a Necronomicon-empowered Freddy wreak *Evil Dead*-style havoc on Crystal Lake. In their first encounter, the dream slasher monologues his entire plan to Ash, who vows to stop him. Freddy cackles at his threat. ("*Stop me?* I did it ten minutes ago.") With that, a giant ripple tears through the town, ushering in a wave of horrors. Smart-Jason notices this and immediately concludes that Freddy has betrayed their agreement. Shortly thereafter, Freddy uses his powers to resurrect Jason's many victims in an attempt to stop him. They burst from the ground to attack the angry titan, who barely manages to escape their assault. Katz writes that these zombie-attackers should be recognizable in order to pay tribute to some of *Friday the 13th*'s most famous kills. Jason's victims seeking revenge from beyond the grave somewhat recalls a similar sequence from the shopping mall finale of the Braga/Moore draft.

DREAMS/NIGHTMARES

Like its predecessor, *Freddy vs Jason vs Ash* is rife with nightmare sequences. The first of these, a waking nightmare of sorts, occurs as the dream slasher taunts his host from within his own mind. To get Jason's full attention, Freddy shows him a vision of he and his mother in passionate embrace. Enraged at this sight, Jason slashes at Freddy with no effect. It's this vision of his mother who eventually convinces him to retrieve the Necronomicon in order to evict Freddy from his mind and bring her back from the dead. Given his low IQ, Jason falls for this trick hook, line, and sinker.

Katz acknowledges in his treatment's notes that *Freddy vs Jason* lacked a classic Freddy kill. To this end, he offers up S-Mart's Dave as a sacrifice to the fans, though the detail of his demise are left open-ended. The scribe writes that his nightmare death "should be something nasty like the marionette guy from *Dream Warriors* or the human cockroach from *Dream Master*."

The story's standout nightmare arguably goes to Ash. To his horror, this plays out inside the cabin from the first two *Evil Dead* movies, a terrifying place for him to return to. Ash is quick to notice that his dream-self still has a right hand, though this reunion is short-lived. His hand once again "goes bad," though differently this time. Painful razor-knives extend from his fingertips, transforming his hand into a fleshy Freddy-glove. The possessed extremity then attacks Ash, wildly slashing at him. History further repeats itself as he retrieves a chainsaw from the workshed and lops it off. The severed hand continues its assault until Ash blasts it with his shotgun. He spins around to see Freddy standing behind him, who reveals his evil plan.

HALLOWED GROUND

In a nod to all three fanbases, Katz stages his crossover across a handful of iconic locations from the parent franchises. The story begins at an iced-over Crystal Lake. The infamous camp has finally been demolished, replaced by new housing construction. We then travel back to Jason's isolated shack first seen in *Friday the 13th: Part 2*. As in that film, he still maintains a candlelit shrine to his mother complete with her badly decomposed head. This treatment finds the shrine updated to now feature Freddy's severed noggin as well. The story also pays several visits to the old Voorhees home which is scheduled for demolition in the new year.

On the *Evil Dead* side of things, the treatment spends quite some time at the newest S-Mart store. Here Katz shows us Ash in his retail element, still employed in the housewares department. Jason's rampage turns the store into one giant crime scene, forcing it to close down. Ash and his co-workers sneak past the police tape for a classic suit-up montage near story's end. As previously mentioned, the iconic cabin also makes a brief return in Ash's nightmare.

During the long final battle, Freddy uses his powers to transform the Voorhees home into the house at 1428 Elm Street, presumably to disorient the heroes. The mailbox out front even changes from "Voorhees" to "Krueger." As Freddy attempts to steal back the Necronomicon from Caroline inside, a bemused Ash "gingerly approaches" the two jump-roping little girls out front as they sing a familiar tune. In a truly *Evil Dead* moment, the two girls turn to attack Ash, choking him with their jump rope. Jason arrives on the scene by bursting through a wall and his fight with Freddy "literally brings down the house around them."

THE ENDING

The majority of the final act is dedicated to a sprawling three-way battle. After destroying the Voorhees mansion, the fight spills out onto the frozen lakebed. Whomever gets the Necronomicon will emerge victorious. Freddy wants the book to maintain his new powers. Ash wants it to send both slashers back to hell. Jason simply wants to kill the other two. Ash brings Caroline along so that she can read a key passage from the Necronomicon as he stalls the other titans. In a humorous nod to *Army of Darkness*, he stresses the importance of proper pronunciation when reciting passages. ("Klaatu Barada... Necktie? Neckturn? Nickel?")

Katz writes that Freddy and Ash are bantering constantly throughout the fighting, making this "the smack talk showdown of the century." He also charges that Jason is so furious by this point that he manages to hold his own against Freddy's new powers. Realizing this, the dream slasher transforms into Jason's mother in an attempt to calm him. As Mrs. Voorhees, he urges the titan to give up this unwinnable fight in exchange for a quick and painless destruction. Smart-Jason sees through the facade and slashes her in half. Ash has used this break in the fighting to retrieve his trusty '73 Oldsmobile, which he crashes onto the ice. It eventually falls through, pinning Jason beneath it on the lake bottom. Caroline, meanwhile, has managed to retrieve the book in the chaos and recite the passage. A portal opens, sucking Freddy and the Necronomicon into it.

With reality having returned to normal, Ash and Caroline speed off in her sports car ("Gimme some sugar, baby.") Katz notes that Freddy's razor-glove now hangs from the rear-view mirror as a trophy. Here the treatment contains a note intended for the *Evil Dead* camp: "If Sam Raimi requests, we can have Ash get sucked into the vortex as well, only to be dropped off in another distant time during our coda." Just before the credits, the camera returns to the icy waters of Crystal Lake where we find Jason still pinned beneath the Oldsmobile. His good eye snaps open! Katz writes, "He's still alive and this lake has to thaw sometime, doesn't it?"

WHY IT DIDN'T HAPPEN

Katz' treatment for *Freddy vs Jason vs Ash* was an explosive, thrill-packed, blood-soaked affair that followed nearly all of the same rules that worked for the Shannon/Swift draft. Michael Lynne and Robert Shaye liked the concept. Robert Englund and Ken Kirzinger were game to reprise their roles. Even Sean Cunningham supported the effort. The only holdouts were in the *Evil Dead* camp. Sam Raimi and Bruce Campbell, while open to the possibility of a three-way crossover, were not particularly enthused for it. The popular story is that Raimi's *The Grudge* remake opened October 22, 2004 to a whopping $39 million opening weekend, just barely cresting *Freddy vs Jason*'s record for biggest horror opening of all time. This was said to have emboldened the filmmaker to immediately suspend *Freddy vs Jason vs Ash* talks in favor of producing an *Evil Dead* remake, which was announced in *Variety* several weeks later.

The truth is that Raimi had pulled out of negotiations even before *The Grudge*'s release, telling *IGN FilmForce* in early October, "I think [New Line] were hoping that it might go. We talked about it, but then the press release came out. I think I would need more control than they would be happy with and I don't want to control some other director. Sean Cunningham's a brilliant director and I don't want to be in a position where I'm trying to protect Ash and the *Evil Dead* story and he's not getting everything he wants. Even though it might have been really great, I'm sure whatever he does next is gonna be great. It just didn't seem like a good position for me to be in. [...] I know that they wanted to do something really cool, but I wanted to keep the option open for myself to make another *Evil Dead* movie without the limitations of what that story may have done. That's really, I think, what it is."

In a 2016 Reddit "Ask me anything" chat, Campbell told fans, "I'll be honest with you. I'm not real interested in crossovers. One of the main reasons why *Freddy vs Jason vs Ash* did not come to pass is because we couldn't control any character other than Ash. That felt like a creatively bankrupt way to go. Not to mention, you're splitting the proceeds three ways with partners you might not even want."

"We tried for two years to make *Freddy vs Jason vs Ash* happen," Katz adds. "That was very serious and very real. We had long negotiations with Sam Raimi's camp on it. That began even before *Freddy vs Jason* came out. The idea was that if they're going to end Freddy and Jason, you may as well have them ended by the one guy horror fans would accept ending them. Everybody was onboard with the concept. Robert Shaye and Michael Lynne were both wanting to do it. We just couldn't make a deal with Raimi despite our best efforts. It got very aggressive towards the end in terms of the dealmaking."

COMIC ADAPTATION & SEQUEL

In 2007, David Imhoff negotiated a deal between Wildstorm Productions, who held the comic book rights to Freddy and Jason, and Dynamite Entertainment, publisher of various *Army of Darkness* comics, to bring *Freddy vs Jason vs Ash* to life. Released as a six-issue miniseries starting in November '07, the comic's storyline was faithfully adapted by James Kuhoric from Katz' original treatment. In 2009, Katz and Kuhoric co-wrote a six-issue sequel called *Freddy vs Jason vs Ash: Nightmare Warriors*. This new miniseries picked up immediately following the last one and saw numerous survivors from the *Friday* and *Nightmare* franchises return including Nancy Thompson, Tommy Jarvis, Maggie Burroughs, Steven & Stephanie Freeman, Tina Shepard, Alice & Jacob Johnson, and Dr. Neil Gordon. *Nightmare Warriors'* conclusion borrowed from the Briggs draft by having an FBI Agent displaced into 1968 Springwood where he forges a signature on the search warrant that previously allowed Freddy to walk free. In doing so, he prevents Freddy from being burned alive by the vigilante mob, thus also preventing the events of *A Nightmare on Elm Street* and *Friday the 13th* from ever happening.

END OF AN ERA

Although unbeknownst to anyone then, *Freddy vs Jason* would mark the last time audiences would be able to see the titans in their original cinematic continuities. The crossover sequel effectively closed the door on two of the longest running timelines in the genre. But what led these franchises to reboot following *Freddy vs Jason*? Certainly not ticket sales - the monster merger clenched the number one box office spot two weekends in a row and towered as the year's highest grossing horror film. They also weren't rebooted due to the filmmakers having written the titans into an inescapable corner. In fact, both Freddy and Jason were left in significantly better standing than at the conclusions of the last several sequels. (Well... Jason was standing, at least.) The answer owes to a then blossoming trend in the genre - the almighty remake. *Freddy vs Jason* may have been horror's highest grosser that year, but second place belonged to New Line's own *Texas Chainsaw Massacre* remake. That film impressively landed just two million beneath *Freddy vs Jason*'s $82 million total, by far a franchise best for Leatherface and the gang.

Did the high profile pairing of Freddy with Jason make future solo-monster films pedestrian by nature? Possibly so, if not only from a financial standpoint. Consider that *Freddy vs Jason* made more on opening day than *Jason X* did in its entire theatrical run. On the other side of the street, consider that *Freddy vs Jason* earned twice the theatrical gross of *New Nightmare* in its first three days. Was New Line reluctant to return to those kinds of numbers? Both franchises were practically limping into the crossover sequel, at least where box office takes were concerned. The lucrative days of *Friday the 13th: Part III* and *Nightmare on Elm Street 4: The Dream Master* were long behind the titans heading into their battle royal.

So in 2009 and 2010, *Friday the 13th* and *A Nightmare on Elm Street* were rebooted. These films had new actors, new continuities, and new sensibilities for a new generation. Neither managed to top *Freddy vs Jason*'s theatrical gross and, if Rotten Tomatoes is any indication, they fared significantly worse with critics than the 2003 sequel. As of this 2017 writing, neither reboot has managed to garner a sequel. The titans appear to be resting... for now. But as long as people love to be scared, they'll keep coming back. Robert Englund even thinks they'll face off again one day.

> **"I'm sure this wasn't the last time anyone will ever see Freddy and Jason onscreen together. They're going to cross paths again someday. It'll just be other actors playing those parts the next time you see them."**
>
> - Robert Englund

"No matter who wins, it'll be a good fight."
- Stephen King in Entertainment Weekly #724

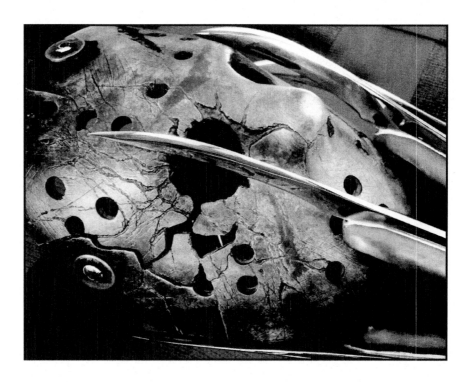

(Photo by Joe Delfino courtesy The Nightmare Museum)

("Battle Damaged VS Mask" created by AUZ, "D400" made by Robbie Atkinson of Terror Gloves)

Appendices

STORY SUMMARIES

The Abernathy Draft: A psycho-cult kidnaps a young girl to marry Freddy so that he can be reborn in reality and take over our world. The girl's sister and her friends team with an ex-cultist to resurrect Jason in hopes he will defeat Freddy and the cult.

The Braga/Moore Draft: The *real* Jason is put on trial for his crimes. A lifelong insomniac, he is given anesthesia for emergency surgery after being shot during the trial. This reunites him with a monster from his past - Freddy - who uses him as a doorway into reality.

The Briggs Draft: Survivors from previous sequels team up with an FBI agent to stop an evil prophecy involving Freddy and Jason on New Year's Eve 1999. The titans are revealed to be pawns of Thanos.

The Reiff/Voris Draft: A psycho-cult kidnaps a young girl to marry Freddy so that he can be reborn and take over reality. The girl's sister teams with a mysterious stranger from Freddy's past to resurrect Jason in hopes he might stop Freddy and the cult.

The Goyer/Robinson Draft: A psychic-teenager helps police capture a Freddy copycat killer. She and friends then take a dream-enhancing drug and head to Crystal Lake. Freddy, Jason, and the copycat all start to appear before them as dream and reality blend together.

The Aibel/Berger Draft: A young girl barely escapes attack by a Freddy copycat killer. She and friends then head to Crystal Lake where their drinks are spiked with a dream-enhancing drug. Freddy, Jason, and the copycat all start to appear before them as dream and reality blend together.

The Verheiden Draft: A young girl begins having Freddy nightmares. After surviving an unexplainable massacre, she and friends head to Crystal Lake while taking a dream-enhancing drug. Freddy and Jason start to appear before them as dream and reality blend together.

The Protosevich Draft: A grad-student writing about Freddy and Jason accidentally draws them to her. Research into her own past reveals a disturbing connection to both killers, which uniquely enables her to defeat them.

The Bergantino Treatment: Freddy devises a scheme to slaughter thousands of souls in a "dream concert," which will empower him to enter reality. *NOES5*'s Dream Child pulls Jason into the dream world to prevent Freddy from accumulating this many souls.

The Shannon/Swift Draft: Freddy resurrects Jason from hell and directs him to Elm Street with hopes he'll drum up enough new fear to bring Freddy back from obscurity. Jason is unable to stop killing, however, and the titans wind up battling over who gets to kill Elm Street's youth.

The Katz Treatment: Freddy tricks Jason into retrieving the Necronomicon so that he may use its power to transform reality into one giant nightmare. Ash also seeks the book in order to send Freddy and Jason back to hell.

SCREENWRITER FILMOGRAPHY HIGHLIGHTS

Lewis Abernathy: *House IV* (Director), *DeepStar Six* (Writer), *Terminal Invasion* (Writer), *Titanic* (Actor), *The Two Jakes* (Script doctor), *Jason Goes to Hell* (Script Doctor), *Jason X* (Script Doctor)

David J. Schow: *Freddy's Nightmares: "Safe Sex"* (Writer), *Critters 3* (Writer), *Critters 4* (Writer), *The Crow* (Writer), *Leatherface: The Texas Chainsaw Massacre III* (Writer), *Texas Chainsaw Massacre: The Beginning* (Writer)

Brannon Braga: *Star Trek: The Next Generation* (Writer, Co-Producer), *Star Trek: Generations* (Writer), *Star Trek: First Contact* (Writer), *Star Trek: Deep Space Nine* (Writer, Co-Executive Producer), *Star Trek: Enterprise* (Creator, Writer, Executive Producer), *Mission Impossible II* (Writer), *24* (Writer, Co-Executive Producer)

Ronald D. Moore: *Star Trek: The Next Generation* (Writer, Co-Producer), *Star Trek: Generations* (Writer), *Star Trek: First Contact* (Writer), *Star Trek: Deep Space Nine* (Writer, Co-Executive Producer), *Mission Impossible II* (Writer), *Battlestar Galactica '04* (Writer, Executive Producer)

Peter Briggs: *The Hunt: Alien vs Predator [Unproduced]* (Writer), *Hellboy* (Writer), *Panzer 88 [In Dev]* (Writer, Director)

Ethan Reiff/Cyrus Voris: *Tales from the Crypt: Demon Knight* (Writers), *Bulletproof Monk* (Writers), *Kung Fu Panda* (Writers), *Robin Hood '10* (Writers)

David Goyer: *Demonic Toys* (Writer), *Arcade* (Writer), *The Crow: City of Angels* (Writer), *Dark City* (Writer), *Blade* (Writer), *Blade II* (Writer, Executive Producer), *Blade: Trinity* (Writer, Director, Producer), *Batman Begins* (Writer), *The Dark Knight* (Writer), *The Dark Knight Rises* (Writer), *Man of Steel* (Writer), *Constantine* (Writer, Executive Producer), *Batman v Superman: Dawn of Justice* (Writer, Executive Producer)

James Dale Robinson: *Comic Book Villains* (Writer, Director), *The League of Extraordinary Gentlemen* (Writer), *Son of Batman [Animated]* (Writer)

Jonathan Aibel/Glenn Berger: *King of the Hill* (Writers, Executive Producers), *Kung Fu Panda* (Writers, Co-Producers), *Monsters vs Aliens* (Writers), *Alvin and the Chipmunks: The Squeakquel* (Writers), *Kung Fu Panda 2* (Writers, Co-Producers), *Alvin and the Chipmunks: Chipwrecked* (Writers), *The SpongeBob Movie: Sponge Out of Water* (Writers), *Kung Fu Panda 3* (Writers, Co-Producers), *Trolls* (Writers, Co-Producers), *Monster Trucks* (Writers, Executive Producers)

Mark Verheiden: *The Mask* (Writer), *Timecop* (Writer, Supervising Producer), *Smallville* (Writer, Co-Executive Producer), *My Name is Bruce* (Writer), *Battlestar Galactica* (Writer, Co-Executive Producer), *Heroes* (Writer, Consulting Producer), *Hemlock Grove* (Writer, Executive Producer), *Constantine* (Writer, Executive Producer), *Daredevil* (Writer, Executive Producer)

Mark Protosevich: *The Cell* (Writer, Co-Producer), *Poseidon* (Writer), *I Am Legend* (Writer), *Thor* (Writer), *Oldboy '13* (Writer, Co-Producer)

David Bergantino: *Freddy Krueger's Tales of Terror: Virtual Terror* (Author), *Freddy Krueger's Tales of Terror: Twice Burned* (Author), *Freddy Krueger's Tales of Terror: Help Wanted* (Author), *Freddy Krueger's Tales of Terror: Deadly Disguise* (Author), *Wes Craven's New Nightmare* (Author), *A Midsummer Night's Scream* (Author), *Hamlet II: Ophelia's Revenge* (Author)

Mark Shannon/Damian Swift: *Freddy vs Jason* (Writers), *Friday the 13th '09* (Writers), *Baywatch* (Writers), *Genie* (Writers)

Jeff Katz: *Freddy vs Jason vs Ash [Comic]* (Writer), *Freddy vs Jason vs Ash: Nightmare Warriors [Comic]* (Writer), *Booster Gold [Comic]* (Writer), *Snakes on a Plane* (Associate Producer), *Shoot 'Em Up* (Associate Producer), *Infernal* (Executive Producer)

* Rob Bottin is not listed here as *Freddy vs Jason* would have marked his screenwriting debut.

FIGHT RESULTS

Results are decided by whichever titan is left standing at each story's conclusion. If both titans perish in the final battle, the last titan to fall shall be considered the winner. This means that while Freddy may take an awful beating from Jason, he can still be declared winner by virtue of outliving his opponent.

The Abernathy Draft	Freddy Wins
The Braga/Moore Draft	Jason Wins
The Briggs Draft	Neither Wins
The Reiff/Voris Draft	Jason Wins
The Goyer/Robinson Draft	Neither Wins (entire story is a dream)
The Aibel/Beger Draft	Jason Wins
The Verheiden Draft	Both Win (script had two endings)
The Protosevich Draft	Freddy Wins
The Bergantino Treatment	Jason Wins
The Shannon/Swift Draft	Tie (both live on as film ends)

FREDDY   JASON
3   5

HEROINES

The Abernathy Draft: Meagan Daniels, seventeen-year-old high school student experiencing recurrent Freddy nightmares.

The Braga/Moore Draft: Ruby Jarvis, Crystal Lake Defense Attorney assigned to defend Jason in court.

The Briggs Draft: Returning characters Alice Johnson (dream powers) and Stephanie Freeman (Jason's great-niece).

The Reiff/Voris Draft: Michelle Barrett, a twenty-four-year-old registered nurse experiencing recurrent Freddy nightmares.

The Goyer/Robinson Draft: Samantha, a seventeen-year-old high school student with psychic abilities.

The Aibel/Berger Draft: Lizzie Daniels, a seventeen-year-old high school student targeted by a Freddy copycat.

The Verheiden Draft: Lizzie, a seventeen-year-old high school student experiencing recurrent Freddy nightmares.

The Protosevich Draft: Rachel Daniels, a twenty-year-old graduate student studying psychology.

The Bergantino Treatment: An unnamed pop star manipulated by Freddy into holding a "dream concert."

The Shannon/Swift Draft: Lori Campbell, a seventeen-year-old high school student living at 1428 Elm Street.

REVISED ORIGINS

Five different revisions to Freddy and Jason's origin were proposed throughout the project's long development. They are briefly summarized below along with the draft(s) that utilized them. Curiously, the Shannon/Swift draft was the only full script that did not attempt to intertwine the titans' backstories.

1. Jason was drowned at Camp Crystal Lake by fellow camper Freddy Krueger.
(Appeared in the Abernathy Draft)

2. Young Jason walks in on Freddy and Mrs. Voorhees having sex. Freddy chases the boy outside and drowns him.
(Appeared in the Braga/Moore Draft)

3. Jason was an Elm Street kid, whom Freddy kills as revenge against his parents for being among the vigilante mob.
(Appeared in the Briggs Draft)

4. Freddy was a camp counselor that molested young Jason, whom he drowns upon telling others of the abuse.
(Appeared in the Reiff/Voris, Goyer/Robinson, Aibel/Berger and Verheiden Drafts)

5. Jason drowns while his camp counselor sneaks away to have sex with Freddy, who helps hide their negligence in his death.
(The Protosevich Draft)

Have we met before?

No. Yes. Maybe.

MEDICATION GUIDE

Dream Dope - A narcotic that, when combined with special flashing sunglasses allows its user to contact Freddy. (Abernathy)

Hypnocil - An experimental sedative used for the suppression of dreams. Overdose can lead to a permanent comatose state. (Shannon/Swift, first seen in *A Nightmare on Elm Street 3: Dream Warriors*)

Hytenexoft - A sedative used for the suppression of recurrent disturbing dreams. (Protosevich)

Imobatine - A powerful tranquilizer given at Westin Hills. Used to tranquilize Jason for transport. (Shannon/Swift)

Mescahedraline Anthropophylax ("Meskie-Mex") - An especially potent hallucinogenic street drug. (Protosevich)

Neurolar - A serotonin-inhibitor that suppresses dreaming including Freddy's new waking-nightmares. (Braga/Moore)

Somnambulene - A sedative that forces sleep upon the user, essentially trapping them in their dreams. Can become deadly when mixed with alcohol. Doing so can lead to dream-sharing and a confusing breakdown in one's perception of reality and dream. (Goyer/Robinson, Aibel/Berger, Verheiden)

Somnazac - A medication that intensifies dreams, empowering its user to access their full imagination while sleeping. Thought to help users defend against Freddy. (Protosevich)

Tetrocaine - A hallucinogen similar to South American tribal drugs that enables its users to share dreams. (Reiff/Voris)

Wake Aid - An over-the-counter sleep prevention mediction, essentially caffeine pills. (Shannon/Swift)

The medications mentioned here are entirely fictional. This information is intended to educate readers about subjects unrelated to their actual health. Please consult your personal healthcare provider before taking these or any fictional medications. Harker Press will not be responsible for the consequences of your decision to utilize the information contained in this book.

(Photo by Joe Delfino courtesy The Nightmare Museum)

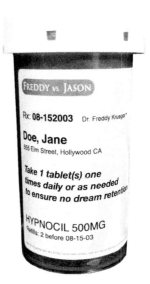

FREDDY vs. JASON

Rx: 08-152003   Dr. Freddy Krueger

Doe, Jane
555 Elm Street, Hollywood CA

Take 1 tablet(s) one times daily or as needed to ensure no dream retention

HYPNOCIL 500MG
Refills: 2 before 08-15-03

A Note About Sources

All interviews and quotations in this book are original except where otherwise noted.

<u>Resources used in the writing of this book:</u>

Fangoria #144, #225, and especially #226

Unmasked: The True Story of the World's Most Prolific, Cinematic Killer by Kane Hodder with Michael Aloisi

Hollywood Monster: A Walk Down Elm Street with the Man of Your Dreams by Robert Englund with Alan Goldsher

Crystal Lake Memories: The Complete History of Friday the 13th by Peter M. Bracke

The Nightmare on Elm Street Companion (Nightmarenelmstreetfilms.com)

His Name Was Jason: 30 Years of Friday the 13th (Documentary, 2009)

Never Sleep Again: The Elm Street Legacy (Documentary, 2010)

Crystal Lake Memories: The Complete History of Friday the 13th (Documentary, 2013)

Acknowledgements

Special Thanks to:

Lewis Abernathy, Lauren Bello, David Bergantino, Brannon Braga, Peter Briggs, Sheila Chambers, David Chaskin, Sean Cunningham, Douglas Curtis, Hannah Dorsett, Robert & Nancy Englund, Jeff Field, Scott Greenberg, David Goyer, Mark Haslett, Chris Heady, Bryan Hickel, David Imhoff, Andrew Kasch, Jeff Katz, Ken Kirzinger, John D. LeMay, Adam Marcus, Ben McGinnis, Tom McLoughlin, Nathan Thomas Milliner, Brad Miska, Ronald D. Moore, Stephen Norrington, Scott Pensa, Mark Phillips, Mark Protosevich, Ethan Reiff, Dustin Sain, Damian Shannon, Mark Swift, Trace Thurman, Lito Velasco, Mark Verheiden, Cyrus Voris, Brian Witten

Phantasmic thanks to Peter Marullo and Kristen Deem for the support and encouragement.
Eternal thanks to Angus Scrimm for the same.

Massive thanks to *Freddy vs Jason* experts Charles Mineo (bottom left) and Joe Delfino (bottom right).

Cover design by the mighty talented George Todoroff. (http://georgetodoroff.com)
Shadow illustrations graciously provided by Rohan Jha.

Love and thanks to my parents, David and Karen, for letting me watch scary movies growing up. Apologies to my sister, Andrea, for all the Freddy-related childhood trauma. Love and thanks to my wife, Lindsay McNeill, for more than I can fit on this page. And thanks to Carly Roberts for always being a fun distraction from research right when I needed it.

Also from Harker Press

"... comprehensive and in-depth..."
- Fangoria Magazine

"Engaging, compulsive reading."
- Bestselling author Brian Keene

"The perfect prelude
to the Tall Man's return."
- Rue Morgue Magazine

"... a glorious retrospective..."
- HorrorHound Magazine

Featuring Set Journals and Introduction by Angus Scrimm!
More than sixty new interviews with cast and filmmakers!
250+ rare set photos, many never-before-seen!
Information on deleted scenes and unmade sequels!
Tips and tricks for better embalming!*

PhantasmExhumed.com

* Just kidding

Printed in Great Britain
by Amazon

79200866R00140